MW00850414

# I'M NOT FAMOUS

*Don't Ever Expect To Be*

Mark R. Genovese

Copyright © 2023
Mark Robert Genovese

Performance Publishing
McKinney, TX

All Worldwide Rights Reserved.
All rights reserved. No part of this publication may
be reproduced, stored in a retrieval system or
transmitted, in any form or by any means, electronic,
mechanical, recorded, photocopied, or otherwise,
without the prior written permission of the copyright
owner, except by a reviewer who may quote brief
passages in a review.

This autobiography reflects the personal experiences and
memories of the author. The decision to use fictitious names is
intentional and is not meant to mislead or misrepresent
actual persons. The author respects the privacy of individuals
involved and has taken steps to prevent the identification of real
individuals by altering details and using fictitious names.

ISBN: 978-1-961781-99-3

PERFORMANCE
PUBLISHING

# CONTENTS

# CONTENTS

# ACKNOWLEDGEMENTS

Thanks to Anthony DiVerniero for showing me the way and to Jodi Falcigno Rooney for her grasp of the English language and her invaluable assistance.

**To my family:**

My wife Caren who is my rock and always there when I need her, and my two children, Steven and Amanda, who make my life whole.

# INTRODUCTION

In 2011, I was diagnosed with Parkinson's disease. This was a huge shock to me. All I could think was the doctors had made an incredible mistake. This simple little tremor was just being caused by stress. I was in the thirtieth year of my career as a police officer. I now held the rank of Captain in the Police Department in North Haven, Connecticut. This was the town I had lived in for my entire life, with the exception of the four years I served in the Marine Corps. I refused to let the neurologist prescribe any medication for me. I was going to beat this on my own.

Like the rest of my life, I did not want any help. I had always hated doctors. All my life, I have been injuring myself or doing something stupid to force me to seek medical attention. I was an accident searching for a place to occur. Now, I had Parkinson's disease, and there was no way around it. I had to face the fact life was going to be different. There was a strong possibility I would soon have issues with balance and coordination. The disease can also affect your memory and ability to speak. I did not want to retire from the police force yet. I did not want to leave the profession I loved that was a part of me. I made the conscious decision to keep it a secret. The only other person who would know would be my wife, Caren.

It was at this point when I decided to write this book. I wanted everyone to know people just like me, who they come in contact with every day, have a story to tell, a life they have lived however long or short it was. I wanted to leave something behind my children could be proud of. I wanted to tell a story about the ups and downs of a person who found a calling as a police officer. I wanted to share with everyone who was interested what it was like to go through Marine Corps boot camp. I wanted to share what it meant to me to serve my country as a Marine assigned to protect embassies in three other countries. I wanted to share how hard it was to become a police officer. Once you have become involved in the field of law enforcement and are a first responder, the difficulties you are presented with on a day-today basis are enormous. The injuries and the deaths, the good days, the bad days, the funny things, and the sad things all contribute to a story that should be told.

The doctors who diagnosed my Parkinson's disease suggested if I read books and wrote about my experiences in life, the effects of the disease might be slowed. I don't know if that is the case, but this is a compilation of events that have occurred in my life. These little incidents are a small sample of what has made me the person I am today. I'm going to keep writing to see if I can keep these Parkinson symptoms from catching me and knocking me off my feet.

I'm retired now. I'm not famous, but I've met some very famous people. I am just a man who stood up for what he believed was the right thing to do. I raised a wonderful family while completing an ordinary career. I could never have made it this far without the love and companionship of my wife, Caren. There were many times my career came between our personal lives: the high-speed pursuits, the altercations with suspects, the police car accidents, the SWAT call outs, and the night shift assignments. But she was always there when I returned home. She is my rock, my guiding light, and my true love.

When you read this book, please realize I was just a simple man doing a simple job, the best way possible. I was not someone seeking notoriety. I was just a Marine trying not to let the Corps down. Then, I was a police officer, just trying to make it home to my family at the end of my shift. When I was a supervisor, it was most important that my troops made it home safely. Isn't all this what's important in life?

# Chapter 1

# ON MY WAY

The hum of the ten tires and the mumbling small talk from the forty young men on this aging bus are all that keep me awake so far. I shake my head in disbelief, wondering what brings me to this bus in the first place. I wipe the sweat beads off my forehead and then rub my eyes. I have just flown in an airplane through one of the most aggressive storms one can imagine. My thoughts drift back to the flight. Seat number 10C is a window seat just in front of the wing of the 707 Boeing jet. As I approach the seat, I think to myself, *Great, I can watch out the window while we are in the air.* I settle into the seat, slide the tab into the buckle, and fasten my seat belt. I determine there are only two seats on this side of the aircraft. I pull the loose end of the belt, so it is tight around my waist. Just then, my mind begins to race. I don't have anything to read, eat, or drink. I start to search the seat pocket in front of me. First, I check over the safety procedure pamphlet. There are two air sickness bags and an in-flight catalog. I have no interest in reading the catalog. My attention turns to the open door where people continue to board, and I simply wonder who is going to sit next to me.

1

I enjoy flying and have been on a couple of planes before this flight. One was a propeller-driven airplane, and two were jets. As I am thinking about my previous flights, my attention is again focused on the aisle. I am soon greeted by this silver haired, well dressed, woman. You know, the grandmother type with the mother of pearl framed glasses dangling from her neck, held in place with a silver chain. She quietly tells me she is assigned to the seat next to me. She prominently displays her boarding pass and points to seat number 10D. She introduces herself and says, "I'm Anna Wright, and this is my seat. I'm 66 years old, and I'm going to visit my daughter and grandchildren in South Carolina." I simply nod and respond, "Nice to meet you. I'm Mark." I do not tell her why I am on this plane or what my destination is.

There is a violent thunderstorm as people board the plane. The raindrops smash into the windows and fuselage and glisten in the different colored airport lights, making it appear a little festive. It is dark outside but not because of the time of day; it is just early afternoon. A flash of lightning briefly lights up the sky followed by the rumble of thunder. This flight will now be delayed.

I seriously wonder if and when we will be able to take off. The thought is answered by the soothing voice of the captain with a southern accent. When the PA system springs to life, he shares that the tower has been kind enough to inform him that due to the current weather conditions outside—meaning this nasty thunderstorm—our flight will be delayed approximately twenty minutes. I look out the window and give a little chuckle. The pilot continues, "The tower has assured me this storm is a fast mover. Thanks in advance. We should be underway to South Carolina in about 20 minutes." The stewardesses walk the aisles attending to the passengers.

After about twenty-five minutes, there is no letup in the storm. Lightening brightens the outside every couple of seconds, as thunder continues to rumble. Surprisingly, the passengers all seem to be content to sit as the storm lingers. The captain then makes a second announcement and tells everyone the delay should not be much longer, and because of the present inconvenience, the stewardesses will be offering complimentary drinks while we remain on the ground.

Anna Wright orders a scotch straight up and drinks the first one pretty quickly. She begins to squirm in her seat as if she is looking for something she forgot at home. The plane immediately goes into party mode. Anna orders another drink as soon as she gets the attention of the stewardess. Our delay reaches forty-five minutes when the captain announces we have been given permission to push away from the gate.

The plane is pushed away from the gate, taxis to a position near a runway, and parks. The storm has only shown slight signs it is letting up. I count twenty-four planes on the taxi runway and can see they are not moving. I look around the plane. I must admit the people and the party atmosphere are kind of interesting. Anna is on scotch number three, and it appears the storm is slowing down with some of the skies clearing.

I am totally not prepared for what is about to take place on this flight. It is obvious old Anna has had a few cocktails and a transformation is taking place. Now, I have never seen this woman before today and will never see her again, but she will live in my memory forever. This flight from New York's JFK airport non-stop to Charleston, South Carolina is about to become remarkably interesting.

The rain and complimentary beverages continue to flow while the plane remains parked. The voice of the captain again quiets the crowd. "Well, ladies and gentlemen, we have a small window here where this plane may be able to take to the air and get out of this airport soon." He gives the normal instructions to the crew to prepare for departure, and then it is quiet. The stewardesses scramble to clear the cabin. They collect the drink cups and move through the aisles, issuing final instructions.

The cups, cans, and waste from all those complimentary beverages are finally collected. The powerful jet engines are all now running as we are in the queue, ready to take off. One by one, the rumble of a jet racing down the runway can be heard. We make our way to the main runway, and the plane makes the U-turn onto the takeoff path. We are finally cleared for takeoff. The engines roar to full throttle, pushing the plane down the runway and into the air. Once we are airborne, the passengers begin to applaud.

Anna Wright springs to life as the landing gear doors close. "Stewardess," she calls out in this shrill old voice. "Stewardess," a second louder impatient scream, and then a third "STEWARDESS," with of course, each one getting louder. I look at her and politely ask if there is any way I can help. That blue haired, old lady grandmother looks me in the eye and indignantly states, "Are you a stewardess?" To which I say, "Nope" while shaking my head in the negative. "Then you can't help me," she proclaims, as a little spittle drips down her chin.

As if to save me, the stewardess arrives. She is this pretty, petite blond with a sweet southern accent. "Yeeess, Ma'am, and what can I do for you?" Anna requests another scotch. As this one is no longer complimentary, Anna begrudgingly reaches into her purse for some cash. She hands it to the stewardess and says, "Now take those pretty little feet and bring my drink back here as quickly as you can, my dear." Anna begins to mumble because the stewardess is not moving fast enough. She speaks loud enough so I can hear her say, "What does someone have to do to get a drink around here?" Anna, the calm little grandma, is gaining altitude right along with the flight as it reaches the cruising height of 30,000 feet. She growls, "This god-damned flight is late," as the mumbling becomes louder. Anna continues, "Now they aren't going to bring me my drink," she says, squirming in her seat.

The plane is starting to roll and bump as it struggles through some turbulence. The storm is not going away. "Stewardess," the screeching voice cries out again. Fortunately, the stewardess is only a couple of steps away from our seats as she arrives with the drink, and grandma is calm again. Johnnie Walker is the savior of the moment.

The ride is now getting much bumpier. I look around and can see the beginning signs of motion sickness in the passengers' faces. It's still raining, and there is the occasional flickering of lightning. A woman two seats in front of me has reached for, and is starting to unfold, an airsickness bag. I can hear a mother trying to comfort her toddler, brushing the child's hair with her hand, whispering, "It's okay, everything is going to be alright." It has now become obvious motion sickness is going to be a big part of this flight. There is the guttural sound of someone dry heaving and then another in a different area of the plane. The passengers are now vomiting. The woman who has just reached for the bag has it opened with her face buried in it. She begins to vomit, one heave, a second heave, and then a third before she is finished. She looks up, wiping the corner of her mouth and lets out a groan. Someone else further back is throwing up.

The flight continues getting bumpier, and the wing of the plane is wagging like a bird as it is trying to gain altitude. We go up a little, bump, and then down we go. My face is pressed against the window, so I don't see what is going on inside. I can see the strobe light at the end of the wing flashing and imagine it is a signal calling for help. The plane is groaning and fighting the weather. I sit calmly, just hoping I do not get sick.

The stewardesses move quickly through the cabin, helping as many people as possible. Anna is calmly sipping her drink and reading a book. Most of the passengers on this plane now have their faces buried in airsickness bags. The complimentary drinks are flowing again in the opposite direction. The plane now reeks of the pungent odor of vomit. I happen to see the woman I had seen filling the airsickness bag. She is trying to make her way to the restroom. I give her a smile as if to say I feel sorry for you.

I unbuckle my seatbelt and start to stand. I grab the two airsickness bags that are in the seat pocket. Anna looks at me in a peculiar way while saying, "You're not sick, are you?" I shake my head no and tell her there are other passengers who need the bags. Anna and I don't seem to be bothered by the ups and downs of this flight. I make my way to the aisle and hold out the bags as if to offer them and immediately see a businessman in a center seat waving to me. He is squirming in his seat, and the bag reaches him just in time. I go down to the galley and inquire if I can help.

The stewardesses have their hands full but tell me to return to my seat. They thank me for the little help I have given. I return but notice most of the passengers have their faces buried in bags. I am beginning to have a different feeling about flying and wonder if this flight is an omen of what is about to come.

Anna screams for the stewardesses two more times before we arrive in Charleston, South Carolina. I feel fortunate not to have gotten sick on this flight. The Charleston airport is the first stop of my new adult life. This is the receiving station where I will catch a bus to take me to the United States Marine Corps training at Parris Island, South Carolina.

People have asked me, "Why would you choose the Marine Corps?" I tell them simply the Corps is already a part of me. My mother met my father while they both served in the early 1950s. I have an older brother who is now serving. I truly intend on making the military work for me for the rest of my life.

After leaving the plane, I am directed to a small receiving area in the airport separate from the main terminal, which has three rows of seats waiting patiently for someone to occupy them. This is my first stop in the Marine Corps.

The airsick passengers have no desire to sit anywhere after that flight. All these passengers are interested in is heading into the closest restroom. All those complimentary drinks wasted. I can't seem to get the pungent odor of vomit out of my nose.

# CHAPTER 2

# I HAVE ARRIVED

There is a Marine sergeant sitting at a desk. Behind the desk above his head is a bright red sign with huge yellow lettering pronouncing: "ALL MARINE RECRUITS CHECK IN HERE." The Marine who is sitting there is dressed in blue trousers with a red stripe running along the outside seam of each leg. A three-inch-wide white belt is around his waist. The belt buckle is a shiny brass buckle emblazoned with the Marine Corps emblem. The uniform shirt is beige with short sleeves and sergeant stripes with crossed rifles. His military creases are so sharp they could cut paper.

I approach this man to hand him the packet of paperwork I was given by my recruiter, Sgt. Philip B. Cease. He instructed me before I departed that this desk would be here. I walk up to this Marine and introduce myself. "I'm a Marine recruit from Connecticut, and here are my recruitment papers." He looks at me while sorting through the papers. He keeps some of them, signs some more, and hands some of them back to me. He states, "So you're here from Connecticut?" but does not give me time to answer. "You are the first one here. Welcome to Marine Corps Recruit Training. As soon as there are enough of you recruits here to fill a bus, I will make an announcement. Until then, you can have a seat right over there." While he points to the empty seats, he continues to speak, "The bus only holds about 40 people, and all the flights will be arriving shortly." He points to a row of vending machines and says, "If you are hungry, the GI Dunk machines have just about everything in them." This is the first time I hear a vending machine called this. The vending machines are lovingly referred to by this name by Marines. It is because of the sound they make when the handle is pulled out and the product is dispensed into the bottom tray. Ah, those good ole GI Dunks!

He finishes checking my paperwork, signs his name on some, and then hands it back to me. He tells me I'm all set, and I take a seat in the back row all by myself. I sit and people watch when a trickle of Marine recruits begins to make their way to check in. A tall black man wearing a green shirt with white trousers is first to arrive. Two guys wearing cowboy boots and Stetson hats are next. Increasingly, more people arrive. One recruit is wandering around aimlessly, staring at the ceiling. He carries a briefcase. The Marine sergeant is not checking any recruits in at this moment, so he looks at the young man and asks if he needs help. It turns out this young man is a Marine recruit. I can't help but listen to the conversation taking place.

This young man is from Texas and has come here with four other recruits. He has been given all the paperwork for all four of them. They have been separated, and he does not want to check in until they are all together again. He is avoiding answering the sergeant's questions by giving evasive answers. He has a thick Texas accent. The Marine sergeant asks him directly, "Are you a Marine recruit headed to Parris Island?" He answers, "Yes sir, I have joined the Marine Corps." The sergeant replies, "What's in the briefcase?" The response from the Texan, "My lunch."

Just then the three friends showed up. All of them are about to get a greeting from an angry Marine sergeant who does not appreciate the sarcastic response he just received from an eighteen-year-old kid who needed his help. The tongue-lashing is just a preview of what we all are about to endure.

Finally, there is the required number of people to fill the bus. Just like on the plane, a public address system grabs my attention. It is the voice of the sergeant who had checked me in. "Will all the Marine recruits please make your way to the exit? The bus transporting you to Parris Island has arrived."

The bus is a non-descript older bus with the destination sign simply proclaiming: "Charter." We all begin lining up to board the bus. There are young men from all over the country. It is a mix of black and white, tall and short, fat and thin, just about any description one can imagine. One of these men will forever stick in my memory. He is a black man dressed in a three-piece crushed velvet suit. The maroon-colored suit is topped off with a white fedora and finished off with a white necktie and shoes. This kind of clothing is something I would never have expected on a Marine Corps Base.

The bus is filled, and everyone is seated. It pulls away to the airport exit. There is not an interstate highway. But the roadway has several lanes, so the bus moves along quickly. I am seated next to a young man by the name of James Jones from New York. We introduce ourselves and talk a little. He never makes it out of receiving into my platoon, and I never see him again. The ride is inconsequential as I sleep on and off most of the way there. This is the last leg of the trip to boot camp. I wake up to the bus driver announcing we will be arriving in approximately ten minutes. I try to wipe the sleep out of my eyes and stretch my arms and legs the best that I can. I look out the window and can see the main gate to the base.

The drive through rural South Carolina from the airport was quiet and subdued. Now that the bus is close to Parris Island, there is stirring in the seats. It is still dark, and most of the men have been trying to sleep. The lights to the main gate are now coming into view.

The inside of the bus is springing to life. Some of the future Marines are running from one side to the other, trying to absorb everything they are about to experience. Many, including myself, are apprehensive about what we are about to learn.

# CHAPTER 3

# PARRIS ISLAND

The main gate has a guard shack in the middle of the road that separates exiting and entering traffic to the base. There are three Marines standing by this guard shack who watch as the bus enters. I read the lips of one of them as we pass, and he appears to be saying, "Poor bastards."

The bus crosses over a bridge, drives on for about two more minutes, and comes to a stop in a large, paved parking area. I can't help but wonder why the Marine at the gate would say "Poor bastards," but I am soon going to find out. There is a large group of Marines milling around outside, apparently awaiting our arrival. People on the bus are making small talk and cracking one-line jokes. Some of them are smoking cigarettes. I can see the expression on the bus driver's face, and it is priceless as he starts to snicker. He stops the bus, announces that we are to remain seated, and then opens the door and gets off of the bus.

This small Hispanic Marine makes his way onto the bus. This man is dressed in forest green slacks with a beige uniform shirt. There are a couple of expert marksmanship badges on it. Above those are about four rows of ribbons. His head is covered with a green campaign hat with the Marine Corps emblem in the center. He is the sharpest dressed person I have seen in my life.

He makes a sharp military right face movement when he reaches the top of the steps. A hush makes its way through the bus, and it is now quiet. Then in a voice that can only be described as the voice used by a drill instructor, he begins to recite a diatribe that will impact my life forever.

"Now that you gentlemen have shut your sucks and stopped running your jibs, welcome to the Marine Corps Recruit Depot, Parris Island, South Carolina. I have some instructions for you, so pay attention. If you are eating, then finish. If you are chewing gum or smoking, stop and get rid of them. If you are in possession of any drugs, knives, guns, or any other contraband, you should leave it behind right now."

"When I call your name, you will answer in a loud clear voice, 'Sir, here, Sir.' You will then run off this bus over to the yellow footprints painted on the pavement in front of this bus. The drill instructor outside will show you exactly which one you will occupy. If you have a coat or a suitcase, take them with you."

He then begins to call off the names listed on his clipboard. "Armstrong, James B." A voice responds, "Sir, here, Sir" and makes his way off the bus. As soon as the first poor soul puts his foot on the ground, he is enveloped by a wave of green and beige with arms waving and instructions being launched in his direction, forcing him to take his position on these strange yellow footprints that have the heels touching on the inside and the toes facing at a 45-degree angle.

"Ashley, Sean J." "Sir, here, Sir." The next name rings in my ears as I watch these men being forced off the bus one by one and then chased onto a position on these yellow footprints on the pavement, where there would not be much space between each man. This formation would be known as "the asshole to bellybutton" formation.

The calling of the names continues and then "Genovese, Mark R." makes me respond "Sir, here, Sir." I am seated in the eighth seat from the door, but I think I make it there in one giant leap. I have only the clothes on my back, and when I hit the bottom step with one foot on the pavement, I am greeted by the blackest face and the whitest eyes and teeth I have ever seen.

I have been watching from inside the bus and know where I need to be within a split second, but I still cannot escape the wave of drill instructors that pursue me, barking out instructions the full 20 yards it takes me to get into the position I need to be in. The hollering and screaming continue until a large enough gathering of men has formed with all the yellow footprints being filled. We resemble some type of herd of humans in a large rectangle. There are approximately eighty of us in this formation. Twenty to twenty-five drill instructors stand around us, still yelling out instructions, trying to make us pay attention to them.

One of them takes charge by getting in front of the formation. He marches us toward a building that is a plain, white wooden structure with green shutters. Somehow, we manage to end up in a single file, entering a door to this building. We are then ushered into a room filled with stainless steel tables with a single red hand painted on them, approximately every three feet apart. These tables are twenty-five feet long. Next to each of the handprints are a piece of stationery, an envelope, and a pen. I could never understand why the red handprint was there or why we had to keep our hand on it.

The drill instructors leave us in this room with one Marine officer who holds the rank of captain. I will learn about his rank insignia later in boot camp. His demeanor is much more reserved than the drill instructors. The room is cramped, and the lighting is poor. The captain explains we are required to write a letter to our parents or our next of kin. This letter is to inform them we have arrived safely at the Marine Corps Recruit Training Facility.

We are now in the processing phase of the training and will be assigned to a training series and platoon within the next couple of days. It takes twelve days before there are enough recruits in our series to begin the training. We are to write this letter while standing with our other hand covering the red handprint painted on the table. There are sample letters on the wall, and he points them out for us to use as reference.

I write this letter as quickly as possible and address the envelope. I fold the letter into the envelope and seal it and then wait for the other recruits to finish their letters. Boot camp will be one of the most life-changing and lifestyle altering events I will ever experience. After everyone has completed the writing of the letter, we are instructed to strip down to our underwear. All our clothing and belongings are then packaged and placed into storage.

I'm now standing in this room with just my Fruit of the Looms, with about 80 other young men. We are then ushered to another room where we remove our underwear and discard it. We take showers, and as we dry off, we move through a line and are given new clothing and uniforms.

The next 48 hours are a blur, but in that time, I have been issued uniforms, some equipment, a bucket, a pair of boots, some sneakers, locks, and a silver-colored helmet liner known as a "chrome dome." We are assigned to the first training battalion, Platoon 180. My senior drill instructor is Sgt. L. Parker, and the assistant drill instructors will end up being Sgt. G. Miner and Sgt. E. Lemmon.

The barracks we are assigned to is a three-story modern building on the edge of the parade deck. I am astonished by the cleanliness and neatness of everything. I will soon learn the base is cleaned as a part of our training. It is close to the central area of the base near the shore. We are herded around the base like livestock, gathering equipment for our training during the first four days.

My family has a tradition of being in the Marine Corps. My uncle was a Marine for thirty-five years; my father, my mother, and my older brother served before I did. Each one of them told me of their experiences while they were in boot camp. They all told me there were things they could not explain. They said there was no way to prepare me for what was about to happen. Each one of them said I would understand once the training was completed.

I am about to understand what each of them has meant. The Marine Corps takes a civilian and completely rebuilds him into something else, a MARINE! So, if you have not been through the training and successfully completed it, you would not know what it means.

I joined the Marines because I just wanted to be a part of something that was important. This was considered the toughest branch of the military services of the United States. I had to prove to myself I had what it took to be a Marine, and a successful one too.

So here I am, this frightened little kid from Connecticut beginning the training to earn the right to hold the title of United States Marine. I haven't really slept in three days. My boot camp experience so far has been nothing like any story I've been told, book I've read, or movie and television show written or broadcast about boot camp I can relate to.

My experience will take me, 18 years old, baby fat, 195-pound weakling and turn me into a tough as leather, highly polished 170-pound man. I would then have the courage and strength to be able to force my mind and body beyond what I previously thought was my breaking point and do things that normally would have been impossible to achieve.

The first thing done by the Marine Corps is to remove your individuality. This is accomplished by dressing every man in the same type of uniform, olive drab green in color. Our heads are then shaved of all the hair. We are formed into a series of four platoons consisting of approximately 100 recruits. My platoon number is 180.

The four platoons are considered a series. Each platoon will compete against each other during the 13 weeks we are at boot camp. There will be a competition for close order drill, final inspection, physical fitness, and the total scores on the rifle range.

The moment you are assigned to a platoon, the training begins. Everyone must speak only when spoken to. Each time you make what is considered a mistake by one of the drill instructors, they instruct you to do some type of physical exercise. The drill instructors of Platoon 180 prefer the bend and thrust. This exercise is a combination of a squat thrust with a push up added.

I participated in high school athletics and considered myself to be in good physical condition when I arrived. Boy, was I wrong. Each recruit is required to submit to a physical fitness test at the start of the training. This test has a minimum passing score, and each recruit is tested in three separate exercises.

Pull-ups are done by grasping the bar and hanging without moving. Then, you are required to pull yourself up so your chin is above the bar. You are not allowed to swing your legs or wiggle your body. A minimum of three pull-ups is required. Each one completed will earn five points. The maximum required is twenty. When you were able to complete twenty, you would earn a maximum score of 100 points. There is no partial credit for attempts and no extra credit if you can do more than twenty.

Sit-ups are done with your knees bent and your hands interlocked and placed behind your head. You are required to complete a minimum of 40 sit-ups in two minutes. The maximum amount is 80 total to achieve the maximum score. The scoring for the sit-ups is one point awarded for sit-ups 1 through 60 and two points each for sit-ups 61 through 80.

The three-mile run is the last phase of the test. The minimum score or time to complete the run is 28 minutes. Completing this run in 18 minutes and under will earn a maximum of 100 points. There is a single point penalty for each 10 seconds increment over 18 minutes until the minimum time of 28 minutes is reached.

The minimum score of 134 is required to continue training with your assigned platoon. When I take this test, I can complete only five dead hang pull-ups. The drill instructors do not count several because I have wiggled or kicked my feet to get over the bar. I can only manage 51 sit-ups. The drill instructor only counts 37 of them, informing me I did not do them the "Marine Corps way." I am stressed because it should have been easy for me to do more of each exercise. I passed the first two phases, but just barely. My score is 71 when 134 points are the minimum passing score. Not passing the run will mean I get sent to a physical conditioning platoon.

In a mile run in high school, I was timed at seven minutes and ten seconds. Doing some quick calculations in my head, I determine at that pace I should be able to run three miles in 21 and a half minutes, which is very comfortable under the required minimum of 28 minutes.

I'm still worried because it has been some time since I have run. Suddenly, my senior drill instructor singles me out of the platoon. With his booming voice, he calls out, "Private Genovese, I thought you were an athlete!" I don't answer, and he continues, "You better run your little Yankee ass off, or you'll be sent to PCP." I know what PCP is because my brother told me about it. PCP stands for Physical Conditioning Platoon. If you are sent to this unit in boot camp, you will be assigned to another platoon and remain here longer. I have no clue why he has singled me out.

We then march in formation to a track, which is a standard quarter of a mile in length and oval shaped. The entire platoon is lined up together at the starting line. I squeeze my way as close to the front as I can when the drill instructor yells out, "Ready, Set, Go." The mass takes off running, pushing, shoving, and maneuvering for position.

A group of about ten recruits break from the pack at a sprint. I head for an outside lane. These sprinters separate from the pack quickly, but there is no way they will be able to continue this pace. I think about keeping a seven-minute pace and move to an outside lane away from the bumping and pushing.

The sprinters continue to separate themselves from the main group, and a third group of stragglers is beginning to form. The platoon begins to stretch out after the third lap. There are three distinct sections running separately. The sprinters, but they have slowed, the main pack, and about eight stragglers. After lap three, I have gotten my second wind. There is a group of about five of us that seem to have a rhythm going and begin to pace each other.

We all begin talking to each other, and it becomes apparent we have some experience running, either from school or as a hobby. We all continue together, encouraging each other to finish strong, mostly to the end of the three miles. To my surprise, the run is completed in a time of 19 minutes 25 seconds, giving me a total score of 92 points for the run.

I am totally surprised and end up with a total score of 163, but I could always run. Running would prove to help me on more than one occasion in the future. This was about 30 points over the minimum acceptable score and more than the minimum for each individual exercise, but just barely.

The drill instructor who singled me out prior to the run does not say anything to me in front of the platoon upon completion of the run or single me out the rest of that day. I am not proud of my performance. I vow it is the lowest score my platoon and drill instructor will see from me. I am beginning to regret not doing more to prepare for this during the summer.

That night before lights out, the drill instructor who had singled me out, has me report to his office. When I report to him, he informs me he has read my file and is aware my family has a history in the Marine Corps, which is why he singled me out. He does not intend on singling me out anymore, but he expects more from me and intends on pushing me harder than most of the other recruits in the platoon. Sgt. Minor then assigns me the nickname "Smiley" because he saw me smiling as I crossed the finish line of the timed three-mile run.

Push me he does, until the final physical fitness test when I complete 15 pull-ups, 80 sit-ups in the required two minutes, and 19 minutes flat on the three-mile run. The final score was 269, not the best in the platoon, but in the top five in the final test before graduation.

The Marine Corps structures the recruit training so every individual experiences the same thing. We are still human beings, and there are two incidents unique to my experience in boot camp. The training follows what every other Marine goes through. When you make a mistake, you pay with sweat and a little bit of pain. The platoon suffers along with you. There is an extreme emphasis on the "TEAM" concept of doing things.

The first incident occurs on the fifth day of training in our barracks. A recruit who should not have been at Parris Island in the first place has a problem with two of our drill instructors. This recruit doesn't know his right hand from his left. He will not follow the drill instructor's orders or commands, and it appears that intellectually he is a little on the slow side. He is instructed to do some simple drill movements and is not able to. The two drill instructors believe he is being belligerent. Then he stops doing anything and begins to cry.

When he starts crying, the two drill instructors begin to yell and scream at him. He tries to run away from them out of the barracks. He claims these two drill instructors beat him when he tried to run away. There is an investigation. I never saw either of the drill instructors lay a hand on him.

When the Marine Corps removes him from our barracks, he is escorted by two military police officers. There are several members of our platoon who are taken away that same day. The other platoon members return later that day. They are all interviewed by a Marine officer about the actions of the two drill instructors and their treatment of the recruit who was mistreated. I will never see him or the two drill instructors again.

The other thing that makes an impression on me is time on the rifle range. Marines are known for their marksmanship. Whether you are serving as an infantry soldier or a helicopter pilot, you are required to qualify with the standard issue rifle at the time of your service.

The rifle becomes an extension of you. Each of us is required to name our rifle, sleep with it, and learn everything there is to know about it. We drill with it, take it apart, and put it back together thousands of times. We do this in the dark, in the light of day, outdoors, indoors, repeatedly, until it is impossible to forget.

This is one more piece of my training that would influence my future profession in the field of law enforcement. All firearms would become important to me. The Marine Corps will train me on several other types of small arms, and I make it a point to learn as much as I can about the M-16a1 assigned to me. She is named Sophia.

As boot camp continues, my body changes. I continue to improve in the physical fitness phase of training. I would go on to earn the maximum score of 300 points three times while serving on Marine Security Guard duty. My time in boot camp is like any other experienced by Marines. This is all I will say about it now. Embellishments regarding boot camp will be brought to light later.

Upon graduation from boot camp, I am promoted to private first class and assigned a Military Occupational Skill (MOS) of 2531, Radio Operator/Repairman. The advanced training takes place at a small training facility by the name of Camp Geiger, Montford Point, North Carolina, near Camp Lejeune. When training is finished, my assigned unit is the Second Tank Battalion.

Prior to reporting to Camp Lejeune, I am given ten days leave, so I head for home. When I arrive home, I learn my weight has gone from 196 pounds to a slim 165. None of my clothes fit me. The Levi's blue jeans that were snug and difficult to get fastened now will not stay up on my waist.

# CHAPTER 4

# THE NEXT PHASE
# OF TRAINING

The stretch waist gym shorts I wear to workout in are useless. T-shirts drape over my shoulders like curtains covering a stage. I can only wear the uniforms issued to me in boot camp. Marine Corps regulations do not allow me to wear my utility uniform in public.

I only go out of the house in the dress green uniform. There are mixed feelings regarding the wearing of the uniform. There is a large segment of the population tired of the war. Many people are also against the Vietnam War. Until I have time to shop for new clothing, I will have to remain in the uniform. I am proud of the uniform and am not ashamed to wear it in public.

I am a Marine and proud of what I have accomplished to this point. My life is about to change for the better, and I am able to drive my brother's car left at our house while I am home. It is a 1964 Ford Thunderbird two-door coupe. The motor is a 389 cubic inch monster with a four-barrel carburetor. It is known to stall on occasion for no apparent reason. The engine easily restarts most times.

The first day I return, I go directly to my girlfriend's house. I pick her up and intend to drive to a store. While we are in the car, there is an intersection that is one of the heaviest traveled in our town. The intersection is Quinnipiac Ave. and Middletown Ave. When we approach the intersection, the traffic signal turns red. As I bring the car to a stop, the engine stalls. I attempt to restart the engine before the overhead signal changes to green, but the Thunderbird's engine will not turn over.

Directly behind me is a carload of high school-aged boys who are anxious to get moving. The driver of that car starts to sound the horn continuously. There are five people in this car, each one yelling at me. They want the T-Bird out of the way. Their shouts start to get louder and are filled with obscenities.

My girlfriend sees I am becoming frustrated and angry at the car for the predicament it has put me in. I know these kids do not know what is going on. I decide to get out and ask for their help. I open the door, and as soon as I do this, Kathleen grabs my arm. She asks me not to do anything to the people in the car. I look her directly in the eye, shake my head, and stand in the roadway.

As soon as I am standing up all the way, I look back at the car beeping the horn. When I do, all of the young men immediately become silent. Each one of them starts to slink down into the seats. I read the driver's lips and see him mouthing the words, "Oh, shit. That's a Marine."

I have no intention of doing any harm to these boys. I simply want their help to push my car out of the intersection. The way they have been yelling at me, they probably believe I am looking for a fight. That is the furthest thought from my mind.

I walk back to his car and simply say to the driver, "My car has stalled. Do you think you guys could help me push it to the parking lot across the street?" All five of them enthusiastically start to exit the car. They are more than happy to help. My girlfriend steers the T- Bird into a nearby parking lot. There is a Dairy Queen ice cream store there. I offer to buy all of them an ice cream, but they refuse. They thank me and quickly leave.

This is my first encounter where the mere fact I am dressed as a Marine has a direct effect on the outcome of the event. I do not know how they would have treated me had I just been dressed in jeans and a T-shirt. It certainly impresses the hell out of my girlfriend.

The Marine Corps has determined I am best qualified to be a radio operator/repairman because I show an aptitude for electronics, or so says my test scores. I reason it has everything to do with the fact every adult male related to me is a commercial electrician, including my father and grandfather.

I cannot stand the thought of electricity or anything involving it. I enlisted in the Marines to separate myself from that family business and career. My future career aspirations are leaning toward law enforcement. Prior to enlisting, some police officers explained to me an option to attending college could be a stint in the military.

The training I receive is the most basic training imaginable in radio operation and repair. I am taught the Marine Corps way to communicate on a radio system. They focus on the accessories, batteries, microphones, antennas, mounts, and radio types, and how to keep them dry and working.

Oh yeah, the most important issue I have learned at training is to hope you never see combat. Radio operators are the most targeted individuals on the battlefield. More radiomen are killed in combat than any other Military Occupational Skill (MOS). Not infantrymen, not 90-day wonder lieutenants; the radiomen are number one. I guess I've finally made it to the front of the line, and I don't really like the view. The training is complete after an eight week-long course.

Radio operators normally receive assignments to a company in the battalion; however, the companies are all at full strength. The radio platoon is a dumping ground and a repair shop. It is the place for those of us who are just starting out in the profession and the short timers to have a place to work.

The repair shop is really kind of useless because Marines who work in battle tanks do not just break something so it can be repaired. Mangle, demolish, destroy, make something unrecognizable, turn something useful into something useless. But just bring a radio or one of the many accessories to be repaired? That wasn't something that would happen very often.

I am working in the radio platoon for about a week when I determine there must be something more suitable and productive in the Marine Corps I could be doing. Our days are spent inventorying radio gear or conducting preventative maintenance on radios.

The way the Marine Corps decides is the most economical way to prevent corrosion from occurring on radio connections is to have the radio operators use pencil erasers to clean the connections. Every morning, I report to work armed with my pencil eraser. Then, I clean antenna or microphone radio connections.

There is an unwritten rule that every Marine learns quickly and knows the rule is "Never volunteer for anything." When a senior Non-Commissioned Officer (NCO) or an officer walk into a room and proclaims, "I need a volunteer" or asks, "Who wants to volunteer?" you should keep your mouth shut, hide if you can, or do whatever is necessary to avoid volunteering.

Well, I have a different plan in mind. I am going to see how many assignments and training classes I can get away with going to and continue to keep my seniority and still receive promotions. I didn't join the Marine Corps to erase corrosion. I am also seeking to avoid military punishment.

The first opportunity to volunteer comes after my second full week of work has been completed. The platoon sergeant asks for a volunteer at the morning roll call. What I volunteer for is a two-week training program that will allow me to obtain a military operator's license for Jeeps and pickup truck-sized vehicles.

This training is conducted in the Second Tank Battalion motor transport area and does not require my leaving. Over the course of this training, I become trained on how to change the tires, the oil, the batteries, all of the fluids, or any bulbs in need of replacement, and how to install the radio mounts.

When I return to the radio platoon because of my extensive training and knowledge, I am assigned to install radio mounts on twelve new jeeps. That assignment lasts for approximately two weeks. The monotonous routine of cleaning and required preventative maintenance of the radio gear takes over.

The first sergeant calls the entire company together after noon chow (lunch) one day and requests to have one man volunteer to receive training as a basic lineman. Not one person in the entire company steps forward to volunteer. This is normal for Marines, due to that unwritten rule. The first sergeant informs everyone he will choose someone to go.

When he dismisses the company to their normal duties, I approach him on my own. I tell him I will attend the training if it is at all possible. The first sergeant looks at me and says, "I am pretty sure you can't be sent because you already have a MOS in the communications field." I suggest he could propose he wants to have his Marines cross-trained to make them better prepared.

I am dismissed from his office and head back to work. Later that week, the first sergeant hands me a set of orders, sending me to lineman training. I will be away from tanks for two weeks back at Montford Point. I successfully complete this abbreviated training and the merry-go-round continues.

I can now wear gaffs (a metal spike you strap to your leg that allows you to climb utility poles) and string wires, but nothing changes when I return to the radio platoon. Every morning after chow, we hold morning muster outside our barracks. We board troop transport trucks that drive us to work. Each company and platoon has their own individual truck, except for the radio platoon.

We have no specific transport due to the transient configuration of our group. One day, there is not enough room for all the Marines to be safely transported. There is now a need to have someone attend training for the operation of the troop transports. I believe it is a waste of time to occupy my day just sitting around, so I volunteer for another two-week training program. And I am now able to drive all the vehicles used to transport troops. A promotion to lance corporal accompanies school graduation. It also carries with it certain fringe benefits.

This turns out to be the last training assignment I am sent on while assigned to the Second Tank Battalion. The troop transportation Marines are able to go to the chow hall early and are never required to clean the barracks or common areas. I always have transportation to go anywhere on base at any time. The only training I receive will be with my entire unit. There will be several battalion training assignments occurring within the next four months.

A little-known fact about the Second Tank Battalion motor transport section is it is the first Marine Corps unit to have trucks painted in the woodland camouflage pattern. One of our trucks is used in a television show with that woodland camouflage pattern, and we are used as extras during the filming of that show.

The entire Second Tank Battalion is scheduled for two weeks at the rifle range. The Marine Corps prides itself on the marksmanship of each individual member. Every Marine is required to qualify with the rifle every year. This is the first time I am required to shoot at a target 500 yards away.

I qualify with the M-16 as an expert with a score of 225 out of a possible 250. I hit the target on all ten rounds from 500 yards. Firearms and shooting will become a big part of my life in the future.

When the training is finished, I go home because it is the weekend of my girlfriend's high school senior prom. I am going with her and will be wearing the dress blue uniform. The Marine Corps dress blue uniform is one of the most impressive military uniforms to look at.

I am the only military person at this affair. Everyone is impressed with the transformation I have made. My girlfriend is now beginning to press me to plan for the future. She starts to talk about marriage and starting a family. I am in love with Kathleen and am at this point in my life planning on marrying her sometime in the near future.

# CHAPTER 5

# SECOND TANK BATTALION

Duration my time at Camp Lejeune, I have grown accustomed to some of the things that make life easier. We have a typical coffee set up for men who consume large amounts of coffee. And I enjoy a good cup of coffee in the morning.

One typical morning while at work, a Marine who is from a southern state, asks me if I would like to have a cup of coffee. I tell him, "Sure, make it with cream and sugar." After 30 minutes, he has not returned with any coffee. I go inside to see what the delay is and see he has removed his boot and sock. He has filled his sock with coffee beans and is smashing them with a hammer. I leave before he notices I am watching him. He takes the smashed coffee beans and dumps them into the percolator. When he finally brings me the finished product, I politely accept it. That coffee never makes it into my mouth. As a result of the way he prepared it, I refuse to drink coffee to this day.

I am settling into the life of the military. The threat of having to be sent to Vietnam has just about disappeared. Life in the Marines is becoming easy. I am summoned to the career planner's office.

It is routine for the military to counsel all the members to keep them satisfied. This career planner has obviously been aware of my volunteering for all the different trainings.

The gunnery sergeant who holds this position at the Second Tank Battalion is one of the saltiest men I have ever seen. His chest is full of ribbons and a set of jump wings, rifle, and pistol expert badges, and his hash marks almost meet his stripes. His hair is in an extreme high and tight hair cut style with no gray hairs. If a human being could be considered the perfect specimen of a Marine, this is the man.

When I report to him, I make sure I am wearing a fresh, starched utility uniform. As I am reporting, he greets me in a way I do not expect. He jumps up eagerly, addresses, and treats me as if I am an officer. He scrambles to his feet with his hand outstretched to shake mine.

The greeting is one that has stuck with me from the moment he said it. "So, Lance Corporal Genovese, what is it you don't like about the Second Tank Battalion, or is it my Marine Corps you are not happy with?" These remarks catch me completely off guard and by surprise. I have been at Camp Lejeune now for almost four months. I have done everything that has been asked of me. There is nothing bad on my service fitness report I know of. I respond, "I like the Marine Corps just fine, Gunny." He immediately cuts me off and asks, "So what do you have against radios? Well, you sure are spending a lot of time away from those radios." Hesitantly I tell him, "You see, Gunny, it's like this. I never thought operating and repairing radios meant sitting for hours with a pencil eraser rubbing the corrosion off brass contacts. That and the fact that radios involve electricity. I joined the Marines to get away from electricity."

He laughs loudly and tells me he was markedly bored during his first year and at his first duty station also. He explains he understands what I am doing, but my tactics could have both good and bad consequences for me. We carry on about what training I've received and my family history. The conversation moves along, and he mentions the Marine Security Guard (MSG) program.

He explains the Marine Corps is responsible for providing security for all of the United States embassies and consulates throughout the world. This is my introduction to the MSG program. This program is reserved for the top 15 percent of the Marine Corps. I am again shocked that the career planner believes I should be considered for a position like this. What this means is I would be considered for a position usually reserved for individuals who are intent on staying in the military for life. I would be considered for a position normally reserved for Marines who have more experience. I have not even been in uniform for a year yet.

The requirements for me to be considered for this assignment are complex, but he is positive about submitting my name for consideration. The major factors to be considered are in my favor, however. First, I must have at least three years left on my enlistment time. Second, I would have to waive the requirement allowing Marines to stay on an assignment overseas for longer than one year. Third, the fitness report scores had to be in a certain range. The final and most important requirement was, when chosen, one could not be or get married in the program.

"When can I sign up?" is my response after this statement is made. We continue the discussion and determine all qualifications are met. There is some paperwork completed and signed. This is an official request for transfer from my unit, which requires more review from my company officers. If I am accepted, I will be transferred to the Marine Security Guard School at Henderson Hall, Headquarters, Marine Corps, Washington, D.C.

He dismisses me from his office, wishes me good luck, and warns me to stay out of trouble. I am not to ask for any further extra training, just return to my unit and do my job! The next couple of months are probably going to test my patience.

It is now May, 1975. There will be some difficult challenges placed in front of me that will certainly test if I am ready for MSG duty. I have officially been given the assignment of troop transport driver. There is not much happening in our platoon until the end of March.

Home and the friends I have left in North Haven are on my mind often. I wonder what most of them are doing while I am working and training as a Marine. I try to stay in touch with them by writing letters. So far, this is nothing like I thought my time would be.

At the present time, the main battle tank maintained and operated by the Marine Second Tank Battalion is the military designation M-48 Patton Tank. The battalion has been scheduled to modernize to the M-60 tank. The entire battalion is to receive training and report to Army Base, Fort Pickett, Virginia. There is no need for me to volunteer for this training.

As a result of my assignment as the troop transport driver, I will be assigned a five-ton truck. I will be responsible for driving this truck to the training. A military convoy will leave Camp Lejeune, North Carolina, and travel for what is estimated to be approximately five hours to Fort Pickett, Virginia.

In May 1975, there are few interstate highways, and most of the roadways in North Carolina are only two lanes. In the early morning chilliness, it is not unusual to have patchy fog most days. Today, the air is chilled, and there is little wind.

Fifteen military trucks now fully loaded with supplies sit parked, while the men of the Second Tank Battalion are joined by ten jeeps that are awaiting instructions in a staging area at the base. The convoy will be led by a jeep driven by Sergeant Louis MacArthur, a southerner from Mississippi. His passenger is a second lieutenant who has been here for less time than I have. He recently graduated from Officer Candidate School in Quantico, Virginia. He is a likable type of person, but Marines with any time in the service and hard corps Marines are absolutely brutal in the way they treat these officers. They commonly refer to them as "Boot Lieutenants," the same as a private who has just come from boot camp. Marines who have been in combat show them the least respect.

There are strict military rules and regulations with regards to the movement of armed troops on roadways located and controlled by local and state authorities. When a military vehicle is being operated within the confines of a base, they operate under the same rules of the road, but there are fewer restrictions.

When off base, we would form into a convoy, which would have a lead vehicle. In our case, it is the jeep that was mentioned earlier. This jeep would be marked on the front and rear with signs that read "CONVOY FOLLOWS." These signs are painted bright yellow and orange, so they are highly noticeable.

The next three vehicles in the convoy will be a standard five-ton military transport loaded with ammunition for the main gun of a standard battle tank. In this case, it is a 105mm cannon round. Each truck is loaded with approximately 50 rounds in the truck and another 20 in the trailer they are towing. The next vehicle in line is the same type of truck, but the payload is thousands of rounds of .50 and .30 caliber machine gun ammunition.

I am the next vehicle in line and have no idea what is behind me. My truck is just loaded with radios and radio supplies. There is one passenger with me, Tommy Boyle, a private first class from Oklahoma, also a radio operator. He is armed with an M-16 rifle because some of the gear I am transporting is classified. There are also two armed Marines in the rear of the truck.

We are formed into sections in the staging area and given orders and instructions. My vehicle will be the fifth truck in the line of the convoy when we mount up and leave. The diesel engines all spring to life with their distinctive whistling sound. All the trucks fall into line as the convoy snakes its way out of Camp Lejeune.

I have mentioned before, on these cool mornings in North Carolina, there is usually a patchy fog. Well, today is no exception. At 0500 hours, most of the area around the base is encapsulated in fog. Most of the base is either surrounded by swamps or marshlands. Outside of the base, there is mostly farmland, and the farmers are always burning brush. This causes the fog to be a thick, dense smoggy mixture.

The convoy has completely left the area of the base making their way slowly through the rural back roads of North Carolina. For a brief period, there is a break in the soupy air, the fog is gone, and the speed we are traveling begins to increase. Suddenly, as if some supreme being covered the area with a thick quilt, there is little light at all. There is also the putrid smell of old tires being burned, filling the olfactory senses.

Visibility has been reduced to inches in seconds. Common sense screams I need to slow down. Suddenly, the brake lights to the trailer and the truck in front of me are illuminated, but there is something wrong. The lights to the trailer are going in a different direction than the lights on the truck. Smoke is billowing from the tires as the brakes are locked in a panic skid. This is not good, and I begin braking and downshifting the truck.

I've also locked up my brakes but still have control heading away from the danger in front of me. I downshift again, and the locked brakes release. The entire time my passenger is screaming, "Oh my God, Oh my God, Oh my God." I downshift one final time and come to a stop. I fear we will be crushed from behind by the next truck in line. I look at my rider screaming, "We need to get out of here NOW!" I ask him if he is all right, and he nods his head in the affirmative.

When I open my door, two Marines run by me in the direction in front of us where the accident occurred. They are now headed in the direction we have just come from. This is commonly known as a "come to Jesus moment," when you realize the only thing about to save your ass is prayer. While the Marine is running by me, he is screaming, "It's on FIRE!" The truck is on fire in front of me.

I bail out of the cab and grab the fire extinguisher under my seat. While this is happening, another Marine runs by. There is an alarm ringing in my head telling me to follow them and get out of there. Yet, something inside of me has made me run towards danger.

It is apparent now a catastrophic accident has occurred with our convoy. These trucks that have been involved in the collision are carrying the ammunition. Don't ask why, but for some ungodly reason, I ignored the fact these trucks were loaded with live ammunition. I run toward the fire and the wrecked vehicles.

The visible fire is in the first truck, and the impact of the collision has dislodged the front axle and ripped off the passenger side wheel. The hood is mangled and open, exposing the engine to the air. The engine is continuing to run but is obviously wounded and close to death. Six of the eight cylinders are still firing as the wires to the other two have been torn away. Small flashes of flame reach up from under the engine, trying to spring to life and grow.

The cab of this dying beast is free of its pilot, and a quick survey leads to my shutting off the fuel and trying to operate the engine shut off lever. Upon pulling the lever on the dashboard, it comes completely free of the truck, with some loose wires hanging on the end. Needless to say, it does nothing to change what is going on with the engine.

My next move is to remove the pin from the fire extinguisher and put out the fire. The moment the cold CO2 fog from the nozzle contacts the engine, it stops running. Now it is dark, as the smog covers us like a curtain blocking the sun in your bedroom.

Flashlights begin to shine through the smog as the Marines try to regroup. A loud request for more lighting is the first order given by a sergeant who has ordered some of his men to get some flashlights. I head to the front of the truck to see what damage is done to the object he has collided with. There is nothing there, no rock, no other vehicle, nothing.

Marines begin appearing at the crash scene from different directions. Not one of them directly involved in the collision is injured. The lieutenant and sergeant who are in the lead vehicle are the last to appear. The smog is beginning to lift, so we shut the road down. Some light is being shed on how this whole thing occurred.

The lieutenant explains the lead jeep had gotten approximately a quarter of a mile ahead of the convoy when the smog reduced the visibility to zero. The sergeant and he had apparently lived their childhood in the same area in Texas, and they were deep in conversation before realizing they were so far ahead. They both had agreed it was dangerous for the convoy to continue in these smoggy conditions. They pulled the jeep over to what they believed was the side of the road, but they had entered a construction zone and had stopped on gravel in the travel portion of the lane. They left their vehicle and had some flares they were preparing to light to warn the convoy to stop, but they acted too slowly. The driver of the first truck was lighting a cigarette at the exact time they were attempting to light the flares. The first truck collided with their jeep.

They were able to wave their flares after the first collision, but the second truck was not able to stop in time and collided with the trailer of the first truck. The third truck stopped, but the trailer jackknifed. The impact of the collision with the jeep resulted in its total demolition. It was launched nose first into a drainage ditch one hundred feet to the side of the road. The operator of the first truck never applied his brakes, and the collision took place at full speed.

Once the smog cleared and the sun came out, we had one jeep destroyed, one troop transport truck totaled, and a trailer damaged. The loads were distributed evenly among the remaining vehicles. The trip to Virginia was not starting off on the right foot. By the time the accident scene was cleared, the only injury of note was the bruised ego of the newly assigned second lieutenant.

We finally make our way to Fort Pickett, Virginia, without any further incidents. When I first receive orders for assignment to the Second Tank Battalion, there are only approximately twenty-four tanks that could be located on the base. In contrast, at Fort Pickett, there are tanks parked as far as the eye can see. Every variation or type of tank in the United States military inventory can be found here. There are rows upon rows of tanks everywhere, like the parking lot of a new car dealership showing off the inventory.

The barracks are old World War I wooden, two-story structures originally used by horse cavalry. They lack furniture, other than the steel racks used for the bunk beds. The plumbing in most of the structures is in need of service. The heads did not work at all.

This is the perfect place to house Marines. What I have come to learn quickly about the Marine Corps is we must make do with second hand, mostly used equipment.

The Second Tank Battalion is just now switching to the M-60 main battle tank which the Army has been using for ten years. It's like we are getting a brand-new toy to play with. The task at hand is to prepare our headquarters and platoon area to make it livable.

Our first sergeant instructs us to set up radio and field telephone communications between the barracks and headquarters. The second lieutenant insists lines be strung through the roof tops and by using the available telephone utility poles. This will require the stringing of thousands of feet of wire between these areas.

I was just a lance corporal at this point of my Marine career. I take orders from people and am not in charge of anything or anybody. The platoon I am assigned to has been made up of four privates, five privates first class, four lance corporals, three corporals, two sergeants, two staff sergeants, one gunnery sergeant, and one first sergeant.

All the staff NCOs have their own quarters already set up. The two sergeants turn an office at the end of one of the barracks into a private room. The rest of us below the rank of sergeant are required to set up the training facilities prior to attending to the barracks or our personal needs.

The running of the wires between the barracks and the headquarters is going to be handled by me and three other Marines. We are led by Corporal Tolfree, a little black guy from North Carolina whose two front teeth are bright gold. He has the attitude he is the best thing the Marine Corps has ever seen. His military MOS 2511, radio lineman, is the equivalent of a telephone or electric line repairman. He finds joy and satisfaction in the fact he could order the three of us "white boys" around because he outranks us. He is very proud of the fact he is from the south, is in charge, and could make us do anything. I have never experienced anything like this growing up. The boys from the south still do not like us Yankees. They still hold a grudge in 1975, so at times it could be a problem with a black man in charge of three white men. Racism never really affects my thinking or interaction with people like it does with him.

Corporal Tolfree has another issue that affects him; he is deathly afraid of snakes. He even lets us know he needs a warning if anyone sees one. We gather all our equipment together on this day and begin stringing a communication line between the barracks and headquarters. The distance is approximately one quarter of a mile between each point. It is a combination of open terrain and woodlands. We are sure to run into some type of wildlife.

I am going out of my way to try and locate a snake I can use to scare Cpl. Tolfree in some way. I find a small, three-foot-long black snake next to the barracks as we begin to string the line. I hide the snake in a green cotton laundry bag and stow it in the battery compartment of my five-ton capacity truck. Private first class Danny Donnelly and I begin to run a line. The wire spool is set onto a stand in the rear of the truck. This allows it to unwind as the truck moves along slowly.

I put the truck into gear and stretch the line from one roof to the next, stopping to stretch it out and secure connections to each building. We come to a small stretch of woods that divides the command buildings from the barracks. When we get to the woods, we unload the spool and tell Cpl. Tolfree he has to climb one of the trees so we can continue to string the wire through the wooded area.

He is the only man trained as a lineman, other than me. Just before reaching the wooded area, Danny Donnelly is still at the pole we used, making sure the wire is attached. Cpl. Tolfree is more than happy to put on a show though. We finish unloading the spool and unwinding enough wire to get up into the tree and through the wooded area.

Once Cpl. Tolfree has gotten his gaffs and safety harness ready, a group of Marines gather to see what we are doing. I believe someone let everyone know I had captured a snake, and this seems like an opportune time to release it. Cpl. Tolfree climbs the tree to approximately fifteen feet. He ascends to that height slowly and deliberately, announcing what he is doing, such as puncturing the tree with a gaff, moving his safety harness up and securing it, and gaffing the tree repeatedly. Each time, he exclaims how good he is at climbing the tree. He finishes stretching and attaching the wire to the tree. While he is doing his work, I remove the snake from the battery compartment.

It is cold in the compartment, making the snake docile and listless. I place it in the area Cpl. Tolfree will land after his descent. As he starts his way down the tree, he again crows about how good he is at his job. He describes each movement as he gaffes the tree and slides his harness closer to the ground.

Where the pistol comes from, I will never know. I didn't know if he could shoot a pistol or if he was a good shot. I never saw the pistol before, and the poor snake had no chance. It is completely blown apart after the first three shots. There is no need for all eight shots of the magazine to be fired, but they are. Eight is the capacity of one full magazine of a Colt Government 1911A1 .45 caliber handgun.

It isn't the reaction I was hoping to get. I figured a little bit of tip-toeing around, screaming, maybe some running around, or possibly climbing the tree again quickly. Cpl. Tolfree shows me how fun and games can become a serious issue. I think some of the dozen or so Marines that came to see my practical snake joke are still ducking for cover. With the smoke starting to clear, I look over to Cpl. Tolfree. He is looking down for signs of life in the obliterated snake, all the time shaking his head and saying, "I hate god-damned snakes, nasty creatures." His gold teeth glint in the sunlight.

Nothing else is said, and we complete the stringing of the communication wires. The Marines who have come to watch simply disappear. It is a day like any other, and nothing is ever said about the snake or the gun. Cpl. Tolfree has made it very clear he is in charge and prepared for any eventuality.

I will never try to play any other practical jokes on Cpl. Tolfree ever again. We spend eighteen days of training at Fort Pickett. I don't know what became of Cpl. Tolfree or his time in the Marine Corps.

The training at Fort Pickett goes as planned after that day. The radio operators are involved with all facets of the familiarization training on the new tanks. We learn how to start them, drive them, and fire the guns, including the main 105mm cannon and the .50 caliber machine gun.

While on the range one day, the tank crews prepare to fire the main gun. Four tanks are lined up on a firing line, ready to send a large round approximately half a mile away. The instructions given on which targets are to be fired upon come from a control tower, located directly behind the firing line. While the tanks prepare to fire, there is a red flag put in place outside the tank, set into one of the radio antennae mounts. When the crew is ready to carry out the phase of instruction being conducted, they will replace the red flag with a green one. The green flag indicates the crew is ready to fire.

At this time, the crews are preparing the main gun for firing. Suddenly, the range master's voice crackles over the loudspeaker, "Marine tank crews on the firing line, with your .50 caliber machine gun lock and load." There is some confusion inside the tanks now. The tank crews are enclosed in an armored box and unable to see that three white-tailed deer have wandered onto the machine gun range. The range master must have thought "live" targets would serve a better purpose right at this moment.

The .50 caliber machine gun is located on the outside of the tank. It has its own turret and is fired by one Marine inside that turret. Hatches on the tanks begin opening, and Marines start loading belted .50-caliber machine gun ammunition into the "Ma Duse." This is the lovable nickname of the famous firearm.

The three deer now grazing calmly 300 yards away have no idea their day is about to change. The red flags have all been replaced with the required green ones. One Marine opens the hatch on the .50 caliber turret, and one opens the hatch on the main turret, next to the .50 caliber turret. One Marine shoots while the other watches.

The voice of the range master again calls out over the loudspeaker, "All tanks appear to be ready, ready on the right, ready on the left, all ready on the firing line. Engage your targets at 300 yards. Commence firing, commence firing."

The three deer have absolutely no chance of survival from the onslaught these four guns deliver. I'm sure it is a painless, sudden termination of their lives. It is not one of the Marine Corps finer moments. It is extremely impressionable to this eighteen-year-old.

Upon our return to Camp Lejeune, the commanders of our battalion are allowed to grant all of us five days off or leave not charged as official vacation time. A small group, consisting of me and four other Marines, plan a trip to Myrtle Beach, South Carolina. It is an impromptu trip and poorly planned. We throw some clothes into a duffle bag and grab a sleeping bag and some cash. We pile into Private Craig T. Felson's Volkswagen Beetle, and we are on our way. We are just going to rough it for those few days.

We arrive late on a Thursday evening, deciding to camp on the beach, as it is allowed to drive one's vehicles onto the beach. We pick a spot on the beach, grab a cooler full of beer, pitch a small tent, and fall asleep early the first day. It is the perfect place to escape for a couple days, and we are pretty wasted. After a quick barbeque and a few beers, we are all asleep.

The next morning, we awake at sunrise and are joined at our little campsite by a group of college students. The party starts and continues until the supply of beer begins to dwindle. All throughout the day, two people will leave at different times to get food or snacks. When the beer is almost gone, Craig, Danny, and I take the VW Beetle to get resupplied.

Around this time, there is a popular television commercial that plays often. In the commercial, a VW Beetle is driven into the ocean and continues to float and go forward. Well, Marines should never be shown anything like this. They should never be put in the position or given the opportunity to test out or participate in such an exhibit, not when there is alcohol involved. Whoever thought of something like that probably was never around a bunch of idle Marines. This is like putting candy next to an anthill and expecting the ants not to eat it. Given the chance with their sick sense of humor, Marines love nothing more than to break stuff. They want to put everything to the test. Is it tough enough to stand up to a Marine? We talk about the commercial and debate if we want to try it for real. We laugh, trying to talk ourselves out of it. The three of us know deep down it is going to happen. We knew before we left Myrtle Beach, the Volkswagen was going for a swim. Nothing else is said the rest of the beer run.

As we are driving back along the shoreline, the waves are gently rolling onto the shore. Craig is driving his car and looks over at me with this wry smile. Without saying a word, he simply turns the steering wheel and drives straight into the ocean. A wave of water flows over the entire car. The motor continues running with the wheels still turning. The Volkswagen is still afloat with all four wheels now off the ground.

We are now in a boat Craig is attempting to steer, but the current and waves are moving us out to sea. I am laughing so hard I am crying. Danny is a big ball of panic, attempting to get into the front seat. My laughing is becoming harder, and I now think my bladder is going to explode. As the S.S. Volkswagen heads out to sea, the engine begins to spit and sputter, slowly dying. Danny is so scared; he is overcome with panic. He climbs over me and opens the passenger side door. The water rushes into the cabin of the VW, and the car sinks almost immediately. The engine is swamped and stops running. The cruise ends just as fast as it has started. The panic-filled passenger is standing outside in waist deep water.

Craig and I remain in the vehicle just laughing, with the water reaching as high as the seats. I reach into the back and grab two beers. Opening the first, I hand it over to Craig. Then, I open one for myself, take a swig and say, "Well, it floated until nervous Norman had a panic attack." It is hilarious, and both of us start to laugh even harder. We laugh for about five minutes and then decide we should get out.

We finish our beer and determine we should see if we can get the car to the shore. There we are, three wet Marines with a partially submerged car. We find out quickly vehicles are easy to move in the water. We begin to push it towards the shore. A large group of Marines and college students join in and help us push the car all the way to the campsite. We all are snapped back to reality because this Volkswagen Beetle is our only means of transportation back to Camp Lejeune. Craig decides to have the car towed. We pool our money and are able to get bus tickets back to base in time to grab a couple hours of sleep before morning formation on Monday.

Once we return to the Second Tank Battalion, I settle back into a routine as I am responsible for troop transport. The ongoing training and work continue to bore the hell out of me. I think about getting transferred all the time. I read articles in Leatherneck Magazine about the MSG duty. Life continues, and we must keep up our readiness. So we train and maintain our equipment.

I spend some of my weekends traveling home. The Marines at Camp Lejeune travel home by a unique way they call "swooping." You can get a round trip ride with some other Marines to New York City for just $20.00. Some enterprising Marines have purchased GMC Suburban vehicles and vans, load them up at the end of the day on Friday, and drive to the Port Authority Bus terminal in New York City.

The trucks are crammed full of Marines, and they drive fast to the city. The ride to Connecticut takes between seven to ten hours. Once I am in the city, I jump on a train and am home in an hour. I do this when we have a Monday holiday or get out of work early on a Friday. I connect with a Marine from Brooklyn who does this as a side business. He works a job on post that has 12-hour shifts, Monday through Thursday. He has two brand new Chevrolet Suburban vehicles that have an extra row of seats installed. I decide to take a chance and try this method to get home one weekend.

I have been dating my present girlfriend since March 1974, my senior year of high school. Kathleen is a senior in high school, and I am in love with her. She is the main reason I want to go back to visit Connecticut. The first time I "swoop" home, I don't tell her I am coming. I want to surprise her and just show up at her house.

When I arrive at her house, it is 11:30 pm, and the house is dark. I do not want to bring attention to myself and am reluctant to even knock on the door. Her parents are proud Kathleen and I are together, but I have never shown up at this late an hour before. It all works out though because her older sister arrives from a date. I am let in. The family is happy to see me, and I spend the night. Staying there for the weekend is a great way to divert my attention from the military.

Our battalion is scheduled to participate in some amphibious assault training that will take place over the next couple of weeks. The first week of the training removes us from the Second Tank Battalion, and we are assigned to an AmTrac Unit. These are tracked vehicles that hold six completely equipped Marines and are used for beach assaults. The AmTrac was developed in World War II, making it easier to get armed troops ashore.

They float in deeper water and get over objects a boat would not be able to. Some are also used as support vehicles for tanks. To say they float is a stretch of the word. Like an iceberg, when they are in deep water, two thirds of the vehicle is under the water. They are loaded onto a large ship and disembark from a ship to assault a beach.

Driving around in an AmTrac is fun in a way but very confining. Swimming around in one is very annoying. You are unable to see outside, and the ride is slow and rocky. One can feel the ocean waves, and some of the Marines become seasick. Which means, yes, there is some vomiting involved. The two best things about this training are nobody is shooting at us, and I get to do something different.

For one week, we load up into the ship, get into the AmTrac, assault the beach against an imaginary army, eat some gourmet C-rations for lunch, do a specific type of training that day, set up camp for the night, sleep under the stars, and then do it again the next day. After the AmTrac training, we are assigned back to assaulting the beach with our tanks and other assigned vehicles. For these assaults, we are loaded onto another type of ship known as an LST or Landing Ship Tank. The Marine Corps uses every possible amphibious landing craft or ship made available to complete its mission. The specialty of the Marine Corps is amphibious beach assaults. On this one day, I am assigned to drive a Jeep with a trailer attached.

We load onto the LST and are given instructions how to drive through the surf and up onto the beach. Two vehicles are staged at the front of the vehicle facing forward. When the boat is close enough to shore, the front doors will open to the water, and we will simply drive into the water and up onto the beach.

My jeep is an important piece of equipment as it is fitted with a radio the size of a refrigerator. It takes up the entire rear of the vehicle. This day starts out like any of the other days at the beach. The ships, LSTs, AmTracs and everyone involved line up in the deep water and begin the assault. I have a confident feeling all is well. The fording gear is properly installed. The water could be five feet deep, and the jeep will still be operable.

This jeep is going to be used for the main communications system of the headquarters of this mock command center for this make-believe war. Today, we load onto an LST from a dock. My jeep with the trailer is alongside a five-ton truck with a trailer. There are three boats and eight AmTracs in our assault wave.

The objective is to get all the equipment safely to the shore intact. Sometimes these assaults take place while under hostile gunfire. There will be no smoke, no explosions, no gunfire. We are simply going to maneuver this boat as close to the shore as possible and go for a ride through the surf onto the beach, then inland and settle in for lunch.

The boats and AmTracs all line up perfectly as they approach the beach. All of them are perfectly synchronized with each boat, slowing to open the gates and ramps together. There is a perfect view of the shoreline as the order is given to leave the boat. The truck and my jeep leave the boat simultaneously with the truck to the left. I am heading to the right. The jeep hits the water, and an enormous wave envelops it. My left foot is completely off the clutch, and the right foot has the accelerator pinned to the floor. My view is totally obscured by the water, and we are going forward but also deeper into the water.

The jeep is in about eight feet of water, and the fording gear is useless at this point. The motor is still running, but the wheels seem to just be spinning. I try to keep the motor running, but it suddenly shuts off. We have driven into a wave washout approximately ten feet from the shore. The other vehicles continue with their assault and hit the beach.

I'm totally submerged, not moving, and the engine is off. I get my seat belt off and swim out of the Jeep and make my way to the shore. The private who is with me makes it to shore also. I watch as the rest of the assault forces drive off. In the short time it has taken me to get to shore, it becomes apparent no one has seen me sink. Everyone is gone, and the beach is quiet.

I stand there dumbfounded as water drips off my helmet. I'm soaked from head to toe. The private starts to pace back and forth, muttering to himself. The boats have all sailed away, the mock war is in full swing, and I'm wondering what to do. Private Michael James and I are the only ones left on the beach. He starts walking in the direction all the other vehicles went. I convince him the best course of action is for us to stay put. I am sure eventually someone will realize we are missing and come looking for us. We debate about it for several minutes, but the funny thing about the Marine Corps is everyone has a rank so someone will always be in charge to make a decision that the junior ranking Marines will have to obey.

I outrank Mike, so we stay put right where the Jeep sank. It takes about fifty minutes to hear the distinctive sound of a jeep heading toward us. The platoon sergeant is driving, and our platoon commander is the passenger. The tide has receded a little, and the roof of the Jeep is now visible. I have been trying to think of what I am going to say the whole time but am at a loss for words. I stand at attention as the jeep pulls up to us.

I am still wet but have my helmet on. I salute the commander when he exits the Jeep. He is a second lieutenant who is very rigid about military bearing. He returns my salute, looks at me sternly, and asks, "Where is your vehicle, Lance Corporal?" Still standing at attention, I point toward the ocean and say, "Out there, Sir." He looks me up and down and glances toward the ocean. He cannot control himself and begins to laugh. "I guess that is the reason you wouldn't respond to the calls on the radio." He laughingly speaks these words and asks me to explain what happened. While I am telling what happened, the sergeant calls for a recovery team to come and remove the Jeep. He and the sergeant speak, threatening to dock my pay until the Jeep and radio equipment are paid for.

When the jeep is finally recovered, it is determined that on the entire stretch of beach, the water is no deeper than four feet, except the one hole I had driven into. This is the last week I am assigned to the Second Tank Battalion, and it is spent in the field, living in a tent eating C-rations. After the third day of these war games, we are on a lunch break, sitting by the communications tent. I have just finished heating up a delicious, military C-rations meal when I notice a Jeep drive up to where my platoon commander is sitting. There is a driver, a captain I have never seen before, and the battalion career planner gunnery sergeant. The officers exchange military courtesies, and my platoon sergeant and lieutenant have a brief conversation with them. They all then focus their attention in my direction and walk towards my group.

The Marines who I am sitting with all speculate what is going on. One looks at me and says, "What did you do now, Genovese?" A second Marine laughs and says, "They're probably here to take him to the brig for sinking the Jeep." I dismiss both and simply say, "They are not here for me at all. It's one of you criminals they are here for."

I barely get the words out of my mouth when my platoon commander calls out, "Lance Corporal Genovese, front and center." I react to the request without thinking, dropping my C-rats. The small hairs on the back of my neck stand at attention. Little beads of sweat form on my forehead. Maybe I am in trouble for sinking the Jeep, I think to myself. I fidget with my uniform while I walk toward them, hoping I am not in trouble.

As soon as I am in front of them, the captain begins to speak to me, "Lance Corporal Genovese, we have a set of orders for you here. Your request for Marine Security Guard School has been approved." I stand silently at attention, at a loss for words. The captain can see I am wondering what this means to me at this moment. He then hands me a large manila envelope that contains a set of original orders. He explains what I need to do as I start to read the first page. Most of what he is saying is inaudible gibberish or like my mother used to say, "The sound went in one ear and right out the other ear into thin air." I did hear the captain say, "Grab your gear, son. We are here to take you back so you can leave."

I am being transferred. I turn and run back to my tent to pack my gear into my backpack. Two of my friends follow me into the tent. We exchange farewells as they congratulate me and help me pack my gear. My wish has come true. I am being transferred out of the Second Tank Battalion. I am no longer going to be sitting in the repair shop with a pencil eraser, cleaning brass connections on radio equipment.

A sergeant from the radio platoon drives me back to the base. Once there, I return my rifle and other field gear and report to the career planner's office. The gunny is waiting for me with my separation papers for my signatures. He hands me a plane ticket and a check. I am required to report to Washington, D.C., within twenty-four hours. The Marine Corps has arranged a shuttle to transport me to the local airport, where I will take a direct flight to National Airport.

This all happens so fast I have no time to contact any family members or friends. My next contact with them is from Washington, D.C., Marine Security Guard Training at Henderson Hall, Headquarters, United States Marine Corps, located in Arlington, Virginia, just outside of the capital city. My experiences and training as a Marine seem a little odd to me at this point. I am thankful I have not been sent into combat. I am especially grateful the Vietnam conflict has almost completely come to an end. I am looking forward to attending the Marine Security Guard training. I know this will be a plus for my future, either as a Marine or a civilian.

## CHAPTER 6

# MARINE SECURITY GUARD TRAINING

U pon checking into Henderson Hall, there is a large contingent of Marines of all different enlisted ranks who are all directed to an auditorium prior to being assigned a squad bay. This is the first day of the training. We are addressed by a squared away tall, blond first sergeant standing at a podium on the stage. He begins his speech by graciously welcoming us to the training. He tells each of us to first look at the person seated to the right of us. He then says to look at the person seated to the left of us.

He says those two people we just looked at probably will not be there on graduation day. The training we are about to undertake will be thirteen weeks long. This will be the most intensive training one will ever receive. My mind wanders a little when I think, Well, I'm sitting on an aisle seat, so my chances of graduating just increased a hair. The first sergeant continues talking. "You will begin each day at 0500 hours, at which time we will fall out for PT." He begins to explain in fine detail how each minute of the day will be filled with class time and exercises.

We will be subjected to inspections three times a day. The first sergeant goes into detail as to when and where these inspections will take place. He ends his diatribe with an explanation of the process for obtaining a Top Secret clearance. The Federal Bureau of Investigation has already begun the process of completing a full background check on each of us. As he is completing the speech, he directs us to a table located in the front of the auditorium. After his directions, he calls out a sergeant and a corporal to report directly to him. We receive our squad and room assignments. The sergeant and corporal are never seen again after having been dismissed from the program.

It is obvious this is not a place for practical jokes or fooling around. There will be no volunteering for extra assignments here. I concentrate on doing the best I can in every facet of this training. After receiving my room assignment, I unload my gear and claim a bunk. The rest of the day is ours to do with as we wish, so I go for a run.

While I am running, my thoughts drift back to being home. I am taken back to the summer before I graduated from high school. I was in a place where my friends and I would spend much of our time just hanging out. It was deep in a wooded area in town, not visible from any house or road. We had stashed some chairs and a table there to use. We would meet there often and build a simple fireplace to have a campfire. A crystal clear spring-fed brook made its way along the edge. It's a place filled with memories where I would go to clear my head. Today, as I make my way along the fence of the Arlington National Cemetery with no destination in mind, I think about North Haven. I am starting something new, but I can only think of the past.

Suddenly, my mind snaps back to my running as a helicopter flies low overhead. I've run about two miles and decide to turn back. The scenery here is much nicer than anything in North Carolina. I get back to the barracks and meet my bunkmate who is a corporal who has been a Marine for four years. He is an infantryman who has seen some combat. His name is Corporal John Butler from Cincinnati, Ohio.

We talk about each other's personal history and how we ended up here, and then settle in. John has just reenlisted for the first time. He completed a four-year enlistment, serving one year in Vietnam. While there, he was in combat and was awarded a silver star and a purple heart. He does not want to talk about Vietnam. I respect his wishes and never ask him about the war.

MSG training is difficult, to say the least. Each day begins with PT (physical training), beginning with heavy exercising followed by a three-mile run. After showers and personal hygiene, we report for morning formation. Each morning, we are required to report in a different uniform. We are inspected and graded in every facet of those inspections as if it were a classroom test. At the end of the inspection, we clean the grounds around our barracks. Class begins as soon as we get back inside.

After lunch, we are required to change uniforms and are again subjected to an inspection. More classroom sessions are conducted until the end of the day when we have our third and final inspection. These inspections are of our living quarters and focus on either our wall locker or our bunk. The staff can inspect any area we spend time in, including the head.

Each day, it seems like there is one less person in the classroom. Another empty seat appears. The attrition rate does not seem possible. Where are these Marines ending up? I keep wondering if I'm going to graduate or end up back at Tanks, humiliated.

During training on the birthday of the Marine Corps, 10 November, the entire class is assigned to a ceremony at the Marine Corps Memorial. There are many important people from the government who are attending this celebration. I am standing as a guard in an aisle leading to a seating area. As the ceremony is ending, the President of the United States, Gerald Ford, walks up the aisle and stops in front of me. I immediately salute him, and he holds out his hand for me to shake. I shake his hand, and he walks away. The encounter is brief, but he is the first politician I will meet that is this important to our country.

The training encompasses a wide variety of subjects, ranging from bomb detection to dining room etiquette. Most of the training is related to security and protection of property and personnel. So, like any training or school, it starts to get boring. I am in week number eleven, nearing the end of the training, and on this day, we are informed as to where we are going to be assigned for duty.

Will it be an embassy or a consulate? Will it be in the free world or a hardship post? Maybe I will get an assignment in an Iron Curtain country? We are all seated in the auditorium about to learn our fate. The first sergeant reads off names with their assignments. I am waiting patiently when he calls out, "Lance Corporal Genovese, Warsaw, Poland."

The American Embassy in Warsaw, Poland, is the assignment that is read to me in front of the entire graduating Marine Security Guard class of December 18, 1975. They celebrate this day as assignment day. Approximately four weeks prior, we had been made aware of facilities around the world that needed guards or that had confirmed vacancies. We were required to complete a form listing the three duty stations that we would prefer to be assigned to. This form was titled "Request of Assignment," commonly referred to as a "Dream Sheet." My requests were Tokyo, Japan; Bangkok, Thailand; and Canberra, Australia.

One reason I applied for a post in Japan or Thailand was my infatuation with Asian women. The reason for choosing Australia was the fact I would never be able to afford to travel there on my own, so maybe the government would pay. I never believed the Marine Corps was going to send me anywhere I wanted to go though.

The first sergeant continues reading off names and assignments. I sit and think about Warsaw, Poland. I know where Poland is, and I know Nazi Germany began World War II by invading there. It is also now a country in the Soviet Bloc, so it will be considered a hardship post. I have been assigned to a post but have not been told the FBI was able to allow me clearance to handle Top Secret material.

I have been in two separate interviews regarding my background check. This forces the Marine Corps to place me on "probation," and graduation is contingent on my clarifying two facets of my past. The first is my criminal arrest history, and the second is my family background.

I was arrested in North Haven, Connecticut, when I was sixteen years old. The State of Connecticut has a court and justice system that operates under a different set of rules regarding what can be considered as an arrest or a conviction. If you were to ask me if I was ever arrested, my answer would always be "yes." If you were to ask the North Haven Police Department if they had ever arrested Mark R. Genovese, their answer would be "no." If you asked the court system of the State of Connecticut if there was any record of Mark R. Genovese being arrested, then there would be certain government agencies that would have access to those records.

I was granted a special probation which was titled "Youthful Offender" that was awarded to any youth who had committed any crime between the age of 16 and 17. The individual would have any record of the arrest erased if he or she had no motor vehicle violations and no further arrests before turning 18 years old. This arrest would be totally removed from my records because I would meet those requirements.

I am now 19 years old, and prior to my arrival in boot camp, I have had no other run ins with the law. My criminal background check turns up nothing. On its first interview, the FBI could not find any record of my arrest, so they thought I was being untruthful and attempting to hide something. They eventually were given access to my arrest record. They were able to determine exactly what happened because a civil lawsuit had been filed against me.

The agents of the FBI or the NSA and the Marine Corps learned the reason for my criminal record was because I had shot a guinea hen with a shotgun. A shotgun given to me by my mother with the intention of shooting that guinea hen was probably one of the most comical reasons for getting arrested. As I am squirming in my chair in the interview room, I try to tell the story seriously about how the guinea hens would walk through the neighborhood and pick on random gardens and destroy them. Well, I hope you get the picture.

The lawsuit was dismissed and considered settled a brief time after it had been filed in court. My father had homeowner's insurance through a nationally known company. The local agent sent the couple, Mr. and Mrs. Carlson, who had filed the lawsuit, a check with no explanation letter for the market value of three guinea hens. He sent a certified letter to the attorney representing them. It explained that the acceptance of the check would be considered as a settlement of the lawsuit. They cashed that check which served as a final settlement prior to consulting with their attorney.

The second reason for the probation and delay of the granting of my Top Secret clearance was just a little bit more complicated. I am related to Vito Genovese who was a reputed crime boss of the New York Mafia. This was a fact I was never made aware of when I was growing up. Apparently, my grandfather was a first cousin. (That will be material for a second book.) The determination is made that my immediate family has no ties to Vito Genovese, and I am granted a Top Secret clearance.

The training here includes handgun and other firearm use. We will carry a .38 caliber Smith & Wesson Model 10 or .357 Magnum Smith & Wesson six-shot revolver while standing watch. This is not the standard issue handgun for the Marine Corps.

This firearm is used because it is considered safer. The real reason is a revolver will not fire unless the trigger is pulled and the hammer with the firing pin attached hits a live cartridge. The standard handgun of the Marines is the Colt Government 1911A1 .45 caliber semi-automatic pistol. It is a difficult handgun to load and unload. Therefore, inexperienced and weaker people can cause the gun to discharge accidentally.

The revolver is not as accurate when firing in a combat situation because more strength is needed to pull the trigger each time. When the trigger is pulled, the cylinder holding the rounds of ammunition rotates as the hammer cocks. When the cycle is completed, the gun will fire. The semi-automatic, on the other hand, is carried with the hammer locked to the position to be fired with a safety holding it in place. To fire, it requires releasing the safety with a thumb and pulling the trigger. The handgun then fires. The slide moves backwards and ejects the spent casing. The firearm then feeds a round of ammunition into the firing position from a spring-loaded magazine. The amount of pressure required to pull this trigger is much less than that of the revolver.

I will also be trained in the use of a 12-gauge shotgun. The most common one used by the Marine Corps is the Remington Model 870, pump action shotgun. These handguns and shotguns are weapons considered as close combat and defensive position firearms. We will be defending a small compound or just a building, so this is the reason these weapons are used.

This will serve me well in the future when I become a police officer. These will be the firearms that will be used by most police departments. Firearms have always been a part of my life and will become more important as my career in law enforcement builds and continues.

We are required to receive a qualifying score for the handgun but not the shotgun. I qualify as a marksman with the handgun. In addition to the shotgun, there are several sub-machine guns we become familiar with, including the Israeli UZI and the German MP5.

I have one week to go to complete this training. The entire time here people are removed from the training almost as a daily occurrence, a failed inspection, a failed test, not completing the morning run, and something in a background check. There is even a Marine dropped because he went to a bar where ladies of the night were conducting business. Whenever a Marine is dropped from the program, we are made aware of the reason he is being removed and all the circumstances involved. The instructors explain exactly why they are relieved. The instructors warn us no position is guaranteed, and it is possible to be removed from the program on graduation day.

In the final tally, more than half of the Marines who were there for the first day of training are gone as we line up to receive our graduation certificates. As we are lining up to receive the diplomas, a sergeant who is standing right next to me is pulled out of line and does not receive his.

I invited my girlfriend, Kathleen, to the ceremony. We have been dating for about two and a half years. I started to date her when I was a senior in high school. The way that we began to date was interesting.

Kathleen approached me one afternoon while we were in high school. It was around the time when the proms were being planned. She stopped me one day and asked if I would go to her junior prom. She was a year younger than I was and a grade lower. My response to her was, and I quote, "NO." We both stood staring at one another as the tears began to well up in her eyes when I said to her, "I can't afford two proms in one year, but I would love to have you come with me to my senior prom." Those tears that were welling up became tears of joy. This would begin a relationship that would continue for a couple years. I would fall in love with her and ask her to marry me. I gave her an engagement ring. I don't believe I was mature enough or ready to get married at this time in my life. This was the point when I believe a rift began between Kathleen and me.

I have made it for now, and I will not be going back to the Second Tank Battalion. I receive my diploma on December 18, 1975. In only a few weeks, I will report to my new duty station as Marine security guard in the American Embassy, Warsaw, Poland.

I am pulled aside the day that we are scheduled to have our graduation ceremony. When this happens, I believe I am being sent back to Tanks. I am informed by my instructors I had finished as one of the top five members of this class. This is the reason for my assignment to an Iron Curtain country.

I have spent the last couple of weeks mostly on leave at home. In retrospect, I should have done more partying. Most of my time is spent with Kathleen. I'm not sure how long we will be able to keep the long-distance relationship going.

While I am in the United States for the last couple of weeks, I reflect on how I have arrived at this point in my life. I truly start to believe that I have made the right decision. I am too young to be getting married. I consider spending the next twenty years of my life as a Marine and making it my career. I have made the most of my time as a Marine. The training that I have received to this point will help me should I decide not to continue as a Marine. I now can drive and make minor repairs on large trucks and diesel engines. I can repair radios and do the work of utility linemen. The experience that I gain protecting the embassies will serve me well in law enforcement.

# CHAPTER 7

# UNITED STATES EMBASSY: WARSAW, POLAND

The trip to Warsaw is an all-day flight with a change of planes in Frankfort, Germany. When I arrive at the airport in Warsaw, I am greeted by the Assistant Non-Commissioned Officer in Charge (ANCOIC), Sergeant Joe Franklin. I am his replacement, and he is extremely happy that I am arriving now. Snow is piled as high as ten feet as we make our way from the airport to the embassy.

The car picks me up and drives directly to the embassy. There is a garage that leads directly into the building. I am separated from my luggage and escorted to the NCOIC's office in the embassy. Sgt. Rademanne is there, and he welcomes me to Poland.

During the ride to the embassy, the ANCOIC advises me this detachment is in transition. The last Non-Commissioned Officer in Charge (NCOIC) has just been relieved of duty and sent out of the country back to the United States. The acting NCOIC is a sergeant named Terry Rademanne. Sgt. Franklin does not believe Sgt. Rademanne will be here much longer.

The Marines in Poland are not a cohesive unit. Something has happened that has fragmented them. The acting NCOIC is dating the ambassador's secretary. He lives with her away from the embassy compound. This was supposed to be forbidden in the MSG program. It becomes apparent just during the ride to my new "home" that the new duty that was described as the best in the Marine Corps has made a lousy first impression.

I see there are soldiers and military vehicles everywhere. A light snow is falling as we make our way through the city. The snow is something that I will get accustomed to, as it will snow most of the time. My first two months in Warsaw are insignificant. Most of my time is spent working or preparing for work. The American Embassy and Marine House are located on a fenced-in compound where I spend 95% of my time.

I mention the Marine House here because there are no barracks that serve to house the military personnel of the United States in Poland. Each embassy that is protected by a Marine security guard detachment lives in what is known as "The Marine House."

Written letters are my only means of communication with home, but the postal system is incredibly slow. I write every day, but the mail pouch only goes to the United States with routine mail twice a week. In April, I receive the first "Dear John" letter of my life. A "Dear John" letter is the letter service men receive from their girlfriends, wives to-be, or wives to inform members of the armed services who get deployed overseas for an extended period of time that they have found someone else and will no longer be waiting for them to return home.

In my case, the letter is from my high school sweetheart Kathleen. I was told to expect this letter, and, in all honesty, I am relieved when it arrives. Telling her I would wait for her and not experience life to its fullest has been the biggest mistake of my life. There have been soldiers who have taken their own lives after receiving these types of letters. That's not the way that I feel about my letter. I have been given a new freedom to live life to the fullest. It is April 1975. Not only will I be celebrating a new freedom, but Saigon, Vietnam, has been taken over by the North Vietnamese, officially ending the Vietnam War.

I am now able to explore the real world and how to get through the hard times and the good ones. Marines who are assigned to embassy duty are the most eligible bachelors in all the diplomatic community. We are young, strong, in great physical condition, and have the sharpest looking uniforms in the world. We are used as escorts and are present at every diplomatic function and event.

When I receive my "Dear John," I send a reply questioning her reasons and the obvious why. I don't get any response from her and do not hear from her directly until ten days before I am to be separated from the service in 1978.

I have now been in Poland for about three months and am settling into the life as a Foreign Service ambassador of the United States. Life at an embassy in a foreign country is not easy to get used to. There are many restrictions placed on us. The people we are allowed to socialize with and talk to are outlined for us. Interaction with a Polish national is not allowed.

American families "adopt" Marines and have them over to family functions and meals. This helps the Marines keep their sanity and feel like they belong here. Three families have adopted me, and they take turns inviting me to dinner. On occasion, I will watch their children so they may attend a social event. This allows me to make a few extra bucks now and then.

Marines assigned to embassy duty are allowed to run a club known as the Marine Bar. The bar is used to run fund-raising events to earn money for the annual Marine Corps Ball which takes place on the birthday of the Marines, 10 November. I'm sitting in that bar after having read the letter wondering how my life will change. I am looking forward to dating again.

The main form of entertainment here at the compound is a game known as platform tennis. Ambassador Davies plays the game almost every morning prior to going into his office for work. It is considered an honor if he asks you to play against him during one of those morning sessions. Everyone is encouraged to get involved and play. There is a tournament during the year, which is loosely run. There is only one court in the entire country. It is the one that was built here by Ambassador Davies. I am entered in the tournament in the men's division and mixed doubles.

My partner in the mixed doubles is an attractive American secretary who is an employee of the State Department. She is an athletic 26-year-old brunette single woman. Her name is Marilyn Esterby, from Long Beach, California. We become friends shortly after my arrival, and I have been her escort to several events already. I don't think of her in the romantic type of relationship in any way.

Poland is depressing, the weather sucks, the country is poor, and the Soviet Communists keep them oppressed. The stores and markets have very little merchandise. There are long lines at the stores every day, and most of the time, you don't know what the line is for. As Americans, we are afforded a big advantage over the local Polish population. There are stores run by the government that accept hard currency. We refer to them as the "Dollar Stores." The selection in these stores is nothing to write home about. The best thing about these stores is that there is a large amount of older American money still in circulation here. I will go to these stores and purchase an inexpensive item and pay with a large bill so that I can search the change. One thing that I will come away from Poland with is a collection of older American money.

Polish money is known as the zloty, and we are encouraged to exchange our dollars and pay for everything with the Polish currency. The exchange rate at the finance office in the embassy is determined by the international stock markets. The current rate is approximately one thousand zloty are equal to one U.S. dollar. This means the Polish currency has little value.

Unfortunately, the most interesting or exciting aspects of being a Marine security guard are classified as government secured information, which I will never be able to discuss or write about.

There are two things common in Poland. Ice and snow. I arrived in January, and there was snow on the ground. In June, there were still piles of snow from the snowplows in some areas. Ice skating and cross-country skiing were some of the recreational activities I became involved in and enjoy.

The country is entertained by a traveling troop known as "Fantasy on Ice," which is like The Ice Capades in America. These ice skaters put on a show while ice skating. When each performance is completed, the American members show up at the Marine bar. Most of the participants are young, single, athletic females.

I became friends with several of these girls because they came to perform in Poland four times while I was there. They would also do a performance in Israel during my tour of duty there. These young ladies have been former Team USA skaters who were either past their prime or actual Olympic and American champions. I mention them now because they will contribute to a story in the future that takes place in Israel.

Poland is a poor communist country. Serving as a guard here is considered a hardship posting. This allows the federal government to pay the Marines additional pay because there are no American military bases located in Poland. Military bases allow for the purchase of the basic needs of a service man at a rate equal to the pay earned by them. Everything the Marines have now, like housing, food, clothing, transportation, and uniforms cost more than all Marines can afford. Everything is shipped to the embassy by air.

Even though the Marine House is located on a compound that is considered U.S. government property, the cost is more than a military base. Marines are given extra pay to help them afford meals and housing. There are thirteen Marines stationed here with this detachment. The Marine House is the first floor of the apartment building located on the compound. Every Marine has his own room, and there is a living room area, kitchen, and eating area. We pool our extra money, which allows us to hire a full-time cook, a house cleaner, and two maids. The pay the staff receives is far less than any pay an American worker gets doing the same work in the United States. There is no mess hall or cafeteria that serves three meals a day. The maids fill that void. The maids shine our shoes, clean and press our uniforms, and prepare them for our duty. They have even been taught how to arrange our shooting badges and ribbons too. We only must worry about cleaning the Marine House when inspections are scheduled. Life is beginning to be nothing I expected as a Marine.

I am nineteen years old, and Poland is allowing me to become a fan of beer. A bottle of beer costs less than a soft drink. Alcoholic beverages flow freely in Poland. It is easier to get, and alcoholic beverages are more readily available than fresh meat.

While being assigned to MSG, there are duties required of us in addition to our guard duties. My assignment is the Mess NCO. This requires me to plan all the meals for the detachment. I am also required to purchase food and beverages. The payments and all the instructions to our cook are also my responsibility.

Shopping for food is a challenge that requires I go each morning. Kielbasa is the standard meat. It is plentiful and served at almost every meal. Fresh vegetables are a rarity, but there is an abundance of root vegetables such as potatoes, carrots, and beets. There is a small commissary in the embassy compound, but selection is limited there. The overuse of kielbasa will make me never eat it again when I finally leave Poland. The last piece of kielbasa that I eat in my life is in early May 1977.

Everyone in the American Embassy and the diplomatic community who spend time at our social events know me as the shy, quiet Marine from Connecticut. So, I propose a "Ladies Night" party for one of the fund-raising events. The party will consist of dancing and refreshments, and each woman who attends will receive a free drink. There will be an appearance from a special mystery guest. This guest will arrive at a predetermined time to perform a special set of songs.

The mystery guest will be me, and I will do a strip tease act all the way down to my jock strap. The Marines advertise it and play it up for weeks. We must get special approval from the Ambassador, and he agrees. He insists I not be totally nude. I must be covered and leave the stage after only a brief flash of skin. We assure him as soon as my shorts hit the floor, the two largest Marines will cover me with blankets and whisk me away.

There is a banquet facility on the bottom floor of the embassy. We set up the room with tables and spend a couple days decorating. There are fancy linens and flowers on every table. The night of the party, we sell more tickets than the capacity of the room. The mystery guest is scheduled to appear at 9:00 pm.

I have come to this party with Marilyn, but she has no idea what is about to happen. At 9:00 p.m., I sneak away and get dressed in a fancy three-piece suit, complete with a scarf, gloves and topped off with a beautiful fedora. We purposefully delay my entrance, and the crowd begins to grow restless. A small chant begins to call for the mystery guest.

Suddenly, our NCOIC acting as a master of ceremonies proudly announces with his microphone, "Now, what you have all been waiting for, our mystery guest. Before he performs, he has requested a special song for the ladies, so all the women grab their favorite man and dance." A song by the band Wild Flower titled "Let Her Cry" is played. When the song finishes, he again announces to the crowd, "Ladies and Gentlemen, your mystery guest."

With that, the music, "Strangers in the Night," sung by Frank Sinatra, begins to play. I have made my way into the rear of the room and am moving toward the front. The lights in the banquet room have been turned down low. All eyes are focused on the stage area as I make my way through the crowd, hiding my identity. I pull the collar of the overcoat over my face. The gloves, scarf, and hat hide most of my features. The music continues playing as a spotlight searches the room trying to locate this mystery guest. There is a simple dining room chair set center stage, and as soon as I make my way to it, the spotlight is focused on me.

When the music stops, I take up a pose with my right foot up on the seat of the chair. The back of the chair is facing the audience. I am bent at the waist with my eyes looking toward the floor. I am shaking, and there is thunderous applause going on. WHY? I haven't done anything but walk into the room yet. I am more nervous than I have ever been in my entire life.

The Marine MC proudly announces, "Ladies and Gentlemen, let the show begin." The music titled, "The Stripper" blasts out of the stereo speakers. The slow wail of those trumpets signal the start of my act. I stand and immediately fling the hat towards the crowd. Sweat is streaming down my back, and I work on removing the overcoat quickly. While bits of other loose or more convenient articles of clothing are sent flying toward the audience, I leave the stage and start to make my way around the room. The scarf is gone. The gloves are gone, and slowly I undo the necktie. None of these clothing items come off easily. The act is working though. I have never done this before, and I did not even practice. I have only imagined how I would get this done or if I was even capable of finishing. I would sit in my room and imagine how to do this act. Everything is going just the way that I had planned it.

My belt slips out of the loops easily and is gone. The jacket comes off, and I saunter over to an Australian woman with beautiful long blond hair and throw the jacket around her. I pull her toward me as if I am about to plant a big juicy kiss on her. I stop and release her just as our faces are less than an inch away from each other. I turn to walk away, and another woman from the British embassy is standing there. She grabs me and plants a full-on kiss, slipping me the tongue. I pull away and walk, working the buttons of my vest. With the vest off, I start to make my way back to the stage. The song is winding down and coming to an end. I am working on my shirt, which turns out to have the most buttons and is proving to be the most sophisticated piece of clothing to remove. Then, it is gone. The ladies have absolutely lost their minds and are clapping, screaming, hollering, and cat calling.

When I return to the stage, the song has almost come to an end. I sit in the chair with my legs spread wide facing the audience. I remove my socks leaving only my trousers for the finale. When I stand up, I grab the chair and fling it aside. I unbutton the top and then drop the zipper. The trousers fall to the floor as the final note of the song makes it through the speakers.

Two gigantic hulking Marines cover me with blankets from each side. They pick me up and haul me away to a back room. I can hear raucous applause and calls for my return. One of these Marines gives me a giant bear hug while heaping a mountain of praise on me. I get dressed and return to the room where I am again greeted by loud boisterous applause. The hugs, hand shaking, slaps on the back, and praise continue throughout the rest of the night.

It is late, but the night is just beginning. I have broken out of my shell. I find Marilyn sitting with some of the other single women from the embassy. She is clinging to me and tells me that she was looking to dance with me when they had played the song "Let Her Cry" because it is one of her favorites. I apologize to her and make sure that our disc jockey plays the song again. Marilyn and I dance to that song to end the party. I am no longer that shy Marine from Connecticut.

Embassy duty in Warsaw, Poland, just improved immensely. Nothing significant happens until the last days of June, 1976. An Air France flight that originated in Tel-Aviv Israel is hijacked after stopping to add passengers in Athens, Greece. The hijackers board the plane in Athens. This incident puts our detachment on high alert because of the Jewish connections here in Poland.

The Israelis pull off an incredible rescue mission on July 4, 1976, while we are celebrating Independence Day. The Israeli Air Force and Army fly a military force to Entebbe, Uganda, and rescue all the hostages except for one. They suffer only one fatality from the rescue team, and only three hostages are killed. Upon completion of the rescue mission, there are many rumors the United States government helped the Israeli government. This causes some tension throughout the diplomatic community.

The embassy in Warsaw is on the receiving end of several threats from anti-Semitic groups. These threats are credible, and the American government believes they will happen. The intelligence gathering agencies have us put on high alert. There is a strong possibility of an armed attack occurring. I write a letter to my parents and family telling them that I may never see them again. The attack never happens.

Vice President of the United States, Walter Mondale, visits Poland in September, 1976. When he arrives, I am assigned to retrieve classified paperwork from his aircraft at the airport. Arriving at the powder blue United States Air Force jet is a treat for me. Upon my arrival, I see the cargo doors are open. There are several Air Force airmen working on different parts of the plane. Secret Service agents are milling around the steps leading into the cabin of the plane.

The plane is in an isolated area of the airport. I notice right away the cargo hold is loaded with American beer, specifically Budweiser and Olympia. When we stop our car and I identify myself to the agent in charge, I immediately negotiate with him to determine if they would like to sell or trade their beer with us. The agent in charge is not prepared to negotiate his supply of beer. He laughs loudly and says, "I should have known the Marines would want my beer."

In Poland, we can obtain all styles and types of beer. German brews and European name brand beers such as Heineken are main stays in our bar. I propose trading cases of Heineken for Budweiser, and he seems to be surprised. I convince him to trade one case of Bud for two cases of Heineken, and I will throw in two free cases of this Czech beer with the name Budvar-Budweiser. We cannot get American beer here in Poland, and by making this deal, we will be able to feature one in our bar for at least a couple months. We end up with twenty-five cases of Budweiser. Our bar makes a large profit from the sale of the beer. This helps with our fundraising for the ball. The visit by the Vice President goes off without a hitch, and life continues.

Vice President Mondale is only in Poland for two days, and like my encounter with President Ford, I am assigned to an area guarding his plane. When he arrives to depart Poland, he walks up to me and shakes my hand. He thanks all of us for our service and boards his plane.

I have now shaken the hands of a sitting President and Vice President of the United States. Both encounters were extremely brief. No other person from my family has ever come close to either of these men.

There are not many things to do in Poland. The restrictions placed on us make it hard to socialize or find ways to be entertained. There is a dart league that consists of teams from different embassies. We are allowed to fraternize with certain personnel from certain embassies. Those included are Canada, Australia, United Kingdom, France, and several others.

The most exciting thing about all these embassies is the employees needed are mostly young female secretaries. Finding a date for any function is simple. This makes the assignment in Poland slightly more tolerable.

There is one tavern in the Old City of Warsaw we are allowed to go to often. It is a restaurant that has been approved by our government. It is named the Warsaw Winery. The drink of choice for us Marines is Russian champagne. I believe it is because it is inexpensive and is a sweet tasting wine. This tavern is exactly three miles away from the embassy.

There are several means of transportation in the city of Warsaw, so you can walk around relatively easily. They have a trolley service on the main roads. Buses are the main means of transportation. Like any other city there are also taxicabs available. The most interesting form of public transportation is the horse-drawn carriages.

On one occasion after a night of enjoying Russian champagne at the winery, five couples – each consisting of a Marine and his girlfriend – all agree to head back to the Marine Bar. Each couple uses a different mode of transportation. The race to the Marine Bar is one way. We Marines have to break up the monotony of the assignment. The couple that chooses to walk arrives first. The couple that took the taxi is the last to arrive and is also the costliest. In the race, I choose the horse and carriage as my mode of transportation. We arrive back at the embassy in third place. I chose the horse and carriage because on days when I was bored, I would go out to the markets and buy carrots to feed the horses. This helped me learn some of the language and history of Warsaw by talking with the owners.

One of the other entertaining things to do is stand in line. This sounds funny, but there are shortages of everything in Poland. When a shipment of anything arrives, people queue up for hours to purchase the new arrivals, no matter what that might be. It is a wonderful way to watch the people of Poland and how they deal with the communist way of life. I stand in these lines on my days off for something to do. Many times, I arrive at the front of the line only to find the store has received a shipment of socks or shoes. Every once in a great while, something good is waiting at the end of the line. One time after waiting in line for over an hour, I am able to purchase a Russian fur hat worn by the soldiers in cold weather. It only costs the equivalent of $5.00 in American money.

I have planned a trip to the former German Army concentration camp turned into a permanent museum. "ARBEIT MACHT FREI" are the words inscribed on a wrought iron sign above the main gate that leads to the grounds of the Auschwitz Concentration Camp. The words are German and, loosely translated, they mean "Work Will Set You Free." This is the site in Poland considered the most infamous death camp run by the Nazi regime during World War II. The Polish government has left it intact and turned it into a museum.

I have always been interested in history and make a point of visiting this place. I have no preconceptions of what to expect as

I enter the camp. The camp is in southern Poland near the city of Krakow. I am accompanied on this trip by Marilyn and one of the Polish national employees from the embassy. He serves as our escort and interpreter. I have made it a priority to visit this ugly piece of world history during my deployment.

Being in this place makes me wonder how one man could determine the fate of one entire religious sect of people. How could one man, one country, been so cruel that they would attempt to eliminate another race of people from existence? The buildings look like military barracks. The railroad leads up to the encampment, and there are loading docks near the front gate. The only way to get inside the camp is to join a tour group. As we are lining up to join this group, my thoughts drift to my high school history lessons dealing with the Holocaust. It is believed approximately eight to nine million people were executed in camps just like these. More than one million in Auschwitz alone were killed, with most of them being Jews.

The day does not match what I am about to see. The sky is a bright blue with not a visible cloud. The grass is a bright healthy green, sprinkled with yellow and white flowers dotting the whole area encircling the camp.

The crowd that is embarking on the tour is quiet and solemn. I feel as though I am attending a funeral and have just entered the cemetery. The start of the tour has us view a short film showing how the German army treated the prisoners they brought here, the selection process used to determine who is to be sent here, and where they are to go after arrival. They are separated by sex and sent to different buildings. The women are transferred to the facility known as Birkenau. Families are destroyed, with the children taken away and parents sent in opposite directions. The film continues with these people being stripped of all their belongings and clothing. The film ends at this point, and the lights are turned on.

As the tour begins, we step into a room filled with black and white striped prison uniforms. The tour guide explains the people brought here are hosed down or sometimes allowed to shower and then dressed in these uniforms. They have been stripped of everything they had which has now been moved and sorted by other prisoners.

As we exit this room, we travel through a series of rooms that house all of these items that the Germans have taken. A room is stacked to the ceiling with luggage, the next room is filled with clothing, and the third room is filled with shoes. The rooms are large, and it is hard to conceptualize how many people have contributed to this. The last room of the tour has large bins that are filled with smaller, more personal items.

The first bin is full of candlestick holders. The second has pictures and frames; some still have pictures of individual people or their families. They continue to become more personal as the next is tableware. Some of the items have the initials or the full names of the original names inscribed on them. There are all different types of brushes, including hair and toothbrushes. Then, there are barrels of human hair, and one is filled with gold teeth.

The tour leaves this area, and then a description of the gas chambers used to exterminate the Jews is given. Leading the group to one of those gas chambers, the tour guide explains what type of gas they used and how effective it was. The final room is the crematorium. I have already seen enough, and the rest of the tour is a blur. I have deep feelings of anger and hopelessness for what happened here.

Marilyn has been clinging to my arm since the beginning of the tour. I haven't really noticed until now. I realize as we are walking towards the car that her grip is getting tighter. When we are seated in the car, it is obvious the tour has had a profound effect on her. She will not let go of me and is crying. We say nothing as the car makes its way back to the hotel.

The next day we take the train back to the embassy and Warsaw. Little did I know my next embassy assignment will be in Israel. Visiting Auschwitz only serves to fuel my dislike for oppressive governments like the Third Reich or the communist one in charge in Poland.

As soon as I arrive at the embassy compound, the Marine on duty informs me three of our guards have been relieved of duty and are being sent out of the country. One has already been sent to another post, the second is on his way to the airport, and the third is packing his belongings and will be gone in the morning. I report to my NCOIC immediately in his office at the embassy. Gunnery Sergeant Streete has only been here for a month. He is a salty old infantry veteran with years of experience, including two tours of duty in Vietnam.

He explains that three members of our detachment invited a group of people into the Marine Bar, which is on the compound of the embassy. They thought they were a flight crew from the Scandinavian airlines they had met in the Old Town Winery, but they turned out to be Russians. It is unclear if they strayed from the Marine Bar, so our regional security officer felt it was in the best interest of the Marines involved to transfer them out of the country. As a result, I will be working more hours, and my time in Poland will be extended.

As a punishment for a breach of security, the three Marines end up in Ireland, London, and Sweden, respectively. My reward for doing my job is a three-month extension in beautiful Warsaw, Poland. The gunny has grown to like me, has given me excellent fitness reports, and has recommended me for promotion to sergeant.

Life returns to normal. Marilyn and I continue to beat up on people in the mixed doubles of the platform tennis game. We even take on some men's teams and beat them. We are becoming the team to beat. Every year, there is a tournament held, and the best teams or individuals get to go to Moscow for a week and compete against their team. Marylyn and I are probably going to be selected.

We easily win every match we are in. There is another team that wins as much as we do. It is a team made up of a husband and wife. The husband is a general in the U.S. Army, and I believe his wife plays because she was ordered to do so. The General and his wife are in their mid-forties and have three teenage daughters. They are both in great physical condition and have played tennis together for years.

Whenever I am working and the General sees me, he challenges my team to play his, and I want nothing more than to accommodate him. I can tell by the way he acts and after watching him play, he is driven to win. He is the type of person who must be the best and will not settle for anything less. We finally get the chance to play each other.

The match is scheduled for a Friday afternoon when all of us have finished work that day. Marilyn and the General's wife arrive before I do, and they warm up together. As I am getting my racket out and tightening the laces to my shoes, the General makes his entrance onto the court. He has on a black with yellow stripes sweat suit with his name and rank embroidered over the front right breast pocket. On the rear are words and the emblem for the United States Army.

We greet each other and have a brief discussion concerning the rules of the game. The General just happens to have a silver dollar he offers to flip to see which team will start the match. We agree to let him flip the coin, and he and his wife agree to allow Marilyn to call it. The match is started with much anticipation, with even a small group of onlookers watching.

Marilyn and I dominate the first set of the match and win it easily by the score of 6 to 1. This does not sit well with the General at all. The General does not want to lose at anything, especially to a twenty-year-old Marine and his girlfriend. He becomes more intense and almost vicious in the next set. He orders his wife around and tries to intimidate Marilyn and me. We still win the second set, although the score is much closer at 6 to 4.

The third set starts with our team serving to open the game. Marilyn serves to the General, and he hits the serve badly, hitting his wife in the back of the head. The platform tennis ball is a solid rubber ball so when it hits her, she is obviously stunned and hurt. We stop play for approximately ten minutes and allow her to gain her senses. We also offer to continue the match later, but the General insists we finish. The third set only gets uglier, and we win by the score of 6 to 2. The General is not happy and is an extremely sore sport about the game. As he is leaving, he does not shake our hands or congratulate us. He ushers his wife away from talking to us and simply says he would like a rematch as soon as we are available. I feel sorry for him and praise his wife.

I do not want to feel the scorn of a General, even if he has no effect or control over my life. Marilyn and I have lunch the next day and agree to have a rematch. We also agree that if the weather conditions are not perfect, there will be no match. There is a neutral party to flip the coin, and we need a referee to call the lines or the match will not be played. The arrangements are made, and the match is set.

I am not one to give in and deliberately lose a game to stroke the ego of anyone. I play every game to win and fight every fight to the finish. On this occasion, I believe the only way for this match to have a positive outcome is for the General to be the victor. He has to be the man with the winning score at the end of this platform tennis match. This way all four of us will be winners in the end.

Marilyn and I play the match as hard as we can play without making it obvious that we intend to let the General win. The match goes five sets with each team winning the exact same number of games. The General's wife makes the winning point in a fifth set tiebreaker with a shot I mishit out of the court. The General is gracious enough to offer us a "rubber" match. He shakes our hands and gives Marilyn a hug. His wife hugs me and whispers into my ear, "Thank you. I know what you've done." Marilyn and I receive the runners up trophy at the ceremony. I never have any dealings with the General again.

Before my assignment in Poland is over, our detachment receives replacements for the three guards who have been sent to different posts. The Secretary of State makes a visit to our NATO allies to negotiate a military cooperation agreement. I have been selected to supplement the security detail at the embassy in Brussels, Belgium. The NATO headquarters is located there, and all the countries that are a part of that alliance will be sending an important governmental representative to the conference.

I will be in Brussels for just five days. Upon my arrival, I am brought to the Marine House. I am ordered to report in uniform for duty immediately to the NCOIC. He issues me a sidearm (the standard .357 Magnum revolver), and I am transported to a facility where I will stand watch for twelve hours. My post is inside a military compound in an office building on the fourth floor, just outside of a conference room. Nothing happens during the entire time I am there. Not one person ever comes to my entry point, other than the Marines who relieve me later that day.

That turns out to be the only day I am needed for guard duty. The conference is cut short for reasons never explained to me. I am able to stay in Brussels for three days as a vacation, enjoying the freedom and the women there. The best thing about Belgium is the food. I have a couple of oranges and eat some pizza while I am there. This sounds trivial. A couple oranges and a pizza are the best part of this trip because these things don't exist in Poland.

My return flight to Poland is interesting. When I am boarding the plane, I am stopped and questioned at length, even though I am in possession of an official United States Government passport. I have no weapons with me and no carry-on luggage. I have been taking Polish language lessons back in Warsaw as a requirement of the duty and can speak and understand common phrases. Two of the airline attendants who are checking me onto the plane are saying nasty things about me as I am boarding. They are both speaking fluent Polish. At this point, I have not let on I know some of the Polish language, and I only respond in English to any question they ask of me. Once they clear me through customs and allow me to access the gate and enter the plane, I thank them for their kindness and assistance in the best Polish language I can muster without an American accent. The red blush on their faces is priceless.

The flight is a short one on Polish Airlines, which is named LOT. When we begin our descent into the airport in Poland, it is obvious something is not right. The engines are operating properly, but the plane takes some very sharp turns and seems to be headed toward the ground faster than any other flight I have ever been on. The plane lands normally, with the engines reversing to slow us down. We begin to taxi around the airport when the plane comes to a stop and the engines shut off.

We sit there for about ten minutes when the tow vehicle normally used to push the plane away from the gate comes out to us. It hooks up to the front and tows the plane to the gate. We are never told why the plane stopped, but it is my belief the plane ran out of fuel.

We have a mascot in Poland. Long before I arrived, a Marine found a puppy while he was on a run near the river. The puppy was obviously abandoned. The detachment adopted this puppy who now is full grown. The breed is a boxer, and he has been given the name D.S. Boot (the D.S. stood for "Dumb Shit"). While I am stationed at the embassy, he holds the rank of corporal.

The dog goes everywhere with us Marines. He runs with us during P.T. He eats when we eat and has a bed in the NCOIC's office inside the embassy. The dog even has a set of dress blues and is a part of our Marine Corps Birthday Ball. One of the Marines takes care of him while I am there.

My tour of duty is coming to an end in April, 1977. The Marine Security Guard Battalion advises each detachment where the vacancies are or where there is a need to send additional personnel. Again, just like it was in school, we submit a "Request for Duty Assignment" form. On this "dream sheet" as we lovingly referred to it , I request Canberra, Australia, as my first choice; Tel Aviv, Israel, for the second, and Jerusalem, Israel, for my final choice.

The Marine Corps will not pay the higher cost to have me transferred to Australia, so I am required to submit a second request. Although this time I am told to select from embassies and consulates that presently are experiencing vacancies. The list is short, and I change my choices to Tel Aviv, Casablanca, Morocco, and Madrid, Spain, in that order.

I am granted my first choice of Tel Aviv and am scheduled to leave Warsaw in May, 1977. In my final month in Poland, there is nothing of importance that takes place. I do not have strong feelings for Marilyn, and since there is no real connection made, there is no need to carry on a long-distance relationship. I have no regrets, as she was a great companion. I only hear from her in one letter after I leave Poland.

# CHAPTER 8

# UNITED STATES EMBASSY: TEL AVIV, ISRAEL

Being in the Marines for over two years now has had a profound effect on me. I am presently recommended for promotion to sergeant (E-5), which is unusually quick in peacetime. I believe this transfer to Tel Aviv will be my final duty station, and I don't feel any desire to make the Marine Corps a career. The pay is not very good, but the training and assignments I have had will serve me well in civilian life. Quite frankly, Poland sucks. I can't imagine serving at other duty stations this bad.

I begin to think about one of the main reasons I joined the military in the first place. I intend to pursue a career in law enforcement; specifically, I want to become a police officer. My thoughts drift back to my hometown and a special person in my life.

My father had partnered with one of his brothers to form a small company in my hometown of North Haven, Connecticut. They were both commercial electricians, and they ran a retail store that sold household lighting. My father was considered one of the best electricians in the area. He was always working which meant that

I rarely saw him, except he insisted our family always eat dinner together.

I would spend many hours playing at the business when I was young. There was one man who impressed me more than anyone in the world when he would come to visit. This man was Officer Hayes Gibson. He was a full-time police officer who worked for North Haven Municipal Police Department. He was appointed to his position in 1955. He is special because he is a black man. In 1955, the Town of North Haven was 96.6% white. He works with my dad on a part-time basis because the pay for police officers is pitiful.

One day when I was just twelve years old, I am at the business. Officer Gibson walks in dressed in his police uniform. His leather and black shoes shine as if he were a Marine. The silver buttons and the bright, shiny silver badge on his coat impress me more than anything. I tell him I want to be a policeman when I grow up.

Officer Gibson looks at me, then bends down so he is on my level. He looks at me straight in the eye. He says, "Son, you don't want to be a police officer. Stay in school, get an education, and go get a good job." He then pats me on the head and asks where my father is. I point to the warehouse because my dad has gone into it. Hayes turns back to me and says, "If you are still interested when you get older, I will tell you what needs to be done."

*Son, you don't want to be a police officer.* Those words stuck in my head. Why would someone who looked so happy and appear to have been put on this earth to be in that profession be telling a young man not to do the same thing? I was at a point in my life where the future needed to be on my mind. My thoughts turned back to the present.

Hayes Gibson was not the only police officer I would see there. Several of the officers worked part-time with my uncle and dad. When they were on duty, they would stop at the light store and visit. They would drink coffee and socialize. It seemed to me that they were just bored and looking for someone to talk to. I would seek the advice of several of these officers while they were in my father's store. However, Hayes would be the person who guided me the most.

I am getting near the end of my enlistment and think about what the future holds. Leaving the Marine Corps and pursuing a career in law enforcement is on my mind.

My tour of duty in Warsaw is at an end. My transfer orders have arrived, and I am on my way to Tel Aviv, Israel. I fly by commercial airlines from Poland to Switzerland and then to Israel. The Israeli security forces have made extreme improvements to the security procedures for anyone boarding a plane bound for Israel.

The Arab nations and terrorist groups are engaging in a campaign to eliminate Israel. These countries do not approve of the taking of the land known as Palestine to create Israel after World War II. The displaced Jewish people want a homeland, so the United Nations parceled off Palestine and created Israel.

The security outside of Israel has been responsible for allowing the hijackers of the Air France flight rescued from Entebbe, Uganda, to board the aircraft there. Israel has added several layers of its own security for any flight into or out of Israel.

Security personnel for Israel are everywhere in the terminal for the flight I will be on. There are clues, or what are commonly known as "red flags," when conducting a security check on an individual boarding a plane who should be considered a risk to the safety of the aircraft or those who should be considered a possible hijacker. I am a single American, traveling alone, from an Iron Curtain country with a one-way ticket paid for by someone else. Each one of these is considered a red flag. I am dressed in a suit and am transporting a diplomatic pouch. I have a certified letter written in English, French, Hebrew, Greek, Polish, and several other languages explaining the pouch only contains sensitive documents being delivered to the American Embassy in Tel Aviv.

The security screening I am subjected to is intense. I am sequestered in a small room with no windows. There is a table and a chair, and my suitcase is on the table. Three security personnel escort me into the room and close the door behind them. One of them is in charge, and he begins to interview me in perfect English with a Brooklyn accent. He begins by asking me, "Why are you going to Israel?" My response goes something like this, "My name is Mark Genovese. I am in the United States Marine Corps, and I am being transferred to the embassy in Tel Aviv as my new duty assignment. I have no weapons with me, and the diplomatic pouch only contains sensitive diplomatic documents. This letter attached to the pouch explains I will cooperate with you completely."

He then asks me where I have come from and why. The explanation seems to relax the three of them. They open my suitcase and search the entire contents. I am searched by hand, from head to toe. He then allows me to get everything back in order. They all help me with my suitcase and paperwork, and we all board the plane.

Israel is serious about the protection and security of the country and their people. I am not an Israeli citizen nor am I a Jew. My story is the truth, but I do not think they trust what I or a diplomatic letter told them. While on the flight from Zurich to Tel Aviv, I am sure there are at least three security personnel on the flight alongside me.

I arrive in Tel Aviv, but prior to leaving the plane, I make sure my suit is in order. I straighten my tie and jacket, check my shoes, and make sure nothing is out of place. I am out of place though because nobody is wearing a suit. Everybody else looks like they are going on summer vacation. As soon as I get into the passenger reception area, I am greeted by eight Marines who are all dressed in shorts and T-shirts and are carrying a cooler full of beer. The NCOIC welcomes me with a handshake. He introduces himself as First Sergeant Fritz and tells me to call him Top. He introduces each Marine as we make our way to the luggage claim. He takes my orders and the pouch as we are walking. We retrieve my luggage, and the small platoon exits the airport. It is about 5:00 p.m. local time.

The Marines in Poland are friendly with each other, but my first impression of this detachment is like no other unit I have been with to this point. The atmosphere is relaxed, but there is an obvious professionalism and team approach here. I feel like I am finally part of the elite unit that the Marine Corps brags about. I never had this feeling in Warsaw.

I retrieve my suitcase, and one of the young Marines takes it from me. We make our way out of the terminal, and while we walk, First Sergeant Fritz is talking to me, "So Corporal Genovese, can you please take that suit jacket and tie off and relax?" He then hands me a Budweiser beer, and says, "You drink beer, don't you?" This is unbelievable I think to myself.

It is May, and the temperature is about 75 degrees. The sun is shining, and people are wearing shorts and short-sleeved shirts. There is a breeze in the air allowing me to smell the salt water of the Mediterranean Sea. The Marines move through the parking lot as if they are celebrities. The Chevrolet van is tan in color and full of seats.

Top explains my room in the Marine House is all set for me to move into, but we will not be going there now. He asks if I can play darts. I tell him yes and point to my suitcase and say, "I have a set of my own darts in there." "Good" is his response. He continues, "Because we are going to play darts right now."

I am not in Kansas anymore as the saying goes. The Marines are now introducing themselves to me one by one. This detachment is different than what I experienced in Poland. I'm starting to sweat because just eight hours ago I was in a country that was 38 degrees. We make our way to a restaurant near the shore and park the van. As I exit, the view is spectacular. The sun is setting with palm trees shading my eyes. Seagulls fill the air, and so do the songs of their voices. It is a sound that has been missing from my ears for more than a year.

I sip on my beer and loosen my shirt, and my thoughts drift back to Poland. I think about the snow there and about how it always had a grayish tinge to it because of all the coal-burning stoves in the city. The sandy shores and dunes here are a light beige color, but they again remind me of that snow.

Suddenly, my senses bring me back to reality. The sun is setting, but it is hot again. The trees are green and full of leaves, life, and aroma. Birds are everywhere, full of color and singing songs. There is so much life going on here I feel like a new person. There is the distinct odor of fresh fish tickling my nose. The waves of the sea are gently slapping at the seawall, releasing its intoxicating perfume. As I enter the front door, there is a cornucopia of fresh fruit on a counter.

Bananas, oranges, lemons, limes, strawberries, apples, peaches, even a pineapple are all within reach. We push quickly by this display without stopping to look for even a second. We end up in a bar that is 65 feet long and packed with people. Everyone cheers as they notice the Marines have arrived. There are two other Marines with a large gathering of Americans in one corner near the dartboards. The little voice we all have in our heads starts to speak to me, "This is beautiful. I must be dreaming." I have not experienced any of these things for seventeen months.

Top grabs me by the arm and leads me to a deck outside and away from the deafening noise of the bar. He explains I am still a Marine and am expected to act like one. He tells me to continue to stay squared away, do my job, don't show up on post drunk or hung over, and don't give him any reason to have to punish me. My record is spotless, and this detachment has been considered the best in the company for the last two years. He intends to keep it that way.

Top then sends me back inside telling me to enjoy myself tonight, and he will meet me at the Marine House at noon tomorrow. The rest of the night is a blur, although I am not drunk when I finally get to my room in the Marine House.

The Marine House that services the embassy in Tel Aviv, Israel, is located approximately nine miles away from the embassy. It is in Herzliya, located on the shoreline between Tel Aviv and Haifa. The ambassador's residence, the American school, and 90% of the American Embassy's employees live here.

The Marine House is in a condominium complex that is gated and within walking distance of the shore. This Marine House is a row of four attached two-story condominiums. Each first floor of the Marine House will serve a different purpose. All the Marines will live on the second floor. Most Marines will have their own room.

Across the street, directly on the shoreline, is a five-star luxury hotel known as the Daniel Towers. Several other Americans live in this complex. There is a pool and a tennis court in the complex.

Condo #1 houses the Marine Bar which has two regulation dartboards, a full-service bar, and an area with tables and seating for thirty people. Condo #2 has a full-size gym equipped with weights, benches, and isolation machines. It also houses a laundry room with washer, dryer, and ironing board. Condo # 3 has a full-service kitchen and dining area. Condo #4 is set up as a library and sitting area. We can see, hear, and smell the beach.

There are three or four duty posts handled by the Marines in Tel Aviv, one to three in the embassy and one at the ambassador's residence. The embassy and the residence are guarded 24/7/365. Marines are given one day off a year to celebrate the Marine Corps birthday. One Marine will volunteer to work on that day so there is a guard still on duty.

I feel rejuvenated after just twelve hours in Israel. Warsaw, Poland, is a distant memory. I have settled into my room, and Top greets me at breakfast. He begins the conversation of the day by asking me what my last detachment was like. I explain it was a bit fragmented and had some issues. I also let him know it was a difficult assignment and really sucked.

Most of what Marine security guards do is classified government information. The general duties are the protection of American government personnel, property, and interests. During the ride to the embassy, Top explains how the work schedule is arranged and the additional duties I am to be assigned. The drive takes us along the shore of the sea. The embassy is located next to a beach.

We turn into a driveway guarded by several Israeli police officers. An electronic gate opens, and we drive down underneath the building, passing by a Marine Guard post. The basement is a parking garage and motor pool. The building is five stories high, including the basement. That is all I will say about the embassy. Top shows me around the building, introducing me to people as we go. Everyone is happy and pleasant, and I notice they are all tan. My skin is light and in need of some sun.

Standing watch and working in Tel Aviv will change my whole perspective on the Marine Corps and life in general. The professionalism, courage, and integrity of the men assigned to this detachment are like nothing I will ever experience again. On this first day, I meet Paul Kalsbeek who will become my lifelong friend.

Israel is basically one giant military base. Every Israeli citizen is required to serve in active duty in the military for two years. There are military vehicles and aircraft visible every day. Soldiers of the Israeli

Defense Forces, the name used for the Army, Navy, and Air Forces of the country, are everywhere, armed with military rifles. They are under a constant threat of invasion from most of their Arab neighbors.

The general feeling here is not worry or fear, but happiness, excitement, and anticipation for what the future will bring. Terrorism and war have taken their toll, but the country is thriving. The recent victory over the Egyptians in a war and the impending peace talks with them has Israel excited about the future. The successful rescue of hostages of an Air France hijacked jet has also made them feel invincible. It all adds to the promise of good things happening for the future in Israel.

As I get used to life in Israel, I feel as though my life has done a complete turnaround. The detachment is a dedicated bunch, closer than most brothers. Standing watch and living in Israel is just what I need to complete my time in the Marine Corps.

One Saturday, I am assigned to work the 0800 hours to 1600 hours shift with Sgt. Paul Kalsbeek at the embassy. Normally when we are relieved, we change into civilian clothing; however, on this day, Paul has a date and is in a hurry. We remain dressed in full Marine dress blue uniforms, including a white cover. We are the only two in the van headed back to the Marine House. Saul Rightman is assigned on the day shift at the ambassador's residence.

These two Marines are commonly referred to as Tall Paul and Small Saul. Paul Kalsbeek stands six feet five inches tall and weighs 225 pounds. His assignment prior to becoming a guard was in the Marine Air Wing. He presently holds the rank of sergeant. Tel Aviv is his second embassy assignment.

Saul Rightman, on the other hand, is only five feet four inches tall and weighs about 150 pounds. He was in the infantry, or as we Marines refer to it as the "Grunts." He presently holds the rank of corporal. Tel Aviv is his first and will be his only embassy assignment.

The drive is scenic, traveling along the shoreline on a roadway known as the Herzliya highway. Today, traffic is very heavy, bumper-to-bumper, and moving slowly. There is a traffic accident that involves a large eighteen-wheel truck that flipped over and dumped the cargo onto the roadway, median, and shoulder. The cargo consisted of cages containing chickens, so there are loose chickens everywhere. There are broken cages, live chickens, dead chickens, confused chickens, hens, roosters, and baby chicks. There are three Arab men trying to salvage what they can and rescue the live birds.

I am in the front passenger seat, and Paul is driving. I look at him and say, "Hey, let's catch one of those chickens and put it in Rightman's room." His response is a simple okay. He then steers his way through the traffic and stops on the shoulder. I am dressed in full Marine dress blue uniform, and without thinking about it, as I exit the vehicle, I put on my cover. The cover is white and loose fitting.

There are several white chickens standing all huddled together in the middle of the road. I decide not to go toward them, fearing that they will scatter and cause major traffic issues. I see a small flock of about half a dozen flightless birds scratching in the grass just off the shoulder. There is the corner of a fence and crate that forms a little trap. I start by herding the chickens in that direction. After a brief pursuit, some squawking, and wings flapping wildly, I have one. It is a beautiful male chicken, a Rhode Island Red rooster.

I gain control of him, tuck the rooster under my arm, and head back to the van. Kalsbeek is screaming, "Hurry up, get in, get in." There are three Arab men headed toward us, determined to stop us from rustling their livestock. We make our getaway without them getting close to us.

The rest of the ride to the Marine House is easy, and we arrive safely with the chicken. Saul Rightman's room is just above the Marine Bar. We take the chicken and let it loose in his room. The van leaves with the Marine who will relieve Rightman, so he should return here in approximately fifteen minutes. We have time to change our clothes, gather in the bar, and wait for his reaction.

Saul Rightman is a corporal who has been in the Corps for about three years. His original MOS is 0311 Infantryman. He was a grunt in a rifle company. He joined the Marines when he was 17 years old. We chose to put the chicken in his room because he was working at the Ambassador's Residence on this day.

There are now eight Marines waiting for Small Saul to arrive. They are all full of excitement, like little children waiting for the arrival of Santa Claus on Christmas Eve. The van pulls up and parks in the assigned parking stall. Saul leaves the van, walking without a care in the world, and then makes his way into and through the bar. He is happy and in a good mood. He bounds up the stairs, skipping every other one.

There is silence in the bar as the Marines shuffle over to the stairway to hear or sneak a peek of the encounter with the chicken. Then, there is the pitter-patter of footsteps running back and forth in the room. There is a loud crash, and Saul's bedroom door flies open. Saul emerges, grasping the flightless bird around the neck. The rooster's wings are flapping helplessly, and the feet keep reaching for something to stand on.

Saul makes his way down the stairs and through the bar. He attempts to wring the neck of the rooster and then tosses it outdoors. As he turns to walk back to his room, he proclaims, "Kalsbeek and Genovese, I know you two put that fucking chicken in my room. I hate you two mother fuckers. Where did you get that damn chicken? That chicken shit all over my room," Every word is said in disgust. I immediately admit it was all my idea and doing. I ask him why he doesn't think the chicken is funny. He replies, "That mother fucking chicken shit all over my room." I am in disbelief because the chicken had only been in the room for fifteen minutes. It couldn't be that bad.

We make our way up to the room to see what it looks like. The rooster had relieved himself at least a dozen times. There is chicken shit on the floor, and the bird had climbed onto the bed and dumped a load there. It was able to get into the closet and defecate on the clothing too. The rooster even made his way onto the window drapes and made a mess on them.

I am laughing so hard I am crying. My thoughts swing back to the chicken. What happened to the chicken? Is he dead? Luckily, two of the other Marines have revived the rooster and are tending to him. The chicken seems to be in shock but is very much alive.

We all pitch in and help Small Saul clean his room. I make arrangements to have his laundry done. We all gather in the bar laughing, drinking, and nursing the chicken back to health.

Chickens drink beer. It's a simple phrase and something I have never imagined I would be a witness to seeing. It's a shame that this chicken can't speak. He has lived a lifetime of adventure in just one day and, ah, the tales he could tell about the day's activities thus far. The night has just begun for this chicken of Herzliya.

Brewster the Rooster is now an official friend of our detachment. One of the Marines takes the rooster with us while we make our rounds through the pubs and bars. The first stop is a bar called "Norman's," a small bar owned by an older couple, with a female bartender from Scotland named Jane. Jane does not appreciate or even like the chicken. We bring the flightless bird to two more bars, showing our friends how he can drink beer. I don't remember him having any accidents with his digestive system during the night. In typical Marine fashion, one of the secretaries from the embassy takes him home at the end of the night and adds him to her hen house. We believe the rooster lived a happy, healthy life after one harrowing day.

The Marines all like to stop at Norman's after working because it is patronized by many Americans and other English language speaking people. Across the street from Norman's is a bar owned by an American known as the BBC or Bernie's Bottle Club.

Both establishments have dart teams that compete against the Marines. The British and Australians can't stand it when the Marines beat them in the dart games. We have taken to the sport and have some particularly good players. It is all in good fun and has become a great way to keep the Marines out of trouble. Jane is beautiful and single. She is one of the reasons the Marines like to go to Norman's.

I'm getting off the subject of the chicken. Now the chicken should be an example for all of us. You can have a really lousy day. You can be involved in a car accident and then get taken to a strange place that will scare the shit out of you. You can be strangled to the point of almost dying. You can be dragged around by Marines to several bars while they force you to drink large amounts of beer. However, you end up in a luxurious home for the rest of your life.

American sports are a big part of my life, and I have always been athletic. In Poland, there were platform tennis, cross country skiing, ice hockey, and running. In Israel, the most popular sports are soccer and basketball. There are more American companies, former Americans, and more influence from the United States. The American School is larger than the one in Poland.

Baseball is the sport I enjoy the most as a fan. In Israel, the closest thing to baseball is fast-pitch softball. The embassy has put together a small team and has entered it in this small league. We are, in fact, the only American team. Mostly, Canadian, Israeli, and mixed teams are in the league.

The differences to American big-league baseball are that the distance between the bases is 70 feet versus 90 feet, the ball is larger than a baseball, the pitcher pitches the ball using an underhand motion instead of overhand, and we let anyone play, man or woman.

Every few weeks there is a fast-pitch softball game. The Canadians always beat the hell out of us because they play it in Canada like we Americans play baseball or football in the United States. We never have a pitcher who can match up with any of the Canucks.

There are many Canadians living and working in Israel. The main United Nations Peacekeeping military force is the Canadian Army. One day, a young female consular officer from the American Embassy asks if her husband can play on the team. Apparently, she has married a Canadian soldier who knows how to pitch. He is added to the team with welcome arms. We are now at least competitive.

Now that our team is equipped with a reliable, competitive pitcher, we ask more teams to play games against us. The Canadian Army has the ability to field the most athletic and talented teams. Our team is good, but we are never able to beat them. We play several games against them which serve to forge a bond between all of us.

We arrange a special trip that allows our entire team, along with families and some of the embassy staff, to have a game played on the Canadian Army base in the Golan Heights. We fill a tourist bus to capacity and make the trip on a Friday night.

The Golan Heights is a barren strip of land that is desolate and lifeless. The base's softball field is beautiful. The bases are perfectly aligned in the diamond shape, and there is a regulation backstop behind home plate. There are two clearly marked foul lines with foul poles in the outfield and an arching fence marking the end of the outfield. Each separate field marks the distance from home plate with four feet high painted numbers. There are team dugouts and bleachers on each side of the field. Each team has its own batting cage and bullpen. There is a manually operated scoreboard in center field, just past the fence. The field is gorgeous, except there is no grass and there are no trees. There is an overabundance of brown and tan. The field is brown from the bench and dugouts all the way to the outfield. The Canadians have used chalk to outline all the features of the field as if it were a diagram in a book.

The game is played without much fanfare, and the Canadians win by the score of 12 to 7. At the conclusion of the game, we are invited to a banquet with all the food one could possibly imagine. The party lasts well into the night. Fast pitch softball would become especially important to me later in my life.

The Marine Bar in Tel Aviv is a center of activity for the Americans living here. There is always something taking place there. We are kept busy raising money and standing watch. The profits from the proceeds are used to pay for the Marine Ball. Life is much better here than it was in Poland.

Sergeant Paul Kalsbeek and I have become very good friends in the short time I have been here in Israel. We seem to be assigned on the same shift most of the time and spend much of our free time together. He is very tall, standing at about 6'5" tall, so dating is somewhat of a challenge for him at times. He has recently found an Israeli girl who he is pursuing for a date. So far to this point, she has stonewalled him and refused.

Paul refers to her as perfect for him as she is six feet tall and put together well. He calls her his "Amazon Goddess." He pulls me aside one evening and proposes I accompany the two of them on a date one night. He asks me to take her girlfriend. The four of us will go to dinner and then to a club.

I have many questions because we both have never seen this other girl. I am faithful to my friend because I know how much of a positive effect it will have on him. I agree to go on the date without ever meeting this woman.

Paul and I arrive for the date at the pre-arranged restaurant. He locates her in the restaurant, and we walk to the table. Paul's Amazon

Goddess is just that. She is beautiful, articulate, and perfect for him. My date is a toad. She is everything I would not expect. I'm totally disappointed with my friend and how the night has begun.

I am the perfect gentleman, however. I made a promise to my friend so he can get his prize. I just came along for dinner and drinks. My date is incredibly quiet as Paul commands most of the conversation. The night is a huge success for Paul and his date. I let him know later there will be a time I will get even with him.

I'm only in Israel for a short time but have become friends with one of the consular officers, Margaret McCoy. She is in her thirties and was here when I arrived. She is attractive and has always been very pleasant to me. I am working at the embassy one day when she approaches me and invites me to her house for dinner. Margaret is a widow who has a young son. Her husband was killed in an automobile accident here in Israel. I respectfully decline her invitation but explain that there is an event being held at the Marine bar that evening that I must attend. I am apologetic and ask her to stop by. Little do I know Margaret has an ulterior motive for inviting me to dinner that night.

Later that evening while the party in the Marine bar is in full swing, Margaret approaches me while I am working. I am acting as a waiter for this function, and the place is packed. The crowd noise is so loud I need to pull her to a hallway to hear what she is saying. Margaret points to a table in the Marine bar where I can see the woman who is the nanny for Margaret's son. Next to her is another woman with her back to me. Margaret speaks directly into my ear saying, "There is someone here I would like to introduce to you when you get a moment." She then points to the table and says, "My younger sister is here visiting me." I happily reply, "Okay, lead the way. I'm right behind you."

We make our way through the crowd to the table. As I walk toward the table, her sister turns to look in my direction. I am now stunned by how beautiful she is. I become a stuttering, blithering idiot. I can think of no reason why Margaret would think this gorgeous woman would have any interest in me. Margaret introduces me to her as we arrive at the table, but my brain has turned to mush. I hear the words, but they do not compute. "Mark, I would like to introduce you to my younger sister, Judy. She is going to be staying here with me for a couple of months." The only word I can get out of my mouth is "Hello."

My mind is racing. This girl is stunning, and that is all I can say. What an idiot. Way to go. Hell of a first impression you are making. I think to myself, "Do something, say something." Then, Judy holds out her hand to me to shake and says, "You must be the Marine my sister thinks so highly of. You have made such an amazing impression on her."

I reply, "I don't know what she has told you about me but thank you for the compliment." She continues, "You obviously look very busy. It was nice to meet you." It sounds as if the meeting is over, and she does not want to interfere. I respond, "Well, then, can I get you anything? Something to drink? Maybe you would like a little snack to eat?" This is all I can think of at the moment. I can't help but worry she probably thinks I am a moron.

Someone from another table diverts my attention away from Margaret and Judy. As I walk away to help them, I plead with the two women to stay until I can return.

The party winds down while I keep waiting on tables and fetching beers. Much to my surprise, Judy remains at the party. She is talking with one of the civilian embassy employees. They seem to be involved in an engaging conversation, which makes me reluctant to interrupt. Suddenly, Margaret is standing by my side. She says, "My sister thinks that you are truly handsome, and she wants to know when you intend on rescuing her from that dolt." I start to laugh. I look her in the eye and say, "I guess now is a good time."

Making my way over to her seems to take forever. I wonder if I should have brushed my teeth first. How does my hair look? Will I say the right thing this time? A million things are racing through my head. When I finally walk the ten feet to her table, I have again turned into an idiot. I look at Judy as she stands up. I ask, "You aren't leaving now, are you?" Her response is "It really is getting late." All I can think to say is "I was going to show you around. Would you like to see our pool and the rest of the Marine House?" After a good chuckle, she politely says, "Not now, but it was a pleasure meeting you. I hope to see you while I'm here in Israel. I am really tired. I think it's a little jet lag." I offer to drive her back to Margaret's, but she declines. With that, she turns and walks out the door.

One of the other Marines is dating Margaret's nanny, and Judy rides with them. I stand there dumbfounded as I close her door, thinking that my first impression did not go over very well. She simply says, "Goodbye." I have one last chance and say, "I hope we get to see more of each other." She responds, "I would really like that." Then, the car drives away."

I am not the type of person who believes in love at first sight, but something about this woman has just grabbed a hold of me. I have just met the second woman who I will fall in love with. I am not scheduled to work the next day, but I get up early and ride with the Marines going on duty so I can be in contact with Margaret as soon as she arrives at work. Now my brain is functioning properly again, and I have figured out why Margaret has been interested in getting to know me. She has always been extremely nice to me and welcomed me to her home. She is now playing matchmaker. Judy McCoy and I connect immediately.

Judy is a tall, slender woman with shoulder length auburn hair. Her eyes are a relaxing natural brown. She is put together like the woman every twenty-one-year-old man envisions to be the perfect specimen to have for themselves. She is intelligent and enrolled in college at Vanderbilt University in Nashville, Tennessee.

We spend a majority of our free time together. Judy is only in Israel for about ten weeks, but in this short period of time, she has stolen my heart. We are made for each other, and I don't want to be without her. When she finally leaves Israel, we both agree we are very much in love with each other. I am more mature than I was when I left for Warsaw and have no intention of losing her like I did with Kathleen.

We agree that if our love is strong enough, when I return to the United States, we will reconnect. I write to her almost every day and call her on the phone. I send flowers on holidays and for her birthday. I am not sure how I will keep the spark going until I finally leave Israel.

When she leaves, I decide to occupy my time by becoming a student of Israel. I want to learn as much as I can about the people, land, and the government. The Israeli government considers Jerusalem as the capital city, but the American government does not recognize it as such. Jerusalem is considered an international city. A consulate operates there, but we have minimal contact with them. There is a small detachment of Marines assigned there. They do assist us with security when we are at the King David Hotel later in the year.

One day while in Jerusalem, we decide to go to the Mount of Olives. This is a mountain outside the walls of the old city of Jerusalem. It is located on the eastern side of the city and is mostly a cemetery. The Mount of Olives is where Jesus Christ is believed to have ascended to heaven. It is one of the holiest sites for people of the Christian faith.

Ironically, located at the top of this mountain is an area that offers camel rides. In my opinion, camels are nasty animals. They growl, spit, and will bite you. When they walk, it looks like their legs are moving in different directions. The ride feels as if you are bouncing like a rubber ball. The camels are owned by native Arab men who dress in the traditional Bedouin style and use them to make a living. The ride is brief and like a carnival ride, but every tourist must do it. I have had a few beers when I decide to do this. It makes my ride on the camel just a tad bit more interesting. Fortunately, I survive without any injury. The most interesting part of the ride is when the camel stands up. The saddle is comfortable and easy to sit in. When the camel stands, it gets to its knees first, then straightens its rear legs and finally straightens its front legs. They rock back and forth until they are finally standing upright. The camel is called the ship of the desert. I think one of the reasons is because when they walk, it feels as though you are riding on waves. Judy takes the ride that day also. She will leave the country for home next week.

The duty is interesting, but since Judy left, I can't stop thinking about the future and what I intend on doing. I remember one of my encounters with Hayes Gibson, the police officer. I would talk to him often. When preparing for my graduation from high school a couple years earlier, we spoke about being a police officer. Hayes, or "Buddy" as he was commonly known, described the profession of a police officer as a lonely, thankless, miserable profession. He said that he would not encourage anyone to become one. He said, "You do not just go out one day and say, 'Hey I think I want to be a policeman.'

There is more to it. The hours are terrible, the pay is lousy, and nobody likes you."

He also said, "You do not simply join a police force and turn into a police officer. A police officer is a calling; it is what you become." The conversation continued with him encouraging me to focus on being the best Marine I could be. He added if being a Marine didn't work out for me, then he would help me in the future. He had made similar statements before to me.

The Marines in Tel Aviv are treated like kings everywhere we go. When we have a new member arriving at the airport, we load up a cooler of beer and parade through the security checks, flashing our credentials. We escort the newest member of our detachment out of the terminal as if they are the United States ambassador to Israel.

The embassy personnel know they can count on us to protect them in an emergency, and they treat us with respect. We are like a family and do everything together. On one occasion, five of us take a trip to Masada, our trademark cooler filled with beer in tow.

The ruins of Masada are a popular tourist attraction. There are three ways to get to the top of the mountain. The easiest is to take a cable car to the top. Then, there is a walking path known as the snake path that winds slowly to the summit. The last and easiest method of making the way up to the summit is from the opposite side. The Romans built a ramp almost the entire height of the mountain. Being Marines, we cannot take the easy route. We have to walk up the most difficult way on the snake path. We always travel with a cooler full of beer, and it is my turn to be in charge of the cooler. I carry that cooler with all that beer up the snake path. It is my turn, so what the hell? That is the best tasting Budweiser I have ever had when I reach the summit. We leave Masada by walking down the side of the mountain, using that ramp the Romans built.

The Marine Ball takes place on November 10, 1977. It is a huge success, even though our new NCOIC attempts to interfere with some of the things we have planned. Sergeant Paul Kalsbeek who is the Ball NCO and Sergeant John Clark who is the Assistant NCOIC handle the plans and the ceremony.

One of the most important institutions that make Marines what they stand for is the attention to tradition. The most cherished of Marine traditions is the Marine Corps' birthday. We don't consider it an anniversary. It is a birthday because it is the start of a life, which is something special. It is an honor to be a guest at a Marine Corps Ball.

The Marine Corps was born in Tun's Tavern in Philadelphia on November 10, 1775. The colonies had not even declared independence from England yet. In today's celebration, the highlight involves cutting the cake, which is done by a sword. The oldest and youngest Marine present at the time use the sword together.

Our ball in Tel Aviv is as fancy as a wedding. The detachment forms a reception line to greet the guests. When everyone has arrived and is seated, there is a brief ceremony. Dignitaries are introduced, colors are presented, a message from the commandant of the Marine Corps is read, the cake is cut, and the party begins.

My date that night is a teacher from the American School. The ball goes off without a hitch. No one gets into any trouble, and everyone makes it back to the Marine House in one piece. When I wake up at 5:00 a.m., Sergeant John Clark is in the kitchen getting breakfast with his girlfriend, Carol. We all agree that the ball was a great time and a fabulous party. Now we need to make sure all the Marines are accounted for, all the rooms are free of females, and everyone is alive. As soon as we finish breakfast, we start in the bar. When we have finished, three girls are sent home by taxi, and the Marines are accounted for. There are nine Canadian soldiers sleeping in various areas of the property, including the weight room and outside on lawn furniture.

We all gather in the Marine bar and celebrate the birthday one more time with a toast. We toast to the friendships we have made here in Tel Aviv, and all agree to try to stay in touch with each other after we leave Israel.

Egypt and Israel are beginning to engage in peace negotiations. The current leader of Egypt, Anwar Sadat, is not a supporter of the Soviets and has engaged the United States as a mediator for peace. The Egyptians took a beating in the most recent conflict with Israel despite some early successes. The embassy in Tel Aviv and the consulate in Jerusalem will soon play a big part in these talks.

The Secretary of State is Cyrus Vance, and he is the main American dignitary acting as the mediator during these peace negotiations. There will not be much time for fun and games during this time. A short time after the ball, we will begin to prepare for the arrival of Secretary Vance in Israel.

Egyptian President Anwar Sadat has planned a trip to visit Israel on November 19, 1977. This signifies the start of the dialogue for the peace talks between the two countries. This is the first time that a leader of an Arab country is going to be welcomed into Israel.

Our ambassador has the only Cadillac armored stretch limo in the country. The United States allows Israel to use this car to transport the two leaders during the official state visit. Ambassador Samuel Lewis is at the welcoming reception. Our Marines are by his side.

The Israeli security forces do not trust the Egyptians. They believe the President of Egypt will not be on the plane coming to Israel. The Israeli Defense Forces believe the plane is going to be filled with an elite fighting force that plans to strike a blow at the heart of Israel. They build an area away from the main terminal of the Ben Gurion Airport, surrounded by a fortress. When the Egyptian plane arrives in Israel, it is brought to this area. Once the Israeli security forces are confident the plane is safe, they will let it make the final taxi to the main terminal.

Anwar Sadat's visit is brief, but the foundation for a lasting peace has been started. Secretary Vance will be in Israel December 10-16, 1977.

The Secretary of State for the United States is an especially important person. The security detail assigned for the protection of both his party and him requires many hours of preparation. Israel, due to the political climate, creates more chaos than normal. Most political visits and negotiations take place in the embassy of the opposing country or the neutral party mediating the talks. The seat of the government of Israel lies in Jerusalem. The embassy for the United States is in Tel Aviv. Egypt does not have an embassy in Israel yet. The Israeli government insists on conducting these negotiations in

Jerusalem. For ten days, the government of the United States sets up a temporary operations center in the King David Hotel in Jerusalem.

Our detachment is divided into two teams. One team stays in Tel Aviv to continue to provide security at the embassy and the ambassador's residence. We have fifteen Marines assigned here. Seven are sent to the detail providing security at the King David Hotel. I am included in this team. The consulate in Jerusalem provides us with three additional Marines.

The week prior to the arrival of the Secretary is filled with meetings to explain what areas we will be assigned to provide security. I am assigned to be at the airport when all the classified equipment arrives. Then, we will escort the vehicles that transport that equipment to the King David Hotel. I will remain at the hotel until the end. We get these instructions about the schedule and plans for the week by both American State Department security officers and Israeli security agents. The coordination between the Israeli and U.S. security forces is amazing. They operate as if they have trained together for years.

We do not wear any uniforms during this visit. All of us are dressed in business suits, and each of us is armed with a firearm. When we are in the hotel or anywhere near the Secretary, we are required to carry credentials provided specifically for this trip. The security also has identified certain categories of people by lapel pins. These lapel pins designate the extent of accessibility a person has. The lapel pins issued to the Marines signify we have access to everything, everywhere. It also lets other security personnel know we are armed. This makes the screening process of a crowd easier.

On the first day of the visit, our team meets the support aircraft at the airport. Our small motorcade consists of three vehicles, all American-made, bearing diplomatic license plates. The first vehicle is a Ford LTD four-door sedan occupied by a driver, our Embassy Regional Security Officer, and a Marine. The second vehicle is a small box truck driven by an employee of the embassy who is an Israeli and an Israeli laborer. The third vehicle is the Marine van, and it has five Marines who are armed to protect the cargo being transported from the airport to the King David Hotel in Jerusalem.

The ride to Jerusalem will take approximately two hours. We travel around Israel freely and have not encountered any problems in the past. On this day, we begin the trip with no reason to believe any harm will come to us. We are equipped with overhead emergency red lights to allow us to get through traffic in emergencies. The three vehicles leave the airport and travel along the highway, making our way to Jerusalem. We are traveling much faster than traffic is flowing. We weave our way past any slow-moving vehicles, and there are no vehicles traveling fast enough to pass us.

The Marine who is in the rear of our vehicle is watching behind us for anything out of place or unusual. We all believe there is nothing in our vehicles except us that would be a target for any attack. The possibility does exist because of the simple fact we are Americans, and there is a group of us together, making us a target of opportunity.

When we are 45 minutes away from Jerusalem, the Marine alerts us to a taxicab attempting to catch up to us. He explains he has been watching it for a few minutes, and it appears to be shadowing us. Suddenly, we become alarmed and go into "Marine mode." Our main function today is the protection of the property and documents we are escorting to the King David Hotel. We have radio communications with the Regional Security Officer (RSO) in the first car. He advises us to go faster at first to determine his intentions. When we increase our speed, so does the taxicab. This makes the whole situation extremely uncomfortable. Each of us inside the van grabs our firearms and begins loading them. Sergeant Kalsbeek is armed with a twelve-gauge pump shotgun and is the closest Marine to the sliding side door.

The taxicab is following us and attempting to catch up. He is alone, and there doesn't appear to be any other vehicles following. The RSO advises us to just keep him behind us. We are not to take any action unless he attacks any of the vehicles. He continues to follow us for 15 minutes. When we approach a narrow winding part of the highway just outside of Jerusalem, the taxicab attempts to pass us on the right side of our van. When he makes this attempt, he slows down when he gets parallel to our van. We don't know what his intentions are at this point, but he is met with an open door. In that doorway are three Marines each armed with a long gun pointed at the taxicab. I do remember his brakes worked well. He never passed us, and we never saw him again. We arrive at the King David Hotel with all the cargo and no injuries. We have the same number of rounds of ammunition which we started the day with.

The rest of the day goes as planned as we arrive at the King David Hotel and unload everything we have. We settle into our rooms and receive our assignments. The Secretary operates explicitly on the sixth floor of the hotel. When I work at my post, I am situated between the stairwell and the express elevator on the sixth floor.

Several members of our detachment spend much of their time traveling with the motorcades which transport the Secretary from the hotel to meetings. My post remains at the hotel. Most of the time is filled with boredom, guarding an unoccupied sixth floor.

On the last night of the visit, I am assigned to the 1500 hours to 2300 hours shift. The embassy staff and Americans who are assisting the Secretary have a party in one of the smaller restaurants in the hotel on the first floor. Upon completion of my duty shift, I am relieved of my duties by Sgt. Tom Dawson. Sgt. Dawson explains to me that he slept in too late to be able to get anything to eat. While I am passing on the orders of the day to him, he asks if I would go and get him a sandwich and a bag of chips to eat.

I leave the post and go to the restaurant where the party is being held. I place an order for the sandwich and chips. While I am there, it takes several minutes for the food to arrive. I drink a beer and socialize with some friends. When the food arrives, I take it from the waiter. The elevator to the sixth floor is just a short distance away. When I arrive at the elevator, there is one hotel employee and two uniformed Israeli police standing in front of the elevator with its door open. I approach them, saying I need to use this specific elevator.

The two police officers explain I am not able to use the elevator. They do not speak English well enough to explain the reason, so I show them my credentials and explain in the best combination of Hebrew and English that I know. I am a Marine with a gun, and I am taking the elevator. The police officers reluctantly step aside and allow me the use of the elevator. The doors close, and slowly, the elevator begins the short trip up to the sixth floor. There is no music in this elevator so I have a brief time to wonder why they would be holding the elevator so no one could use it.

With that, I reach my destination, the sixth floor, and the doors open. As the doors are opening, I know I should have found another way here. Much to my surprise, I am greeted by the United States Secretary of State Cyrus Vance, a television crew, and several photographers, snapping photographs with flashbulbs going off. There I stand with my sandwich and bag of chips. The only thing I can think to do is press the fifth-floor button and proclaim, "I must be on the wrong floor." The elevator door closes and makes the short trip to the fifth floor. I exit the elevator and make my way to the stairwell. I deliver the sandwich and chips and see the reason I should have taken the stairs in the first place.

Menachem Begin, the Prime Minister of Israel, has arrived to visit the Secretary before he leaves Israel. Life in Israel will soon return to normal. After the departure of the Secretary, we all return to duty at the embassy. The peace negotiations will continue for years. An accord will be reached and signed by both countries in March 1979.

My friend, Sergeant Paul Kalsbeek, has broken off his relationship with his "Amazon Goddess." The time has come for payback for the blind date he arranged for me. The ice-skating girls who I met in Poland and had become friends with are now here to perform in Israel. The Fantasy on Ice will be here for about a month.

These women are beautiful, athletic, and built. He does not know any of them. I am working in the embassy one day when two of the girls arrive. We immediately recognize each other, and I make arrangements to meet them that evening. I telephone Sergeant Kalsbeek and ask him if he will be a pal and double date with me. He believes it is "get even" time. He blows me off and gives me some piss poor excuse for not coming.

I have four other Marines meet the ice skaters. We all eventually end up with these women at the Marine bar. When Sergeant Kalsbeek arrives, they are preparing to make their way back to their hotel. Paul and I both agree there are no hard feelings. The two of us will laugh about these two "dates" for the rest of our lives. He believes I had planned to set him up with the ugliest girl I could find to get even, which was not true.

March 10, 1978, is the date of the terrorist attack that will become known as the "Coastal Road Massacre." It is carried out by Palestinian terrorists against Israel, and it is close to the Marine House. Due to the timing and location of the attack, the detachment is split into separate groups. The Israeli Defense Forces have determined there are several small groups of attackers who have made their way to Israel by boat.

At this time, our NCOIC is out of the country, and his assistant Sgt. John Clark is in charge at the embassy. By the luck of the draw, I am the senior sergeant away from the embassy, so I take responsibility and charge of the Marines here. Here would refer to the ambassador's house, the Marine House, The American School, and all other important American Embassy personnel residences located in this area. My main concern is the protection of the ambassador's family and residence. The Israel Defense Force (IDF) has their hands full and is unable to provide adequate security to our ambassador's residence.

The town that these sites are in is known as Herzliya. It is now under Marshall Law, and only military and emergency vehicles are allowed on the road. The information provided to us concerning what has occurred is approximately twenty to twenty-five terrorists have hijacked a tourist bus and have taken hostages. They are driving the bus and at least one other vehicle along the coastal highway. These terrorists are heavily armed and equipped.

The Israeli police have engaged them at a hastily established roadblock, approximately three quarters of a mile east of the Marine House. A firefight is taking place, and gunfire is heard distinctly from the area. We have limited communication with the embassy, but they keep us informed using a radio. The embassy staff informs me the ambassador's residence has been confirmed as a target of this attack. The residence is located on the shoreline; however, it is located on the top of a large cliff that is difficult to climb. There is a six foot high wall encircling the property. There are two guard houses on the outside of these walls, located at opposite ends of the compound and manned by an Israeli security officer, each armed with an Uzi sub-machine gun.

The Marine guard at the ambassador's residence usually consists of just one man. Today there are three, and they are Sergeants Parre and Dye and Corporal Rightman. I hold the rank of sergeant, and I am the senior NCO here. The assistant NCOIC has assigned me to inspect these points of interest and concern. The ambassador's residence will be the first site that I will inspect.

The Israeli guards are walking around the perimeter of the compound and are not in the guard houses. The Marines unlock the gates and front door to let me into the residence. The Marines are in uniform because we want to make sure they are easily recognizable to the Israeli soldiers. There are several security measures in place to gain entry to the residence.

These three Marines are younger than I and are obviously nervous when I explain the situation. The ambassador is not at home, but his wife and children are. The residence has a hardened area they can hide in when under attack. I explain there is the possibility of a heavily armed force coming to attack this compound. The Marines cannot count on help from the Israeli Defense Forces. I ask them if they understand and if they need to ask any questions.

Corporal Rightman looks at me and in an articulate, apparently rehearsed, speech says,

"Sergeant Genovese, I'm armed with a .357 Magnum revolver loaded with six rounds of ammunition and a 12-gauge pump shotgun with five more rounds of ammunition." He pauses and then continues, "What can be expected of me? What can I do against an AK-47 or an RPG?" Without hesitation I look him straight in the eye and say, "We are Marines ... Make it count. If they come over that wall, you shoot to kill."

We received many hours of training on the use of deadly force and how it was only to be used as a last resort. I tell these Marines to forget all they have been taught. The room is deathly silent when I say, "Understood?" The response is simultaneous "Understood" from the three Marines. It is obvious to me this Marine is in fear for his life, and he believes it is unnecessary. I know we have been given a hard task to complete should an attack occur. There is nothing I can do other than make him realize that he may not survive. There is nothing he is going to do about it except to go out the best way possible.

I then give them their orders and advise them we will relieve them as soon as possible. As I begin to leave the compound, a UH1 Huey Helicopter comes in low over the compound, flying slowly, just about 75 feet above our heads and hovering over the compound. My eyes meet the sunglass-covered eyes of the door gunner. I hold up a sign written in Hebrew and English that says "United States Marines" and has the American flag and the eagle, globe, and anchor on it. I receive a "thumbs up" from the other two IDF Soldiers sitting on the deck with their boots on the landing skids, both armed with guns in hand. The white and blue Star of David emblem, out of place in the desert camouflage pattern that is emblazoned on the helicopter, is something I will never forget.

I make my way back to my vehicle and begin to head to The American School. This is a wasted trip because the school has been totally evacuated, locked, and left abandoned. That causes me to head back to the Marine House. Many American families have made their way here. Sergeant Kalsbeek and Sergeant Seymour have been assigned there and have turned the night into a party.

This entire time, I decide I will not be armed. The reason is two-fold. First, I do not want to become a victim of friendly fire. Everyone in Israel who can handle a gun is ready and willing to use it right now. The second reason is I need those firearms at other locations.

This is the closest I have come to being under fire or in a combat situation in my four years in the Marines. I sleep very little during those next 48 hours. The Israeli Army believes up to four of the terrorists have escaped and fled into our neighborhood. This turns out not to be true, as the firefight at the bus has resulted in the killing of all of the terrorists, except for two who have been taken prisoner. The Israeli police had set up a roadblock at the intersection of Glilot Road and the Coastal Highway. This intersection is one block south of the intersection leading directly to the Marine House. The bus was driven off the roadway and into a field there.

The bus exploded at one point during the incident. The Israelis claim the terrorists exploded it with grenades which ignited the fuel tanks. The two surviving captured terrorists claim an Israeli helicopter ignited the fuel tanks by firing at it. The burned-out skeleton of the bus remains there for about a week. A total of 38 civilians are killed during the attack.

We are allowed to observe the burned-out wreck of the bus. The IDF and the Israeli police force still believe there are terrorists in the area. The first victim was an American citizen. The Ambassador tours the site the next day as a representative of our government. Fortunately, all the bodies have been removed from the scene.

Life returns to some semblance of normalcy in Israel. I am not interested in having a steady girlfriend but continue to date when I am able. Communication with Judy is mostly through written letters. She questions me about each date. She still wants to be with me when I return to the United States.

Just before I left the United States, my father handed me a folded $100 dollar bill. He said to me, "Take this and hide it in one of the pockets of your wallet, and only use it in an extreme emergency or as a last resort. You will know when you need to use it. Be disciplined enough to know it is there, and you will have it when it is needed." I would do as he said and kept it there for years without ever having to use it. Then one day while three of us Marines were out on the town in Israel, we stopped to get a drink at a restaurant a little on the expensive side.

In Israel in 1977, one-hundred American greenbacks are quite a bit of money. We enter this restaurant and take our seats at the bar. The bartender and the maître d' are extremely rude to us. When we order our drinks, they ask to be paid in advance. Normally, I would have been insulted, angry, and ready for a fight. I have heard many positive reports about the food and atmosphere at this restaurant, so I am quiet. My response to the rude treatment is to simply pull out my folded one hundred dollar bill and lay it on the bar. I then ask, "Is this enough?" The rest of the night is very pleasing. The dinner, drinks, and atmosphere are much more than I ever imagined. We are treated like royalty. The picture of Ben Franklin on American money speaks volumes in that little restaurant that night.

Israel leaves a permanent and indelible mark on my life. I have been a part of the peace process between Israel and Egypt. I have witnessed an attack by a hostile force that resulted in the deaths and injuries of many people. I am part of a military unit ready to fight even though the odds are greatly stacked against us. I remain connected to the Marines of Tel Aviv, and they will be my friends for the rest of my life.

Marines have been known to spend countless hours in bars and taverns drinking beer and just having a good time. Occasionally, there would be some type of confrontations during these bar hopping events. The Marines in Israel are no different than any other Marines. There was one night while we were competing in the dart league when a fight broke out.

One of our Marines had the nickname "Fast Eddie." His real name was Eddie Pierce, and he was from Alabama. He spoke with a noticeably thick southern drawl. On this evening, Eddie was drunk, and he tried to pick up one of the Israeli women sitting at a table in this bar. Eddie was asked politely by the young lady's boyfriend to leave her alone. Due to the extent of Eddie's intoxication on this night, he did not heed this request.

The boyfriend became angry with Eddie and threw him across the room. The rest of the Marines present immediately came to Eddie's aid. I positioned myself between the enraged boyfriend and Eddie. I did not want to turn this into a bar room brawl and attempted to reason with the boyfriend. He had his back to the bar and was yelling in a mix of Hebrew and English. He was obviously furious Fast Eddie's behavior.

I tried to play the part of peacekeeper. I started a conversation with him, explaining that we, the rest of the Marines, would take care of Eddie and would like to make a peace offering by buying him and his girlfriend a drink. His first response to me was "Fuck you, Americans." I responded by saying, "Hey, there is no reason to insult my country. It has nothing to do with this." I again offered to buy them a drink or two. He became a little more aggressive and said, "Fuck you, Marines." I took a deep breath, looked him in the eye, and said, "Now, that is not necessary. We don't want any trouble, but now you're getting personal." He poked me in the chest with his right index finger while saying, "Fuck you, too!" I looked at him and said, "If that's the way it's going to be," spread my arms apart, and punched him as hard as I could with my right hand clenched in a fist. The punch landed right between his eyes on the bridge of his nose. I punched him about five more times, and there were a couple other Marines involved in a fight, making it a real bar room brawl. We all escaped without injuries, and the Israelis lost the fight. As we were walking away from the bar, Sergeant Miller looked at Sergeant Kalsbeek and told him, "You can take the dart out of your ass now." Sergeant Kalsbeek had a dart embedded in his buttocks, but he had such an adrenaline rush, he had not even felt it.

This was another night when our group of Marines were vastly outnumbered but were able to win the small battle in a bar in Israel. It will not become as famous as Belleau Woods or Iwo Jima, and there is no historical monument. There are five Marines who have each other's backs and always will, for as long as they all live.

After this bar fight had taken place, I came to realize there were many times when I would just sit down and think that life was good while I was in Israel. The United States is a staunch supporter of Israel and what it stands for. There are many fancy receptions and dinners taking place during my time here.

Jerusalem is considered the birthplace of three of the major religions of the world. Jesus Christ was arrested and crucified in the city. Muhammad is said to have ascended to heaven from there, and the "Wailing Wall" is considered the most holy of Jewish sites.

The entire city and surrounding areas are now under the complete control of the Israeli government. The city was under the control of Arab countries until the war of 1973, known as the Yom Kippur War. There is an enormous military presence in Jerusalem. Fully-armed soldiers and vehicles are everywhere. Officers of the embassy must travel almost every day to Jerusalem because the Israeli government seat is there.

State dinners being held in the Tel Aviv area are very rare. Most of my work assignments become limited to just standing watch at the embassy or the ambassador's residence.

It is March, 1978; I have been in the Marine Corps for three and a half years. There are approximately six months left of my enlistment. I have made it clear to my NCOIC, Gunnery Sergeant Clowney, I have no intention of re-enlisting. The Marine Corps has a book of regulations that is extremely strict. The Corps very seldom waivers when it comes to the regulations. One of those regulations is to attempt to have members who are eligible to re-enlist and have them do it as they reach the six months to separation mark.

Your supervisor must sit with you and attempt to convince you to remain a Marine. On this day in March, I am working in the embassy, and each time the gunny passes by me, he reminds me I need to meet with him before leaving to go to the Marine House. I spend the entire day thinking of how I intend on leaving the Marine Corps and starting a career in law enforcement. I know he is going to talk to me about re-enlisting. My only thoughts are what I can say to get away as quickly as possible.

When my shift is finished, I report to his office and casually take a seat in front of his desk. He is reading through some official Marine Corps papers. He looks up at me and addresses me. "Sergeant Genovese, you have received orders, and you are going home." My reaction to this statement is, "Yes, Gunny, my enlistment is up soon."

He then hands me a large envelope and says, "I have just received orders for you to report to Washington, D.C., Henderson Hall, Headquarters, Marine Corps no later than March 30, 1978." He continues, "Sergeant Genovese, you have always been one of the best Marines here, and you have been chosen for a special assignment. The Marine Corps is just as impressed with you as I have been since the first day I met you. You are leaving Tel Aviv in three days. You are being assigned to re-open the embassy in Havana, Cuba". I look at him and say, "So I guess you are not going to try and talk me into re-enlisting?" He chuckles. I ask him quickly if I am required to go or if there is an option to stay. He lets out a loud belly laugh and tells me to go back to the Marine House and start packing.

We both stand and start to walk out of the embassy together. He explains the orders he has been given. He jokingly says he no longer must give me the re-enlistment speech. When I get to the Marine van to ride home, Sergeant Kalsbeek is waiting for me patiently. He can see I am concerned about something. I explain to him that Gunny had just given me the re-enlistment speech, which is an obvious lie.

I am just a little surprised by this sudden change in my duty status. Sergeant Kalsbeek and I have become close friends since we began serving together here in Israel. He knows I am not being truthful, and he prods me the entire ride home. I break down and tell him I am being transferred. He wants to know the details as quickly as I can tell him. We learn as I read the orders. He is pissed because he was scheduled to leave before me.

We both know that this means no going away party. I will not have any time to let him know where I will end up. He is not supposed to know where I'm going, but we read the orders together. I have no idea where he will be after he leaves Israel. He will have no idea where I will be after I leave Cuba.

CHAPTER 9

# SPECIAL ASSIGNMENT: HAVANA, CUBA

The United States Government is attempting to normalize diplomatic relations with the island nation of Cuba. The American government has not had a diplomatic mission such as an embassy or consulate there since 1963. President Carter wants to re-open the embassy in Cuba. As a result, there is now an immediate need to have experienced Marine Security Guards assigned to that post.

I have been chosen for this detail because the assignment will be temporary and last for only three months. The Marine Corps is assigning members who have six months or less on their assignments in the MSG program. I do not want to go, but that choice is not up to me. I am glad my tour of duty overseas is finished, and I am going home. I am apprehensive about being assigned to another embassy.

The first thing my orders require is that I am not to discuss with anyone where my next assignment is located. I cannot call anyone in the United States. As far as my family is concerned, I can only tell them I am returning to Washington, D.C. The first telephone call I make is to my girlfriend, Judy McCoy. She is obviously excited and pleased that I am heading home. When I telephone my parents, my mother believes I have done something wrong.

That evening, the NCOIC in Tel Aviv holds a meeting of the detachment to inform them I have been transferred and will be leaving in three days. The Marines who are remaining have the duty roster modified by removing me from standing any watch over the next three days. These next three days in Israel seem like three hours.

My flight takes me from Israel to London, England, and then directly to Washington, D.C. I arrive at Henderson Hall at approximately 10:00 a.m. EST. This is the second time in my career I have been transferred here on a moment's notice. I report directly to the MSG Battalion, dressed in one of my finest suits. The person who greets me is a captain. When he calls me into his office, he treats me as if I am a long lost relative of his.

After he finishes welcoming me, he explains what my next five months are going to be like. I am being sent to Havana, Cuba. However, before I make my way there, I am to go home. While at home, I am to become a civilian. He instructs me to let my hair grow longer and grow a beard and a mustache. I am to try to loosen up a little. I am going home on leave for five weeks.

The United States is going to attempt to normalize diplomatic relations with Cuba. The plan is to re-open the embassy building which has been closed since 1961. The building is presently under the control of the Swiss government. Upon completion of my five weeks of leave, I will be required to turn in my military identification and dog tags. They will be kept here until my assignment is complete.

The Cuban government is allowing security personnel to be assigned to the embassy. They do not wish to have Marines as the guards though. I ask him if we will be armed and what the exact duties will consist of. He explains the duties will be the same as any other Marine Guard. But the difference is this is a new embassy, and there is a limited staff. He then informs me my housing will be in a hotel. I will be required to make my own meals and take care of my own laundry. There will be no facilities at the embassy. Before I can question him about it, he gives the best news of the day. The government will pay a per diem rate to me to cover the cost of the hotel and other expenses.

I am issued a wall locker in Casual Company and secure my uniforms in it. He issues me a large folder of orders and instructions, and I am free to leave. I am back in the United States for the first time in over two and a half years. I gather my belongings and telephone a cab. I will take a train home to Connecticut.

I read the orders on the way home while on the train. The per diem pay is $ 289.00 each day and starts the second that I arrive in the United States. I can also claim all my expenses and be reimbursed for most of them. I have not let anyone know I am here and heading home. The train ride home will take about four and a half hours.

The last four days have been a blur. I went from standing watch in the embassy in Tel Aviv to London, England, and I will soon be home. I make my way to the train and settle into a seat. I have not told my mother I am on the way home, intending to surprise her. She lives in a condominium along with my youngest brother Andy, who is twelve years old. It will be just a little before 11:00 p.m. when I arrive at her residence.

I can think of nothing but weddings and marriage during the entire train ride to New Haven. I remember how shy I was in high school. Kathleen was the first woman I ever felt in love with. She was the one who initiated the relationship. I had other girlfriends and had been on plenty of dates, but something was different with her. She was the woman I thought I was going to marry and settle down with to raise a family. She had recently sent me two letters attempting to apologize for not keeping her promise to remain my girlfriend. She wanted to try and ignite the feelings of love we had felt toward each other before I left for Poland. These random memories are racing through my head as the train winds slowly back to Connecticut. The past is now coming back to me. Each stop the train makes and every time a new female passenger gets on the train I think about Kathleen.

Then my thoughts turn to Judy. She has intimated to me in her letters that marriage may be in our future. I have thought about it, and I am very much in love with her. I will make it a point to visit her during my leave in the United States. Should I start to seriously consider marriage during this transitional time in my life?

As the train makes its way up the eastern seaboard, I wonder what has changed. How much have I changed? Will my friends still be around? When this Cuba assignment is over, will I get a job? What am I going to do in Cuba? So many questions ... maybe I will get some answers.

The train finally makes it to New Haven, and the cab ride to Wallingford is a simple one. When I arrive at my mother's condominium, it is just about 11:00 p.m., and it takes a few minutes for her to get to the door. When the door opens and the realization it is really me finally sinks into her brain, I am greeted with a hug and kisses that can only be given by a mother to her son who has been deployed overseas with the Marine Corps for almost three years. Mom is happy to see me. I make my way to my room with plans to go to bed, but I telephone Judy before going to sleep. The phone call lasts more than an hour. We try to catch up on everything since we were together in Israel. I just want to hear her voice.

The next morning is Saturday, and I had difficulty sleeping through the night. I am dressed early and am eating breakfast when my youngest brother, Andy, gets out of bed. The second he realizes it is me, he runs towards me. I have just enough time to stand up when he jumps into my arms. My brother is obviously happy to see me. He screams my name and hugs me tightly.

My time spent at home is too short. The only thing on my mind is seeing Judy. While I am home, I make arrangements to fly Judy to Connecticut to spend a weekend with me. Three days is all we can arrange before I am required to report to Cuba. She is still attending classes at Vanderbilt, and it is the end of the semester. I want everything to be perfect when I see her. I plan a romantic weekend for the two of us. For the first night she arrives, I plan to cook dinner. My menu is to include chicken cutlets that I will prepare Italian style. I buy these at a local butcher shop in my hometown when I run into a high school classmate. This is one of the most ironic things to ever happen to me. The classmate is Caren Mally. I will end up marrying her.

Judy flies from Nashville to Hartford on a Friday morning. When I pick her up, it is obvious we are still very much in love. I rent a hotel room for the time she is here. Our weekend is spent together, and we are never more than a couple inches away from each other. It is difficult for me to separate myself from her when she boards her plane on Sunday night.

My leave ends, and I return to Washington, D.C., where I am issued a new passport. The captain has me surrender my dog tags and military identification cards to him. There are no direct flights from the United States to Cuba. My flights will take me to Canada as the first stop and then a flight on Air Canada to Mexico City, Mexico. From Mexico, I board an incredibly old propeller-driven airplane owned by Aero Mexico, a direct flight to Havana, Cuba.

Upon my arrival, I am picked up from the airport in Havana by a consular officer from the embassy. There is no large welcoming party like the one I received upon my arrival in Tel Aviv. I feel as though I have stepped back in time here. The streets are filled with vintage American-made automobiles. None of them is newer than the model year 1963.

There does not appear to have been any new construction in over a decade. There are tanks and military vehicles everywhere. Some of those tanks are dug into defensive positions on the shore. We make our way along the shoreline towards the center of the city. The scenery on the drive is beautiful.

The American Embassy is located on the Caribbean shoreline. The embassy is surrounded by an eight-foot-high chain link fence, and the perimeter is guarded by eight Cuban soldiers. The feeling I get is one of total disgust. I have just four more months of my enlistment left and have to spend it here. I haven't been here for an hour yet, but this makes my decision to leave the Marine Corps a done deal.

Once inside the building, I am greeted by my new NCOIC Staff Sergeant Minor. We know each other having both served at the embassy in Warsaw, Poland. The building had been abandoned and locked up when the United States severed diplomatic relations with Cuba in 1961. Dwight D. Eisenhower was the President of the United States at the time. When the American personnel left the country, they did so quickly. The NCOIC greeted me and explained the expectations for this assignment.

Many of the offices and areas of this building are locked. Our initial assignment is to gain access to all those areas. We will then collect and secure any valuables, classified material, and identifiable personal items. This building is enormous and is six stories high. When we complete the opening of the offices and securing of all the items, the embassy will be staffed and officially opened. This process began in September 1977. There had been several delays, and approximately half of the offices in the embassy had been opened by the time I got there. The NCOIC explains it is a slow process because they have uncovered substantial amounts of classified material.

The living arrangements are then explained to me. We live in a hotel. There is no Marine House here. There are no other living quarters available to us yet. We are not allowed to go anywhere on our own. We cannot go for a walk or a run alone. There must be a minimum of three of us together every time we leave the hotel or the embassy. Everything we do will be done on a strict schedule, and each day will be specifically planned out by a member of the embassy staff. The host country has made it clear to our government they do not want American military members here. There will be no individual free time spent outside of the hotel grounds alone.

The Marine Corps has really made my life difficult. I take a little time to ask about the payments. The NCOIC explains the per diem payments will be paid directly to each of us individually. The hotel bill is in our name and must be paid each week. We are required to pay for all our own food. I am an employee of the Swiss Embassy, living in Havana, Cuba, now. During this time, the U.S. doesn't have diplomatic relationships with Cuba, so we are "The American Interest Section of the Swiss Embassy." We are considered employees of the Swiss Embassy. The Cuban government does not want U.S. military personnel in Havana.

I settle into life in Cuba quickly. On my first day at work, we open the section which served as the library for the embassy. Not a single person has been in this room since 1961. A portrait of Dwight D. Eisenhower hangs above the main desk. The title "President of The United States" is engraved on a brass plate attached to the bottom of the picture frame. Chairs and tables have been moved into the middle of the room and stacked up. There is a cash register on the main desk that is bolted to the floor. The shelves once filled with books are empty and stacked in a corner. There are stacks of boxes in another corner of the room. There are four filing cabinets next to the main desk that are all double locked. The NCOIC has an envelope of keys that are supposed to open all the locks.

The first thing that we open is the cash register. To our amazement, the cash register is filled with money. Each denomination of bills, from one dollar to twenty dollars, is in the tray. Each tray for the coins – penny, nickel, dime, and quarter – has some coins in it. There are also rolls of coins and bundles of bills in the available spaces in the cash register. There are thousands of dollars in this cash register. This is the first significant find in the embassy, and it is just the first day. We complete an inventory of everything in the cash register and secure it. Next, we open the file cabinets. There are only a few classified documents found in these cabinets. The rest of the day goes slowly, and nothing of significant historical or intrinsic value is located.

I am extremely interested in the cash we have located in the cash register. All the cash had been issued prior to 1961 when the embassy was closed. It is all uncirculated, and I am interested in obtaining some for its collectability. The bills are what interest me the most.

We continue to open locked rooms for a couple more weeks, and there is not much of interest located. There is a second cash register found in the commissary. There is only approximately $600.00 cash in this register, and it has been in circulation.

I had hoped we would have located evidence connecting the United States to some of the incidents leading to the Cuban Missile Crisis or the Bay of Pigs, but nothing I read shows any connections. There is no hidden treasure, no gold bars, no silver bullion.

While we are busy securing the locked rooms of the embassy, a construction crew is working to rehabilitate the rooms and make them functional. The embassy is being totally refitted and remodeled. There is some political business being conducted. A consular section has been constructed on the first floor, but very few people use it. While I am here, the first through the third floors of the building are all unlocked, and the old furniture and cabinets are removed. The first and second floors are completely rehabilitated by the time I leave Cuba. There are three highlights from my time in Cuba.

1. I was approximately ten feet away from Fidel Castro. A small contingent of our embassy staff was invited to a dinner where he was present. He was dressed in his military uniform and was seated, talking to two younger women. Our eyes met as I walked past him to get a drink. I never spoke to him or shook his hand.

2. We were allowed to visit Ernest Hemingway's residence in Cuba. It was located just a short distance from Havana. The Cuban government has maintained it, and they allow tourists to visit the house. It's a small thing, but I have always been a fan of his writings.

3. The Smothers Brothers made a trip to Cuba while I was there. We spent an entire night in the hotel bar, drinking and exchanging stories. Tom and Dick Smothers were an extremely popular comedy team and had their own television variety show for several years. They were allowed into Cuba to film an adventure fishing show. We met them in the bar of the hotel one night, and much to their surprise, we were Americans. It was tough for us to not disclose we were Marines in Cuba. I spoke with Dick for over two hours, with him constantly trying to make me confess that I was a Marine. I never admitted I was, but I am sure he knew.

I am able to save a healthy sum of money. Cuba is not good for much more. My relationship with Judy has ended. Apparently when we were together in Connecticut, I said something that hurt her feelings. I am not sure what it was that I said. We had exchanged several letters while I was in Cuba. One of them had the tone of a "Dear John" letter (my second).

I just believe that long distance relationships don't work. There is nothing like being able to hold on to the person you are in love with. Talking with them face to face rather than reading a letter over for the fourth or fifth time just does not work. If I had come home for good, there may have been a different outcome.

The tour of duty in Cuba ends on August 15, 1978. I again fly a roundabout way to get to Washington, D.C. I fly from Cuba on

Aero Mexico to Mexico City, and then change planes and catch an American Airlines flight to Dulles International Airport. I am supposed to complete my enlistment on September 2, 1978. I spend the rest of my enlistment listening to re-enlistment speeches and getting medical clearance.

I am assigned to what the Marine Corps refers to as Casual Company. It is generally reserved for those men who have committed a crime or have done something that has caused them to be dismissed from the Marines. There are no other facilities available to house me. I should not be here, and it serves as one more factor to ensure I will not re-enlist.

Each day, I am required to report to duty with the officer of the day. On occasion, I am given some menial assignments, but most days I have the day to myself. There is one day I am going to a medical appointment and had two hours to wait. I am dressed in my utility uniform. I had removed the shirt and hung it on my bunk. I then lay down on the bunk, without turning down the bedding. This normally is a no-no and contrary to Marine discipline, especially in a Casual Company setting. I am being honorably discharged and should not be here. I should have my own room, and then this would be overlooked. While I am lying on my bunk, a corporal in charge of the five other people in Casual Company observes me in this position. This corporal assumes I am a member of Casual Company and sneaks up to my bunk, kicks my feet, and begins to yell orders and instructions to me. He is loud and obnoxious and does not give me time to answer. His last order is for me to report to the captain in charge. This is the same captain in charge of the MSG battalion.

I dress in my uniform and report to the Captain as ordered. When I arrive, the corporal and the captain are having a discussion outside of his office. The captain looks at me curiously and asks why I am there. I explain the reason for reporting to his office. He looks at the corporal and motions both of us into his office. He closes his door and takes a seat, shaking his head. There are two chairs in front of his desk, where he orders each of us to sit.

The corporal mistreated me when he kicked my feet. I also outrank him as a sergeant. I had been given permission to occupy my bunk in the manner he found me. The captain wants to know if I am going to pursue the issue and bring charges against the corporal. We all agree it was a perfect teaching moment for each of us.

CHAPTER **10**

# OUT OF THE MARINE CORPS

The next time the three of us are together is September 8, 1978. The corporal signs me out of the Marine Corps, ensuring all my paperwork is in order. The captain salutes me and shakes my hand. He sends me off by saying, "Good luck out there, Marine."

I have a car and am going to drive home to Connecticut. The last two items I load are my sea bag and the envelope holding my records and separation papers. I cannot believe this day is finally here. Four years in the Marine Corps have come to an end. I drive out of the front gate and wave goodbye to the two Marines standing guard.

The Marine Corps has prepared me for the future. It has taught me what it means to be a leader of men. No university could have prepared me for what I am about to endure. I was able to serve in a military organization known for strength and the ability to fight. I have been a part of an organization considered the best of what it means to serve America.

I am now a civilian again, and my service to my country is complete. I decide on my way home I am going to drive through the center of Washington, D.C. The drive takes me along the east side of Arlington Cemetery. Traveling north past the Pentagon and then across the Potomac River to the mall, I drive past the Lincoln Memorial, the Jefferson Memorial, and the Washington Monument. There is a distant view of the White House, the mall surrounded by the many museums, and at the end, the Capitol Building.

I make my way to the Baltimore/Washington Parkway and the jumble of roads to Connecticut. The drive home is insignificant, but I have hours to think about the future. My thoughts drift to the past. My mom was a single child, born and raised in Romulus, Michigan, a very small suburb of Detroit. The town was best known as the home of Detroit Metro Airport. My mother grew up on a small residential street with an interstate highway serving as the border of their backyard. My grandfather was a hard-working, bigoted mid-western "Made in America" white man. He had worked in an American Motors Corporation factory for thirty years.

Aenon Rehkop made refrigerators and learned about how they worked. He had retired from the factory and now had his own personal refrigeration repair business. We affectionately referred to our grandfather as "Bumpa." He was originally from St. Louis.

My mother, Donna Mae Rehkop, joined the Marine Corps immediately after she graduated from high school in 1951. She joined the service because she felt it afforded her the best chance to get away from her parents. Her father expected her to marry a local boy, settle down, and raise a family. My mother wanted to spend many years in the Marines until she met my father. She was stationed at the Marine Corps Air Station in Cherry Point, North Carolina. They were both supply clerks who insured that planes were properly loaded. Mom and Dad both held the rank of sergeant when they left the Marines. Mom wanted to stay in the Marines, but she wanted to be married more. In 1951, female Marines had to remain single and could not be pregnant.

Family history and tradition steered me toward joining the Marines. Now I had to decide where the future would lead. My thoughts were leaning towards becoming a police officer. I knew the assignment I had just completed was best suited for pursuing a career in law enforcement. I needed to seek out Hayes Gibson as soon as possible.

Nothing of importance occurs on my trip home. I soak in the scenery and check off the landmarks on the trip. I am determined to contact Judy when I return home and try to reconcile. If it does not work out, my focus will be on finding a place to live and somewhere to work.

The next phase of my life is about to begin. The town I live in is considered a small town in Connecticut. North Haven is a suburb of New Haven and is located north and east of that city. The connection to the city is minor because of the geography of the area. A large hill known as East Rock and the mouth of the Quinnipiac River separate the two. North Haven has become the upper middle-class suburb of New Haven.

My father was raised in New Haven. He established an electrical business along with two of his brothers. There are two facets to the business: a retail store known as "Lights Incorporated," with the contracting business side known as "Triangle Electric."

My father is an electrician by trade and has a reputation of being one of the best in the trade. I hardly ever see my father when I am growing up. He leaves for work six days a week before I am out of bed. He has dinner with our immediate family every evening. Dinner is the biggest extent of our interactions, but he is home most Sundays. Four or five nights a week, he works as a part-time bartender.

Life in North Haven is simple while I am young. My mother is the main parent handling our discipline. She takes the responsibility of raising four boys and my sister. The first ten years of my life are filled with many medical emergencies and injuries. I was born with a common affliction in the mid-fifties known as pyloric stenosis. The valves in my stomach would not work properly. This allowed for food to be ingested to a point, but not pass through. This caused me to vomit everything back up. Emergency surgery was done, and the problem was corrected.

Some of the other medical incidents include my older brother feeding turpentine to me at the age of one. This led to my stomach having to be pumped out. A short time later, I took a tumble off a couch and suffered a broken collarbone. At the age of two, a toe caught in the spokes of a tricycle, resulting in stitches and a broken toe. The injuries and broken bones will continue well into my life.

My family will live in two residences during my childhood. The first is a small Cape Cod style home, located in the northeast section of North Haven, a post-World War II housing development. This subdivision served as housing for the workers of a jet engine construction factory located in this area. The second house is constructed by my father and his friends in the southeast section of town and is a large colonial style residence. We move into this house when I am eleven years old. It is built in an area that is surrounded by woods, with a trout stream flowing through the backyard.

Most of the land and property on this side of town is used for farming. The land directly across the street from our house is used to grow vegetables. Working on these farms will serve to build much of the character my brothers and friends gain in our childhoods. I will always have money in my pocket that I earned.

My thoughts shift back to the drive home because I reach the George Washington Bridge in New Jersey. This is the main crossing of the Hudson River into New York City, and it marks the home stretch of my trip home. Another hour and a half and I will be back in North Haven. I pay the toll and immediately move into the right-hand travel lanes. I exit the highway as soon as I get to the other side of the bridge. The Henry Hudson River Parkway helps me skirt the center of New York City. It will eventually lead me to the Hutchinson and Merritt Parkway and a direct route home.

My mother has moved back to North Haven, having sold her condominium in Wallingford while I was in Cuba. She now lives a block away from the house I was raised in. The rest of the drive home is filled with anticipation of finally getting back to a normal life. When I arrive, it is late, and only my mother is at home. I empty the car, exchange niceties with Mom, and head to bed.

In September of 1978, there are no cellular telephones. The computer is not yet a personal item. There are very few people who have a telephone answering machine. Telephoning someone out of state costs money, even if you don't make a connection.

Judy McCoy lived in Tampa, Florida but attended school in Nashville, Tennessee. I believe she graduated from Vanderbilt University, and she may be living anywhere. After several attempts to contact her, I speak with her sister. Carol explains to me that Judy has moved on and has no interest in reconciling the relationship. The last contact I have with her is a letter wishing me the best in the future. I am sorry we cannot work things out, but now I can focus on finding a job and a place to live separate from my mother. I have no job, and I've taken up residence with my mother. This is not going to work very well. I spend most of my time filling out applications for employment. I have no real skills I can use or any experience that will be useful to me, having just been discharged from the military.

Most police departments require a long application and testing process. I have begun the application and testing process in five separate towns for the entry level position of police officer. I decide to visit Hayes Gibson at the North Haven Police Department. I walk into the police department without making an appointment to see him. The lobby of the police department has two sets of double doors that lead into a large room. The duty officer who is either a sergeant or lieutenant is seated behind a window with a hole in it so that they may talk with individuals who come in. I approach this desk and speak with a sergeant who I do not know. Sergeant Tom Mele stands and asks if he can help me. I respond by saying, "Hi, my name is Mark Genovese, and I was wondering if Hayes Gibson was working." With that, he turns to the side and yells, "Captain Gibson, are you here?"

I did not know he now held the rank of captain. His office is located directly to the side of this desk. A door opens to my left, and Hayes Gibson stands there. He says, "Mark Genovese, why don't you step into my office." I walk to his office, and he grabs my hand firmly, shaking it while welcoming me in. He points to a chair and asks me to have a seat.

He starts the conversation by asking about my family, and this takes up a considerable amount of time. We eventually talk about why I have stopped to visit on this day. I explain I am interested in becoming a police officer. I ask him what is required, and if there are any employment opportunities here. Hayes explains the town just went through a testing procedure to hire a police officer in August. He is angry and asks where I was at that time. When I explain about Cuba, he just laughs. He is disappointed because the police department will only hire people when someone resigns, retires, dies, or is fired, and then the vacancy is filled. On rare occasions, there is a new position. That normally happens when a new yearly budget is submitted.

Hayes is enthusiastic I am looking to start a career in law enforcement. He lets me know he will contact me when there are any employment opportunities available to me. He advises me to start thinking about taking some college courses. Many police departments are beginning to require that newly hired police officers possess a degree from a college or university. I finish the meeting with him, and he reminds me of what he said to me years ago. "You should have listened to what I told you and gone to school to get an education. Now, we will see if it is a part of you. Did you get the calling?"

I leave this meeting feeling hopeful but apprehensive. I must think about finding some place to work so I do not waste my savings. The Marine Corps is in my rear-view mirror. While leaving the building, I meet Officer Steve Smith who my family and I know.

Officer Smith has been a police officer for over twenty years. He was the investigating officer of a motor vehicle accident that involved me at the age of eleven. The accident occurred on a Saturday morning at approximately 9:00 a.m. as I was riding my bicycle northbound on Pool Road. My family had recently moved from this area of town to the residence on Mill Road. I was riding my bike to the old neighborhood to play baseball with my friends. The ride was about three miles, and I had just about reached the park. I had just traveled under the overpass of Interstate 91 and was approaching Fairlawn Drive, a side street. I was traveling in the same direction as the traffic and needed to cross to the other side of the road. I checked in front of me. There was a car approaching, but it was far enough away for me to cross safely. I checked behind me by glancing over my left shoulder. The roadway at this juncture took a slight jog to the left. This caused my view to be somewhat obstructed. There was a car approaching that I had failed to see. I turned my bike directly into the path of that vehicle.

As a result of the collision, my bicycle was bent at a perfect ninety-degree angle, and both tires were flattened. I became a missile and was launched from the seat to a point directly above the windshield on the driver's side of the vehicle. I landed there with my chest and left arm in full contact with the car. My body slid and then rolled off the roof onto the ground. I was conscious the entire time and landed on the roadway on my backside. When I landed, my first thought was, "Oh shit. That is my brother's bike. He is going to be mad." I felt a sudden sense of panic and made an attempt to get up and run away. When I tried to get up, it was obvious that my left ankle was broken. I wasn't going anywhere but back down on the pavement.

The driver of the car turned out to be a North Haven Elementary School principal. He attended to me and had me sit on the curb. A neighbor telephoned the police department, and Officer Smith and Officer Oertel arrived. Since my injuries were minor, the police did not call for an ambulance. I was more nervous that my parents were going to be angry with me. The emergency medical personnel and ambulance drivers during these days were volunteers and would not be called unless there were serious injuries involved. My broken ankle was not considered life threatening or in need of immediate attention.

I had just been fitted with a permanent tooth cap that had taken months to complete. That cap had been knocked out of my mouth. I tried to tell all the adults about this tooth because I could see it lying in the street. They failed to understand what I was trying to tell them. I sat on the side of the road and watched as a curious passerby stepped on the cap and crushed it.

I was not thinking about my injuries. The most important items of concern to me were the tooth and my brother's bicycle. That I might have just been killed never entered my mind. The injury to my leg would heal. The question of how I would replace the bicycle was repeated in my head.

Steve Smith knew my family personally. He picked me up off the street and loaded me into the rear seat of his police cruiser. He placed my damaged bicycle in the trunk and drove me home. When we arrived, he held me in his arms across his body. I explained how he could open the doors and where the keys were located. When he opened the door, he called out my mother's name – "Donna" – as he stood holding me in the front foyer. My mother was lying down sleeping on the living room couch. As she got up, trying to wipe the sleep from her face and straighten her clothing, she looked at Steve. "Why is there a policeman in my house?" were the first words out of her mouth. "Donna, Mark was involved in an accident, and you are going to need to take him to a doctor," Officer Smith said, still holding me. Now my mother was flustered and started to point him in the direction of the couch to put me down. While she was pointing, she was questioning Officer Smith about the accident. He made his way to the couch, placed me on it, and quickly explained what had happened. Officer Smith and my mother continued the conversation about my injury for a few minutes. He then left, and my mother took me to the hospital. My ankle was splinted, and this was one of the injuries that will continue to be a part of my life story. The cap to my tooth was easier to replace than I thought it would be. I did not suffer any other injuries because of this collision.

After exchanging greetings and a handshake, Officer Steve Smith and I reminisced about the accident, and he asked why I was at the police department that day. I explained my desire to start a career as a police officer. He also offered to assist me in any way that he could. As I was leaving, he handed me his business card.

The next year would prove to be complicated and a challenge. The path to becoming a police officer would take some time to accomplish. The world, especially the field of criminal justice, was experiencing extreme changes. The application and hiring process for becoming a police officer are complex. I start the process at six different municipalities like North Haven, while looking for other employment in the meantime.

After three days, I find employment with friends who have formed a small landscape construction company. Working for this company helps me appreciate the time spent at the completion of my tour of duty with the Marines. I am a laborer. We construct driveways and sidewalks, plant trees and grass, build retaining walls, and grade yards. My job is all manual labor. The work is difficult and requires physical strength and endurance. It helps me stay in good physical condition, but it is exhausting. I work for them for about eight months.

## CHAPTER 11

# TRYING TO JOIN THE POLICE DEPARTMENT

The process for becoming a police officer will take some time. Hayes advises me to apply to as many municipal police departments as I can. The procedure is much the same in each town. Applications are comprehensive and include submitting historical background information about me. There is a series of tests required once you meet the pre-requisites of the application.

The first test is a written general knowledge exam covering everything from sentence structure, grammar, spelling, and mathematics to memory and more. The second test is a physical agility test but is not difficult in any way. The hardest part is the requirement to run a mile in under twelve minutes. These tests are given a pass/fail score, and each applicant must pass each phase to continue to be eligible for employment. Once these are completed and scored, the municipality selects as many people as they want to comprise a list of possible candidates. Some will just pick them in the numerical order they finished, while other towns will use different criteria. North Haven ranks candidates by their respective test scores.

When these tests are completed and your name is put on a list, that list is transferred to a civilian police commission. This commission is comprised of five civilians elected to office by a public vote. Each commissioner holds his/her office for two years. North Haven has been run predominantly by a Republican majority for most of the town's existence. The present commission consists of a three to two majority in favor of the Republicans. The commissioners normally hire the candidate recommended to them by the Chief of Police. The Chief of Police at this time is Walter T. Berniere. He has taken over the title from his brother Leno after his retirement. Leno was the first full-time police chief in North Haven.

At this point in my life, I am naïve to think that by doing my best and presenting myself as the best person for the job, I should be hired. I have no experience with politics. I know many people who hold positions in town government. My father is well known and socializes with many of them. I do not contact them prior to the list being sent to the commission.

The commission determines who to interview for the position. They can use any criteria they wish to claim as a valid reason. In 1979, there are no female officers on the police department. The commission makes it a priority to interview females for the open position.

I do not get an interview, and three officers are hired, including a female. The list will be valid for a year. Several police officer positions become available in the next year, but I am not offered one. I continue to take tests and make my way onto several lists. This is the start of a year-long waiting period.

Within a month, Hayes Gibson unexpectedly telephones me one day. The purpose of the phone call is to offer me a position in the police department. It is a position designed to introduce high school graduates to law enforcement and is titled "Police Cadet."

The candidate must pass a series of tests to determine if he meets the criteria to become a police officer. The candidate must also apply to a local university, be accepted, and begin a course of study there. The individual will be considered a police trainee and assist police officers in their daily assignments.

The original design and purpose of the program was well intentioned, but North Haven has different plans. The program is made available to the town through a grant from the federal government. When the grant expires, municipalities are required to take on the expense of the program. The town turns the cadets into emergency dispatchers, which is something I didn't want. Taking the job as a cadet proves to be one of the worst decisions I make in my entire life.

Captain Hayes Gibson paints a fabulous picture of how, if I take this position, the next police officer position which becomes available is guaranteed to me. The profile of the standard police cadet is an eighteen-year-old high school graduate with no employment history, holding a driver's license, and willing to enroll in a university criminal justice program. I, on the other hand, am twenty-two years old, have four years of experience in the Marine Corps, and am already enrolled in a university criminal justice program. I have a healthy bank account, but I am still living with my mom, which I dread.

Hayes Gibson believes it is important for me to get recognized by "getting my foot in the door." It is his intention to take me under his wing and be a mentor. He is trying to give me an advantage over any other person who might be seeking the same position.

We work a rotating shift, requiring us to work two weeks of a shift on days, two weeks of a shift on evenings, and two weeks on a shift of midnights. The pay for these 40-hour weeks is $100 with all the appropriate fees and taxes taken out. We are not allowed to join a union, and the time spent in employment does not count toward retirement or tenure.

There is a night out that will not be good for me personally or professionally while I am employed as a cadet. I have only been discharged from the Marines for a short time. My friends consider my behavior too rigid and disciplined. They try to get me to relax and have some fun.

On a Saturday at the end of August, we gather a large amount of ammunition and guns and spend a day just shooting and blowing shit up. The day does not end at the range. We all go out to dinner and then bar hopping. We spend the night at three drinking establishments in North Haven. The night ends at a lounge in the northeast section of town. When the six of us get there, it is only 7:30 p.m. After drinking just one beer, four of my friends decide they need to get home, each making their own excuse or reason they need to leave.

Tom Murray and I are the only two left in the bar. We have not seen each other since I went away to the Marines. We talk and eat for another hour, and I'm sure we have a couple beers. The bar is full, and the waitresses become busy. We both decide it would be easier to walk to the bar to be served.

I volunteer to buy the first round of drinks. I walk from our table to the service area. When I walk through the crowd, I notice there are six or seven men wearing motorcycle "colors." These colors signify which motorcycle gang or club the individual who is wearing them is affiliated with or belongs to.

These particular colors are an outlaw motorcycle club organized in Connecticut. This gang is known for committing crimes and dealing drugs in the area. They are a "Hells Angels" spinoff. I know they should be avoided.

I make sure not to have contact with any member while walking up to the bar. I place my drink order and wait to receive and pay for the two beers. The bartender hands me my change and places the two bottles of beer on the bar. I put my change into my pocket and grab a beer in each of my hands. When I turn to go back to my seat, one of the men wearing the colors is standing in front of me, blocking my way. I should have known something was about to happen, as I have let my guard down. When our eyes meet, he smiles wryly at me. I politely say, "Excuse me, sir." (I still have that Marine mentality and call everyone "Sir" or "Ma'am.") He simply obliges and steps aside. I take one more step and am again blocked by a man wearing colors.

I realize these men wearing the colors have encircled me. The short hairs on the back of my neck start to stand up. I say to the next person that now stands in front of me, "Excuse me, please." He looks at me and says, "What did you say?" My response is simply, "Excuse me. I would like to get by." He then sucker punches me. I saw it coming so I am able to react and not take it full force. His fist glances off my right cheek.

My thoughts are only one thing. "I'M FUCKED." There are at least five of them. They obviously have planned this, and we are in a confined area. My reaction is to try and take out the first asshole as quickly as possible. I spread my hands as wide as I can and then, still holding the bottles of beer, slam them into the sides of his head.

The beer bottle on the right side shatters and gouges a deep laceration on the side of his face. The second beer twists over the top of his head, showering the crowd with Budweiser. He is stunned, his eyes are glazed over, his knees buckle, and he stops throwing punches. Suddenly, I feel punches from behind me and from the left side. I am being assaulted by at least three people. They are not landing any blows that hurt me up to this point. I am able to grab hold of the one man in front of me by his hair. I attempt to use him as a shield from the others who are punching me.

The bikers start to shout at me, and other people start screaming. The man who I am holding goes limp and falls to the floor. As he is going down, a beer bottle is smashed across the top of my head. My thoughts are to just fight my way out and escape. There is no way that I can fight and beat six people. I am now being punched and kicked from every direction.

There is an exit door and a jukebox about five feet to my right. I grab another one of them around the waist as if I were playing football and am about to tackle a running back. When I do this, I get kicked directly in the nose. This is extremely painful, and it breaks my nose. I watch the boot connect with my face. I was just kicked in the face, dazed, bloody, but I am still fighting. I drive the man into the jukebox, and as I do this, I hear Tom's voice. He has come to my aid and is in a fight with two of the gang members. We separate from the fight, get out the exit door, and make our way to the car.

The motorcycle gang has parked close to where our car is. I see they are coming out toward us and go to confront them again. Tom is holding me back at this point because he believes I am seriously injured. There is a laceration across my nose that is bleeding. My first thought now is to get to my car and get one of my guns. Then it occurs to me I had allowed one of the friends who left earlier to leave in my car.

Tom convinces me my injuries need medical attention. I am angry and cannot understand why they chose to attack me. The gang members are rushing to get onto their motorcycles and leave. I get one last blow in by knocking over one of their motorcycles.

Tom pulls me to his car and convinces me to let him take me to police headquarters. When we drive out of the parking lot, we can hear sirens in the distance. These turn out to be police cars and the fire rescue unit responding to a report of this fight.

Tom has a small first aid kit in his car, but the bandages are not of any use. They are just too small. We use an old towel to wipe most of the blood off my arms and face to determine the locations of my injuries and their severity. When we arrive at the police station, the officer seated at the desk is Lieutenant Anthony Saccavino. The moment he looks at me, I know I look bad. He yells to the dispatcher to have medical personnel sent to the lobby. I receive medical attention by fire personnel and am brought to the hospital by a police car.

My injuries are a broken nose with a laceration across the bridge that requires 25 stitches to repair. I also have a laceration on my wrist that requires 18 stitches to close and a small cut on the top of my head closed with a couple of butterfly bandages. The biggest injury is my pride. Here I am, beaten and bloodied, sitting in the police department in which I am trying to become a police officer.

The police arrive at the lounge after the motorcycle gang has left. When they try to learn what has happened, the employees of the lounge are not very cooperative. They don't tell who the members are or how the fight started. I am released from the hospital at approximately 5:00 a.m. the next morning. A police officer transports me to an old church building that is now the motorcycle gang's clubhouse. We sit parked in the police car and wait for the occupants to wake up. Members of the New Haven police department are attempting to wake them by knocking on the doors. Three members of the motorcycle gang who fought me are there. They are arrested and taken into custody. The other three are not there. It takes several weeks to identify two more members of the gang who were involved. The detective assigned to investigate this case is Steve Smith. Our paths are connected again.

This fight is probably a factor keeping me from being appointed a patrolman. I did nothing wrong technically, but the perception I was in a bar at night fighting just does not sit well with the chief of police. This is a hard lesson learned.

The other critical lesson I learn as a cadet is how political influences can be the driving force to how or if things are done in this type of government employment. Your experience and education are sometimes secondary to the people you know. I am not happy that Hayes Gibson talked me into taking this position.

I resign my position as a cadet because there were several police officer openings filled by people who were not in the cadet program. When I resign, informing the police chief with a note giving two weeks' notice, he immediately requests that I meet with him in his office. When this meeting is held, he explains he is disappointed with my resignation and wants me to reconsider. I ask him why I have not been hired as a full-time officer. He does not give a reason why I was not appointed and will not guarantee I will ever be appointed a police officer. He talks about life, politics, his career, and employment in general.

I explain to him that I believe the cadet program has become a roadblock to my becoming an officer. The hours of work and expectations of being a student make it impossible to comply with the requirements of a cadet. The pay is not enough for me to pay my bills. I am engaged to be married and would never be able to support my future wife on the pay of a cadet. I make it clear to him that my leaving as a cadet does not mean I am not interested in a police officer position.

I end the meeting by telling him I have been offered a position as a part-time police officer in Madison and let him know I am going to accept that position. I know it is a policy of the North Haven police to not allow any of the employees to hold two badges of authority from different police departments. The position in Madison is part-time, and I have no powers of arrest as a cadet. I ask to be allowed to continue as a cadet due to the Madison position being part-time. That is the only way he would be able to convince me to stay as a cadet in North Haven. He does not agree to this, so I resign.

The most positive thing to have happened to me while I was employed as a cadet is that I begin to date Caren Mally, who I will end up marrying. She works for the Parks & Recreation Department in North Haven. We attended high school together, graduating the same year. I had run into her several months ago when I was still a Marine; yet I never had any intention of contacting her after that chance meeting.

During the summer of 1979, the fifth-year class reunion for my high school class is held. I attend, and Caren is also there. While we were in high school, we were friends, and our hobbies were similar. She was always dating some other guy, and I was pretty committed to Kathleen. The thought of dating her had never crossed my mind until the reunion. We had spoken and exchanged phone numbers when I was dating Judy and before I headed to Cuba, but I did not believe she was really interested in me.

I was attracted to her but did not immediately follow up on that feeling. When we were younger, she was always a little more sophisticated than I was. We were different. She lived on the wealthy west side of town, while I lived on the less fortunate east side. She was Jewish, and I was Christian.

Since we work in almost the same building, I finally get the nerve to ask her out on a date. I am working as a cadet on the midnight shift, and we agree to go to the beach during the day after I get off work at eight o'clock in the morning. We go to a beach where I fall asleep and get sunburned. The date is a disaster, but I survive to get a second one. I will fall in love with her, and we will be married.

Caren's mother, May, doesn't really take to me right away. I believe she wants her daughter to marry someone within their religious beliefs. She accepts me more when she learns that I spent some time in Israel. She accepts her daughter's decisions and eventually accepts me.

On November 2, 1980, we are married, and neither of us are employed in a position we wish to be in. I am working for a landscaping company mowing lawns. I still hold the part-time job as a police officer in Madison. Caren's position has been eliminated, and she has returned to taking classes at a local university.

Caren is the third and final woman I will fall in love with in my lifetime. We will live the rest of our lives together. After we are married, I tell people I have fallen in love three times. Kathleen was my first love; with Judy, I experienced real love; and, in my wife, I finally found true love. Caren will be with me for the rest of my life.

Right now, I no longer have full-time employment. I begin to wonder if the decisions I am making are from my heart or my head. The Marine Corps was a large enough organization where I had options. I could volunteer for training or request a transfer. The real world is much different.

I end up taking a job with a small landscaping company. Six days a week, I mow lawns for minimum wage. The workday begins at 7:00 a.m. and ends most days at 5:00 p.m. The days are long and tiring, and the work is hard and boring. The company I am working for is a small mom and pop operation. While I am working for this landscaper, I continue to pursue positions in different police departments. I find the process painstaking and slow. Mowing lawns turns out to be good for me because I lose weight and get back into good physical condition. This helps me in my overall appearance and ability to take on the agility phase of the testing procedure.

I only work mowing lawns for about three months. I find employment with a construction landscape company that pays more and has more diverse work. This type of work involves difficult manual labor. I am allowed to drive trucks comparable to those I had driven in the Marines.

We construct anything involving outdoor landscaping. One of the more difficult places we work on is a recently constructed building on the side of a hill. The field is almost one acre of land in front of the building and has a pitch of approximately 80 degrees. The company wishes to plant mature trees and sod on this hill. Mature trees are usually twenty feet tall and have a root ball that weighs about four to five hundred pounds. The holes are normally dug by a backhoe type of machine, but because of the degree of the slope, it is impossible to dig the holes mechanically. Each hole has to be dug by hand. We dig twenty-two holes for these large trees to fit into, manually, with picks and shovels. There are six men on this crew planting these trees, and we finish the tree planting in three weeks. Then we are required to lay sod where there has not been a tree planted. The sod is staked to the hill with ten-inch-long nails holding it down until the roots begin to grow and take hold. We make it work somehow. Every tree survives the planting, and the sod takes root in just a couple of weeks.

This kind of work is considerably harder than anything I have ever done. Most of the construction we do has some type of difficult twist to accomplish it. The city of Bridgeport is in the midst of beautifying the harbor. The boardwalk had recently been fitted with large wooden planters that will house trees. They need to be loaded with topsoil before trees and shrubs are planted. The boardwalk is supported by concrete support legs that have been driven into the ground, and it extends over the water. It is made of pressure-treated lumber, two-by-ten planks that vary in length. One can drive onto the boardwalk because there is an access ramp.

The truck I am driving is a three-quarter ton dump body Chevrolet. It is equipped with dual tires in the rear. The capacity in the dump body is four yards of topsoil. The gross vehicle weight is well over two tons. There are four planters that need to be filled so the trees can be planted properly and begin to grow.

My boss tells me I can drive the truck right onto the boardwalk and dump the topsoil directly into the planters. I do not believe the boardwalk will support the weight of the loaded truck. I tell my boss I believe the truck will fall through the wooden planks. We argue for about ten minutes when he says to me, "I want you to drive the dump truck onto the boardwalk and fill the planters. Do it now, or you are no longer employed by my company." I do as he says, and I begin to back the truck onto the boardwalk. As I am doing this, I can feel it swaying. The noises the boardwalk make sound as though it is bearing the weight of the world on these planks of wood. I believe it might hold if I can keep the wheels traveling over the crossbeams and support columns. The creaking and groaning give way to snapping and cracking as the wood breaks and gives way to the passenger side dual rear tires. They crash through the boardwalk, and I am now stuck. My boss is watching the entire time. He has two wheelbarrows and some shovels and hands them to me. He apologizes by only saying he is sorry. My partner and I now must unload the topsoil manually, shoveling the dirt from the truck to wheelbarrows.

I am a part-time police officer while I am working as a full-time landscaper but am having financial difficulties. I bought a brand new Pontiac Firebird when I left the Marine Corps. I was just married, and my wife had been laid off from her position with the town and had returned to school. The prospects for becoming a police officer do not work out the way I thought they would.

CHAPTER **12**

# PART-TIME POLICE OFFICER

My first experience dealing with death and dead bodies is presented to me during my third weekend of training as a supernumerary police officer in Madison, Connecticut. It is early evening on a Friday in the spring, and I am riding with a patrolman who has been a police officer for about ten years. We have received a citizen's complaint regarding a missing man.

Madison is on the shoreline of the Long Island Sound in Connecticut. The residence we have been dispatched to has a view of the water and is within walking distance of the shoreline. The house is an old colonial style two-story residence with a three bay attached garage. There is an unattached workshop in the back yard.

The workshop is located approximately seventy-five feet from the residence, and it has a front door and one full size window on each side of that door. The property is approximately two acres. Large oak, grey birch, and maple trees provide a canopy of shade. The lawn is a dark green color, thick, and manicured as if it were the infield of Yankee Stadium. The front of the residence has flowering foundation shrubs.

As we enter the paved driveway, there is a van with commercial writing on the sides parked in the driveway. One garage bay door is open, and the rear end of a newer model Cadillac is visible. My partner advises the dispatcher of our arrival, and we both exit the police cruiser.

We are greeted at the door by the missing man's wife who introduces herself as the woman who telephoned the police. She describes her husband's general appearance and explains all of his keys, wallet, and other personal items are on the counter. She describes what he was wearing when he left for work that morning. She explains she looked around the house and in the workshop, but could not find him.

My partner pulls me aside and commands me to take a walk around the yard to just make sure he is not out there. His exact words are, "Make sure he isn't dead somewhere out there in the yard." I am eager to help in any way possible, so I go outside immediately.

I check the van, inside and out. Then I walk completely around the house. Finally, I make my way to the workshop. The door is open, and power tools are on the workbench. I see a box of bullets in the center of the workbench, but it is closed. It does not seem to be important or out of place. I go to the rear of the building. It is still light out so as soon as I go around the corner, I see a man sitting on the ground. He startles me a little because I am not expecting to see him.

He is sitting with his back against the wall of the building. His legs are stretched straight out with the left foot crossed over the right. His right hand is on the ground by his side with the fingers and palm facing up. His eyes and mouth are both wide open. He looks relaxed as if he is staring at the spectacular view of the water.

Thinking there is nothing wrong I say, "Hey, buddy, everyone is worried about you, and your wife called us." He doesn't move or give me a verbal response. I first think he doesn't hear me. Then I wonder, "What is this guy's problem?" I reach down and touch his shoulder. When I touch him, it becomes immediately apparent he is DEAD. He is already stiff because rigor mortis has set in. As I push on his shoulder, his body slides to the left, and a rush of feelings go through my body I have never felt before. All my senses are awakened at once. He is dead, and I now see the gun lying in his lap.

I gather my composure and look around. The gun is a small caliber handgun, and it is sitting in his lap. He does not slide down the wall that much, so I simply grab onto his shoulder and pull him back to the position he was in when I first found him. I now notice the wound on the side of his head and realize he has committed suicide.

I make a mental note of everything I have observed. I walk back to the residence and speak to the police officer. I do not want to alarm the wife. When I get to the door, I get his attention to speak privately. I start to quietly explain to him I found the husband, and he is dead.

When I utter the words "I found him," he interrupts me and in a voice that can only be explained as a "cop voice," he questions, "You found him?" While I am attempting to have him keep his voice lower, he continues to talk and says, "That is great! Where is he?" I attempt to have him stop talking by bringing my index finger to my lips in the "SHH" sign, trying to keep him quiet. I tell him the man is dead. The patrolman then hustles me out of the house.

When we get outside the residence, he tells me I should have just asked him to come outside to talk. I do not argue and just explain where he is and what I observed. I had already determined there was no way I could have handled this differently. Once I went to the door and he opened his mouth, there was no way that he was not going to embarrass himself.

I explain where the husband is and what apparently has happened. Since I am a trainee, he questions everything that I tell him. How do I know he is dead? What did I do to determine he was dead? Did I check for a pulse? Did I see if he was breathing? Why didn't I try to do CPR? The questions just keep coming as quickly as he can spit them out of his mouth. I answer each question as it is asked.

While he is questioning me, the victim's wife is close enough to hear us. I attempt to show some compassion and keep the talk to a whisper. While we are walking and he is questioning me, another officer arrives and is listening to the conversation. The first officer stops talking to me. The two of them walk away toward the police cruiser. They are whispering so I cannot hear them.

They contact police headquarters using the car radio. In what seems like a matter of seconds, there are two detectives and a sergeant on the scene. One of the detectives comes to me and asks me to show him where the victim is. We go to where the victim is seated, and the detective now goes into "Cop Mode."

The police officer I had come with and the other one begin to act different to before. It is obvious to me they are on a mission. The detective reaches down and places his fingers on the victim's neck, checking for a pulse. He looks at me without saying a word. He then bends down and looks at the gun. He is checking to see if it is semi-automatic and needs to be made safe, as I would learn later. It is a blued steel revolver. There is no need to move it now.

After everyone looks at the victim, the detective assigns individuals different tasks. I am standing alone with the detective. He looked me in the eye and says, "This exactly how you found him?" I admit when I first touched him, he slid down. I tell him the position he is in now was the way he was when I first saw him. He starts to laugh and then assures me it made no difference. He explains how everything will take place. They need to locate a suicide note as a priority, and there is no need for me to remain at this scene. I am picked up by another officer working that evening and finish my shift a few hours later.

I learn the man had a home remodeling business which had fallen on tough economic times. He was losing money, and one of his vehicles was being repossessed. He left a note on his bedroom pillow explaining to his wife he thought he was a failure. For that reason, he took his life. He was the first human I saw dead before anyone else, but he would not be the last.

I drive home wondering what I had just been a part of. Is this the way policemen conduct their daily lives? When I was a cadet dispatching, there were at least five or six incidents each day that dealt with death or serious injuries. My first impression was these officers were cold and callous. The death of a human being seemed to have little impact on them. Each one of them had to see the man though. Was that curiosity, or was it part of the work? Was it necessary for as many as half a dozen police officers to look at this man in this way?

I wonder why there is not more damage done by the handgun. Shouldn't there have been more blood? Why is there only one hole and no exit wound? How come the gun ended up in his lap and not to the side? Why did his eyes not close? I had all these questions, and no one to answer them.

I will learn death will be all too common of an occurrence, even as a part-time police officer. I will be working and observe something that will never be forgotten. It will make me understand why the police officers initially seemed so cold and callous.

May 29, 1980, will bring death into the family I know as the thin blue line. One of the North Haven police officers I am friends with will be involved in a one car accident, and it will cost him his life. He will be the first police officer killed in the line of duty for the department.

The profession of being a police officer is a dangerous one. Every year across the United States, officers are killed while on duty for a variety of reasons. Car accidents are one of the major contributing factors. Speeds are higher than normal driving speeds. High speed pursuits are common now with few standardized guidelines. Police chase or pursue offenders even for petty motor vehicle violations.

The North Haven officer was attempting to stop a motorcycle because it was not registered properly and should not have been on the road. He was chasing this motorcycle in his police cruiser, lost control, and collided with a tree. His name was Timothy Laffin, Sr. He had initially survived the collision but was in critical condition. He was married and his wife was pregnant with their first child. Again, I experienced the death of someone. This one would have tremendous influence over me during the rest of my career.

Shortly after Tim was laid to rest, I continued my part-time police work with the Madison PD. One summer evening, I am dispatched to check a small cemetery in the northern section of town. There is a suspicious vehicle that has been left in the cemetery for two days.

It is a summer day, late in the afternoon. There is no description given of the car. The dispatcher just gives the location of the cemetery and orders me to check for any vehicles. When I drive in the entrance, the entire cemetery is visible. There is one vehicle parked there, facing toward the front entrance, but approximately one hundred yards away from any of the gravestones. The windows are all closed except the driver's side front window, which is slightly open. I cannot immediately see if anyone is in the car.

I park close to the car, staying on the paved road and radio the description and the marker plate number to the dispatcher. I get out of the police car and walk over to the car. As I am walking, there is an odor I have never smelled before. The closer I get to the car, the stronger the odor becomes.

"This is not going to be good," I think. When I look inside the car, I see the figure of a man. The window is cracked open about half an inch, and the smell now is overwhelming. The figure of this being is wiggling and moving ever so slightly in place. The features of any possible face are indistinguishable and are mostly white.

Maggots! This body is rotting and is covered in maggots. I don't go any further. I walk back to my car and call the dispatcher for assistance. I use a police radio code and tell them that I have located a dead body. The first question they ask on the radio is, "Do you need medical assistance"? My response is "No, I am going to need a supervisor, and he will determine what is needed. It is a possible homicide."

When the sergeant arrives on scene, he smiles at me and starts to joke with me. "What's the matter, rookie, don't you know the right codes to call in?" Then, I notice the odor from the decaying body reach him. His tone of voice changes instantly. "Where is the body?" are the next words out of his mouth. I just point toward the car and say, "In the driver's seat."

He reaches into his pocket and grabs a handkerchief. He wets it down with a bottle of water and holds it over his nose and mouth. He gestures to me to follow him, and we both walk to the driver's door. The sergeant then opens the door. The clothed decomposing, maggot-covered body of what resembles a human being is seated in the driver's seat. The sergeant's face becomes ashen gray as he forces back dry heaves. As he turns, I feel his attitude concerning my experience has just changed. I stand looking at the inside of the car without covering my nose or mouth and do not feel nauseated. I proclaim, "Well, Sarge, I guess he has been there longer than two days, and I think the radio code I used was correct."

No other words are spoken that day about my being a rookie. The sergeant turns and walks back to his police car. He sits in the front seat and gathers his composure. It is only moments after he speaks into the radio microphone that two full-time police officers arrive on the scene. When they arrive, they have to see the body. One of them leaves his lunch there.

The entire cemetery is now considered a crime scene. The investigators have the gruesome task of removing the body and preserving any evidence that may lead them to question if any foul play was involved in the death of this person.

Identification is difficult due to the condition of the body. There is a large amount of circumstantial and personal identifying documents and articles that will most likely confirm the identity of this person as the owner of the car. He had been reported missing eight days earlier by his daughter. The owner is a 68-year-old man with a history of heart problems. The description of the clothing he is found in is similar to what he was last seen wearing. There is a wallet in the pants pocket that matches the owner of the car. Eventually, the dental records confirm his identity.

While I am sitting there, my thoughts drift back to Marine Corps boot camp. During the first week at Parris Island, the drill instructors broke out a folder of gruesome dead body pictures. These pictures are of recruits who attempted to leave the island by swimming. They all ended up drowning and washing ashore. This body in the cemetery is just as gruesome.

I only work at the Madison PD police for 93 days over a span of thirteen months. I accept a position as a police dispatcher in Cheshire. I have taken several police exams and have made my way onto half a dozen lists. I still have not secured a position as a police officer.

I resign my position as a part-time police officer and believe my career in law enforcement is in jeopardy. I am involved in an incident and am advised to resign so I am not fired.

I am working as part of security and crowd control at the Madison High School varsity basketball game. They are playing against the crosstown rivals, Guilford. The gym is filled to standing room only. The game is close in score the entire time. The fans are into every aspect of the game as time is running out. Guilford is holding onto a slim four-point lead with about four minutes left in the game. There is no shot clock, and Guilford has possession of the ball. They are attempting to use as much of the clock as possible and have gone into a stalling offense. At this point in the game, a Madison player steals the ball and begins to break away for an easy layup. The Guilford player responds by punching the Madison player and knocking him to the floor.

With the punch, the players on the floor rush to their fallen teammate and the assailant, and a fight begins. The benches empty, and the referees lose all control of the game. The students in the gym enter the fight, and it is total chaos. The bleachers empty, and it is obvious there are not enough adults to stop the fighting.

I call for assistance on the portable radio and begin separating people who are fighting. I come to two teenage boys exchanging blows with each other, and I separate them. I am holding one, and the other runs away. I order the student to stop, and he agrees. But I know it is a useless request. As soon as I let him go, I see him run to another confrontation. I grab a second student and throw him to the ground while ordering him to stop. Almost simultaneously, I grab for another combatant who turns and attempts to punch me. I am able to duck out of the way, but he knocks the hat off of my head. I get hold of him and place him under arrest by handcuffing him. When I complete this, I now arm myself with my nightstick. I am holding onto the student I have handcuffed, and a girl hands me my hat. Two other students are fighting next to me, and I strike one in the shoulder with the nightstick. He immediately runs away. Another student comes toward me as if he is going to assault me, and I use the nightstick to defend myself, hitting him on top of his shoulder. As a result, he falls to the floor.

It appears the entire brawl ended at that moment. I notice there are more police officers in the gym. I briefly tell them what has happened, and we all agreed that in addition to the student I had in custody, two other arrests will be made at this time.

The game is declared over, and the people are sent home. The three arrestees are transported to the police department. The officers who come to my aid are satisfied with my performance and stand behind my assessment of what happened. Each officer insists every action I have taken is legal and should have been done.

When we arrive at the police department with the three arrestees, everything is progressing the way it should. The process of completing the arrest is being conducted by the full-time police officers. The three have been charged and advised of their rights. They have been fingerprinted, and all the corresponding paperwork required by the police department and the Connecticut court system is being done.

The chief of the Madison police department arrives at the police station, not a normal occurrence. He addresses the group of us and orders the arrestees be released. No reason is given for the release. I have only been involved with law enforcement for a little more than a year, but this action appears unusual to me.

I have no idea what has just happened. Under what authority is the chief allowed to release the three individuals who have been arrested? Once an arrest is made by a police officer, the only way he or she can be released is per the order of a judge. The police officers are at a loss for an explanation as to why these people are released. I am simply told to go home and wait for the administrative officer's telephone call.

I leave the police department for what turns out to be the last time. The incident took place on a Friday, so I had the entire weekend to wonder if there was anything I had done wrong. On Saturday morning, I telephone one of the police officers who had been there to help.

Officer Bob Stimpson explains the people I arrested were related to some important political figures connected to the First Selectman of Madison. They are claiming there is a possibility I used excessive force in affecting this arrest.

My concern for what action is going to be taken against me overwhelms me. My future as a police officer could be significantly affected if a claim of excessive force by me is made, investigated, and confirmed. Officer Stimpson assures me the police union will back the action I took because it was proper. Officer Stimpson has great concern for the action the chief of police took. None of the police officer's opinions or the union's support means anything to me. I was on my own and at the mercy of whatever the police chief had in store for me. It does not take long for my fate to be determined.

On Monday morning, I am contacted at home by a lieutenant from the police department who informs me there is a question related to my conduct on Friday night. One of the arrestees claimed I used excessive force in arresting him, and the department is investigating the matter. He is going to ask me a series of questions about the night. I explain the incident exactly as it occurred. He tells me at the end of this phone call my version is the same as all the other persons involved. The lieutenant doesn't believe there was any use of excessive force or any other impropriety. He ends the call with an assurance I have nothing to be concerned about.

At noon, I receive a second telephone call from the same lieutenant. I can tell by the tone of his voice and the way he is talking to me something has changed. He is now speaking in official terms and advises me the chief is going to charge me, or I can resign my position and nothing will be done.

I end the conversation with him by saying, "I guess I have no other choice but to resign my position as a police officer." I know there is no way this is going to end well for me. I decide without consulting anyone I will just resign. I know any type of publicity involving me in this incident will be bad for my future. A resignation with no discipline recorded and not being terminated makes more sense than a fight to keep a part-time job.

The lieutenant has a resignation letter typed in my name. He drives to my home to obtain my signature. I return my badges and equipment. I learn the incident is just an ugly memory for everyone involved. Political interference causes my resignation and may affect my future career in law enforcement.

Approximately a month later, I accept a position as an emergency dispatcher in Cheshire. The testing for police officer is starting as I am employed as a dispatcher. The position is the same as a cadet was in North Haven, except the pay is higher. I have promised my wife this is temporary, and I will accept the first police officer position offered to me. My hope is that the position will be in my hometown, but I am resigned to the fact it may not be.

I start work in Cheshire in the summer of 1981. While in Cheshire, I regain my confidence and composure. Nothing of note or any major incident occurs while I am working there. I continue my studies at the University of New Haven. My wife has secured an internship at the Connecticut Mental Health Center. Life is beginning to head in the right direction again.

One day while at work as a dispatcher in Cheshire, the chief of police calls me into his office. My first thought is, "What did I screw up now?" I am extremely nervous while sitting in the chair just outside his office and next to the secretary. I don't know why I have this feeling, but I cannot get it out of my head. He walks out of his office and invites me in. He motions me to sit in a chair in front of his desk. As he points to the chair, he blurts out, "What are you doing here as a dispatcher? Why aren't you a police officer yet?" All I can say is, "Maybe you can tell me." Chief George Merriam is a young man who has been the head of the department for just a couple years. He states, "With your experience in the Marines and the scores you achieved on the tests, you should have, at the minimum, been offered a position." My response is, "I don't know the answer to that question. Maybe you can shed some light on the subject."

He asks me about the incident in Madison. After I explain what happened, he does not offer an opinion one way or the other. He just asks, "Do you think it is what is keeping the departments from hiring you?" I tell him I don't believe so because it just happened. The conversation ends with him telling me I am someone he would like to have working on his police force.

I remain employed as a dispatcher in Cheshire until September 11, 1981, when I receive a telephone call from North Haven Chief of Police Walter T. Berniere, notifying me I have been given a conditional offer to become a police officer. I must pass a physical and mental examination. I will then be assigned a date to attend the Connecticut Municipal Police Training Council Academy. The training will be conducted over a thirteen-week period beginning in November, 1981.

CHAPTER **13**

# FINALLY, A NORTH HAVEN POLICE OFFICER

T he swearing-in ceremony is conducted on September 15 in the lobby of the North Haven police department. It is quite different from the pomp and circumstance of the Marine Corps when a ceremony was held for any reason.

This is where I wanted to be from the start. I am satisfied and will be sent to the police academy just after the first of the year. Many changes have occurred in my life since my last day in the Marines in September 1978, and now I am where I want to be. I am going to be the best police officer my department has ever seen.

I thought about when I was a child and when I had occasion to be around a police officer. Hayes Gibson came back to mind. He is a very well-known man in North Haven. He has been in my corner from the start. I will finally be working with him. My thoughts drift back to earlier years. One of the things he would do when he came to visit my father's business was to take care of our dog. The family owned a Doberman pinscher named Vince, and Vince was kept in the businesses' warehouse as a deterrent to thieves. Vince was short for

Vindicator, which was the full name given to this dog. His disposition was not all that pleasant. Hayes had a way with Vince, and the two got along well together.

On occasion, Hayes would pick up Vince and take him for a ride in the police car. If you did not know any better, you would think that Hayes had a police dog with him. Vince enjoyed his trips in the police car until one day he attempted to bite Hayes. Hayes stopped taking him for rides and would not even play with him when he came to the business. After he attempted to bite Hayes, he was taken out of the warehouse. He eventually would bite someone and was euthanized.

Now I am working with Hayes Gibson. When I join the police department, I am the forty-forth officer appointed. The North Haven Police Department was organized in 1943. The department leader holds the rank of chief. The rank structure consists of the chief, a deputy chief, one inspector, two captains, four lieutenants, eight sergeants, four detectives, and twenty-three patrolmen. The police cadets are being replaced with four civilian dispatchers. There are two secretaries and three civilian records clerks.

The department operates 365 days a year, twenty-four hours a day. The schedule of work is what is known as a New York two-week rotating shift. Officers work a five-day-on day shift followed by two days off and then five-days-on day shift and three days off. Then they switch to the evening shift, following the same schedule as days and finally the same for a midnight shift.

The rotating shift was invented to give all employees covering assignments over a twenty-four-hour period equal time off and equal time on each shift. It did not consider that police officers are subject to being held over or called in early. The extra hours are due to emergencies or personnel shortages.

The captains are the commanders of divisions in the department. The divisions are the Patrol Division and Records Division. There is an equivalent rank of inspector in charge of the Detective Division. Hayes Gibson is the captain in charge of the Patrol Division. I am immediately assigned as a dispatcher as soon as I start work. There is a vacancy, and I am used to fill the position because of my experience as a cadet and the position in Cheshire.

The Municipal Police Training Council (MPTC) is the governing body for the police academy in Connecticut. All police officers are required to complete a thirteen-week course of study started within one year of the date of hire to be a certified police officer. I am assigned to the 160th session of the MPTC Academy. When in the academy, the staff assigns two positions of authority to recruits. These are recruits charged with making sure rules are adhered to as well as to have leaders in the trainee ranks. These positions are referred to as the sergeant and corporal of the class. I am appointed as the class corporal.

There are several awards the academy bestows to individuals of each class. They are given to recruits who excel in certain areas of requirements for graduation. They include the high shooter, best academic average, and top physical fitness score. I didn't achieve any of those but am chosen by my peers to be the Speaker of the Class. I will give a speech upon graduation from the academy.

I hate speaking in front of a crowd. I believe the reason I hate public speaking is the way I was treated when I was in the fifth grade. My fifth-grade class had been selected to perform a song at a Christmas pageant at my elementary school. The song chosen by my teacher was the "Twelve Days of Christmas." In the performance, I am assigned to sing a solo of the "Five Golden Rings" part. Each time it was my turn to sing, I was loud and did it with gusto. The audience laughed each time I sang my part. When the song finished there was loud applause and people hugged and patted me on the back. The only thing that I took away from the night was people were laughing at me. I was embarrassed and stopped singing in any organized way. I even stopped playing a musical instrument because people were laughing at me.

I write a speech and recite it at the graduation ceremony of the 160th training session of the Connecticut Municipal Police Academy. I have no problem speaking in front of my peers and the family members who are there to attend the ceremony.

The transition from being a Marine and becoming a police officer will be a challenge. Police officers are charged with protection of property and the saving of lives. As a Marine, the protection of property and saving of lives was part of the mission. The main mission of the Marine Corps is to fight wars. They are a force used to kill the enemy and destroy their capability to fight. They are part of the most sophisticated military force in the world.

I served in the Marine Corps but never came under fire or went to war. I never fired a weapon at anyone. I did not witness any death or injuries because of combat or hostile fire in combat close up. The terrorist attack in Israel was the closest I had come. I did observe some of the aftermath of that fighting.

There is no enemy when you are a police officer. Police officers are charged with the protection of every person and their rights. They are commonly referred to as the thin blue line. I would soon learn that the "bad guys," those people who chose to break the law, had enumerable rights. There are people who want to hurt and even kill police officers.

There is no enemy, but there is nobody who likes what you do or what you stand for. I say this "tongue in cheek" because a police officer believes the battles they fight will never end. They believe everything they do is scrutinized, analyzed, made up, thankless, and unappreciated.

The criminal element can commit crimes, be arrested for those crimes, and be walking on the street the next day. This is true regardless of the seriousness of the crime. The basic premise of our law states that a person accused of committing a crime is innocent until proven guilty. This is the case no matter how overwhelming the evidence is.

I have begun to learn police officers are societies' garbage men. All the worst things that happen to people are investigated by the police, which means everything a human being can think of: traffic accidents, downed wires, where anything is located, when events are scheduled, controlling wild and domestic animals, where all the town boundaries are located, who has jurisdiction on certain roads, and the list goes on and on.

I will lose friends because they do not agree with what a badge stands for. They don't understand that as a police officer, I will need to set the example and be in tune with the law and abide by it. I can't look the other way when something is illegal or unjust.

Dealing with death and injuries changes you as a person. I will appear emotionless after years as a police officer. At this point in my career, I deal with it by trying to find humor in what I have seen. Or I think when they have passed away maybe their pain is over, and they are in a better place.

Most of what we do as police officers in North Haven involves motor vehicle violations and accidents. There are very few homicides that occur during my thirty-five-year career. My first day assigned to the patrol division after graduation from the police academy is interesting.

On my first day of work, I am assigned to the 4:00 p.m. to midnight shift, and the commander of the shift is Lieutenant Ed Halkovetz. There is a period of time known as "roll call" that takes place prior to going out in the patrol car. Officers are advised of areas and people of interest they should be aware of. Changes in orders or new laws and procedures are discussed also. During this roll call, I am introduced to the other officers who are working. At the end of roll call, the lieutenant hands me a set of car keys and proclaims, "Sonny Boy, these are the keys to your police car. You are assigned to patrol # 3 tonight. Go out there and drive around your patrol area. DON'T call us; we'll call you."

The town is divided into five separate patrol sectors, or areas of the town for which one officer is responsible. Patrol # 3 is located on the southeast side of the town. It is mostly rural, residential, and farms.

I grab my gear and walk outside to my police car. The cars are parked at the rear of the building. Each officer has his own personal equipment they take on patrol with them each shift. They park next to their personal vehicles and load this gear at this time. While I am loading my equipment into the police car, the three other officers assigned to the shift come over and welcome me to the shift. I drive the police car to the area of town I am assigned to after loading my gear for the shift. There is one officer assigned to each patrol area during each shift. That officer is responsible for handling all complaints and incidents that occur in their respective patrol area. When an incident requires more than one officer, the commander or dispatcher determines who that will be.

Nothing happens during the entire shift in my patrol area. I do not handle a single complaint or assist on any other incidents. I do not stop any cars for any violations. When I finish my shift, I wonder if this is what Hayes Gibson was trying to warn me about.

The North Haven police are considered first responders, meaning the police are required to respond to each medical emergency and motor vehicle accident that occurs. Death and injuries to human beings are an almost daily happening. Crime is not the priority I thought it would be. There is little criminal activity that takes place in town.

I have to quickly get used to blood, broken bones, and death. On my third day working, I am sent to check on an elderly man who has not been seen for two days. I find him in his bedroom face down on the floor. He was 92 years old and lived alone. It is determined he has died of natural causes.

There is absolutely nothing out of place in his entire residence. The house and all the rooms look like a car detailed for a car show. Everything is neat and orderly. He did not even make a mess when he fell on the floor. He was prepared to die and had notes on his desk explaining where every important document could be found.

I will not forget this day because of this and a second incident I have to attend to. Approximately one hour after finishing the first incident, I am parked in the police car and am dispatched to a medical call in a residential area that was going to take me at least three minutes to get to. The dispatcher advised me to respond using my lights and siren because there was a possibility the victim was not breathing.

Just turning on the siren of a police car has an effect that gets adrenaline and blood flowing. I am driving fast with lights and a siren headed to an emergency for the very first time in my life. My mind is racing, and most of the vehicles I approach move to the side of the road as I approach them. There is one car in front of me for about a quarter of a mile that slows but will not pull to the right. I swear, scream, and wave my arms at them. Eventually, the road allows me to pass them and continue.

I arrive at the residence to find fifteen people there. They are in a long line directing me to a bedroom in the rear of a large colonial style residence. In the bedroom, lying on the bed is an elderly man. His wife is hugging him and crying. He is not breathing and looks to be dead. I am told he said he did not feel well and told his wife he was going to lie down. The time he has been here and not breathing is unknown. I explain to the wife she needs to leave the room. I quickly check for his vital signs and determine there is no pulse, and he is not breathing. I have been trained in CPR but never had to perform it. I ask the crowd of people if anyone knows how to perform CPR, but there is not one.

I can hear the sirens of the ambulance and fire rescue vehicles as they are getting closer. I need to start CPR. I pick the man up under his shoulders and lower him to the floor. I make sure there is enough room to do chest compressions and deliver mouth to mouth resuscitation. I make sure his airway is clear and tilt his head in the position to give rescue breaths.

With my first breath into the man's mouth, I am greeted by him vomiting into my mouth. This is not how this is supposed to be going I think to myself. All I can do is start to upchuck myself. I throw up about four times, and as I am looking for something to wipe my mouth out, the firefighters walk in the room.

I ask them for water as I am retching and trying to spit the debris out of my mouth. They begin to laugh and crack jokes referring to my being a rookie. They believe I'm throwing up because I am not used to seeing the dead. When I explain what has happened, I get some sympathetic treatment. Partially digested food that has come from some other person is the most disgusting thing I can imagine being in my mouth.

The fire and ambulance personnel do what they can to save the life of this man, but he does not make it. I get myself back in order and have a little composure. The police officer who arrived to assist me has been kind enough to gather the information needed to complete my report. He informs the family to go where the ambulance is taking their loved one. This saves me from having to inform them their loved one has passed away.

Being a police officer is physically demanding, but it is nothing compared to the emotional stresses experienced over the spectrum of the duties we perform. This first incident requiring me to attempt CPR and having such a catastrophic outcome is not good for my overall confidence. The firefighters are making jokes about my technique.

I can't help but wonder what I did wrong. I drive around that day trying to retrace my steps. I can't get the smell out of my nose. I can't get the taste out of my mouth. I laugh as I remember my flight to boot camp. Vomit seems to be a theme for me when I start something. I laugh as I remember the day, I did not get sick. I leave work on this day feeling relieved I survived the day. There is a strong possibility it will be a long time before I attempt mouth-to-mouth resuscitation on anyone again.

Each day of work starts with a roll call, and at the end, the lieutenant hands me the keys to the police car and proclaims, "Sonny Boy, here are your keys. You are assigned to Patrol # 3. Don't call us; we'll call you." On the fifth day before I leave the building, I am ordered to report to the captain's office.

I report to his office and wait for him to finish a phone call. He motions me to sit in a chair in front of his desk. The captain is Hayes Gibson. He is now my supervisor. He completes the phone call and greets me in his office.

"Well, Patrolman Genovese, congratulations!" This is the first time I have seen him since I graduated from the police academy. I respond by standing, saluting, and extending my hand. He does the same, and we shake hands. "So how goes the battle?" he asks. I tell him everything is fine and that there is a tremendous amount to learn. He laughs and continues the conversation. He asks, "Is there anything you need help with yet?" I tell him no.

Suddenly his tone becomes serious. "Well, I was just wondering if they taught you in the police academy how to write tickets or how to arrest people?" I have not stopped a car or investigated any crimes yet during my first week. I look at him and tell him I haven't been sent to anything where it was necessary. He then proclaims, "When you drive around, you don't see any cars speeding or breaking some other law?" I don't want to tell him the lieutenant told me not to stop any cars. I respond with, "I will work on that tonight, Sir. I've just been trying to learn my patrol area." He tells me the lieutenant does not like to make waves and is lazy. He wants me to be aggressive and enforce the law as I feel it should be. He tells me he expects I will start to conduct enforcement activity today.

The day starts out like all the other days that I have been on patrol by myself. All four days, there is not any activity in the area I am patrolling. The town is quiet, and there is not much crime. Motor vehicle law violations will become my way of finding the criminal element.

I decide to act on a simple violation of the law that is of personal concern to me. I drive to the neighborhood that I spent most of my youth in. The intersection of Clark Avenue and Moulthrop Street is located off the beaten path. It is an area that is residential but close to a business and interstate highway entrance. The intersection is controlled by a stop sign.

This is what police work consists of in the early 1980s. I am going to sit and watch to see if people driving their cars stop at the stop sign. I know just about every family in this neighborhood. I can't immediately focus on looking for violations because I am visited by many of the residents. They are friends of mine. Most just want to congratulate me and are socializing. They are pleased with the fact a police officer is in their neighborhood.

Eventually, I watch as a car drives west on Moulthrop Street and fails to stop at the stop sign at the intersection with Clark Avenue. This is the first crime I observe as a police officer. I put the police car in drive and am ready to give chase. The emergency overhead lights are activated, and I proceed. The vehicle is a blue Chevy Camaro. The car turns left and then right into the second driveway on Clark Avenue. I'm committed, and I pull into the driveway behind the Chevy. I know the family who lives at this address. The driver of the car has no idea I am behind her. She is an elderly woman who is gathering her belongings. This is her residence, and she has just returned home from work. A young man walks out of the front door of the house and approaches me.

I have just executed my first motor vehicle stop, and I feel like I should have stayed home. I have stopped the mother of a friend who I went to high school with. We have been friends for as long as I can remember. I immediately turn off the lights and start to laugh. My friend and his mother walk toward me happily proclaiming how nice it is to see me.

After we exchange niceties for a few minutes, the question is raised as to why I am here in the driveway. I explain I observed his mother fail to stop for the stop sign. The mother proclaims that it was about time that somebody enforced the law. She apologizes for her mistake and surrenders her license and registration information. I use my police discretion and give her a verbal warning.

As I leave their house, it becomes apparent working in my hometown as a police officer will be interesting. Eventually, stopping cars will become second nature. Knowing what is acceptable to ask the occupants will take many years to hone those skills. The arrests that are custodial and turn a motor vehicle stop into a criminal investigation will become more common.

Murder is not a common occurrence in our town. There is, however, a very famous triple murder that did take place here when I was in high school. On August 13, 1972, Guillermo Aillion allegedly murdered his wife, mother in-law, and father-in-law. He was convicted of the murders but appealed that decision and was awarded another trial. He would have three trials.

He was charged with the stabbing deaths because his wife had filed for divorce, and they were separated, which served as the motive. The night the murders were committed, he was stopped approximately three blocks away from the scene for a motor vehicle violation, which would serve as the opportunity. The murders were not known to have been committed at the time of the stop. The bodies were discovered the next afternoon.

The patrolman stopped the vehicle because the muffler on the car he was driving was considered louder than acceptable. This officer did not determine anything was out of the ordinary, and he allowed him to leave after issuing a written warning him about the loud muffler.

The vehicle again was stopped by a second police officer in a different area of town, approximately ten minutes later. This officer observed a knife in the rear seat that had what appeared to be blood on it. The patrolman was not confident about what his authority was with regards to this knife. He requested the assistance of a supervisor.

The knife was the type used in the kitchen or the food service business. It was one generally not believed to be used as a weapon. The supervisor who arrived was Hayes Gibson. He held the rank of sergeant. The knife was wrapped in some sort of a towel, and both had what appeared to be "dried blood" on them. Mr. Aillion said he had been at a cookout and had been cutting steak with the knife. This knife was approximately a foot long with a serrated blade.

Sgt. Gibson questioned the suspect at length regarding the knife and the suspected blood. The patrolman and sergeant agreed that his story wasn't the best they had ever heard, but there was nothing to disprove it at the time. They allowed Guillermo Aillion his freedom. He drove away with a possible murder weapon in his possession, coming from the scene of the crime.

When the bodies of the murdered victims were found the next day, the police obtained a search warrant to search the car. The police believed it was possible that the knife that the police had observed on August 13, 1972, was in fact a murder weapon. The blood substance could be tested to determine if it was human.

When the police search the car, they do find a knife. This is a different knife than the one observed by the police officers. Each of the officers noted that the knife they saw during the stop had a serrated blade. The one recovered from the car has a straight edge.

The third trial was taking place while I was a patrolman. Many officers were called to testify at that trial. Captain Gibson (he had been promoted) had to testify again about his actions. He sat me down on two occasions to reinforce that he could have, and should have, taken the bloody knife the night it was found.

Taking the knife would have been justified under the law. He could also have charged the driver with a crime unrelated to the murder. The knife, because of its length, was considered a weapon under the law, and therefore, could have been seized and held as evidence. The claim it was used for lawful means could have been a legitimate reason a court would allow it to be transported in a motor vehicle.

Guillermo Aillion was arrested on August 18, 1972, for the murders of his wife, mother-in-law, and father-in-law. In an ironic twist, I will be arrested on that same day for the killing of three uncontrollable guinea hens. One of the most infamous criminals is being arrested at the same time by the same police department on the same day.

This is the arrest that almost keeps me out of the Marine Corps and is the incident that slows my obtaining a Top Secret clearance. I will be cleared of all charges. Guillermo Aillion will serve the rest of his life in prison.

Captain Gibson was making sure I understood the law. He wanted to make sure I knew how to use the law to my advantage and was making sure that I did not make the same mistakes he had made. He told me the story of the "bloody knife" so I would take possession of any knife that I find in a car that the owner did not have a legal reason to possess.

He was taking me under his wing. I appreciated all the help any of the police officers would pass on to me. By the end of my career as an officer, I had a collection of approximately fifty knives, none of which involved an arrest. I would explain why I was keeping the knife, citing the triple murders, tell the person they could come back to get their knife in a week. None was used as a murder weapon, and none of those people ever asked to have their knife returned.

Police officers work and spend most of their time alone. They are almost always on their own. A "beat cop," as they are commonly referred to, is assigned to handle an area in a town or a city, and they are responsible for what occurs there. They start the day in a group of people and may be assisted on certain assignments. The individual police officer determines how he will conduct the business of law enforcement.

Each police officer is guided by rules and regulations of the departments for which they work and the states they work in. They must also work under the laws and statutes of the United States considering the rights guaranteed by the Constitution. The states can be more restrictive than the federal government. They are the determining factor on how aggressively law enforcement is carried out. State law requires a sworn officer to arrest all people who commit violations or break the law. The chances of observing a crime being committed while you are driving in a black and white car with all these red and blue lights on it are very slim.

There are motor vehicle statutes that existed though. Observing violations being committed by the motoring public is easy to spot. Therefore, most police officers who work in small municipalities generate activity or make arrests by enforcing the motor vehicle laws vigorously. I would learn the most common violations and would be active in stopping vehicles committing these common mistakes.

The supervisors are happy with officers who arrive for duty on time each day, complete required paperwork in a timely fashion, and are active in enforcement of the law. I am a patrolman who makes his supervisors happy by doing those three things. I am an aggressive police officer who believes enforcement of minor violations would have an overall effect on the attitude and perception of what would be tolerated in North Haven. The police department and the town have a reputation of being fair to those who committed violations of the law. There is very little crime in town.

The department is considered a capable reactive police organization. I would learn as much about motor vehicle law as possible. In the early years of being a police officer, not much of significance occurs. There is the occasional suicide or house burglary. My time is spent on routine patrol, learning how to do the job properly.

In 1981, police officers are poorly equipped in comparison to when I retire in 2015. The individual portable radio is heavy and has limited range, with an extendable metal antenna. These radios are not practical, and only the supervisors use them. An individual officer depends on pay telephones, call boxes, and the car radio. When I am away from the patrol car, the only communication is my voice. I am disconnected from the police headquarters.

Officers are at the mercy of the public and the person they are stopping. There is no requirement to record or report every car that is stopped. Notification is not required when a vehicle is stopped for minor violations, no action being taken or just a verbal warning. The instructions of "don't call us; we'll call you" was how we operated.

I am equipped with a .357 Magnum Smith & Wesson Model 19 six shot revolver, two individual sets of handcuffs, a nightstick, and an ammunition loop with twelve extra rounds of ammunition. We are allowed to carry a blackjack in our trousers. That was all the equipment my department allowed. No shotgun, no bulletproof vest, no mace or cap stun container, no backup firearm, and no knife.

Stopping cars and issuing tickets for motor vehicle violations became routine. I am assigned to the same patrol for the first couple of years. I'm involved in no significant incidents. There were no homicides in the first couple of years I am a patrolman.

I am settling into the work when I have my first problem with a civilian disagreeing with the way I investigated a motor vehicle accident that she is involved in. North Haven is bordered on the west side by the town of Hamden. The town line runs down the center of a main roadway that is five lanes wide.

This will cause issues regarding the jurisdiction of police agencies. On this day, I will be dispatched to investigate an accident that has occurred at the intersection of Whitney Avenue and Skiff Street. This is a shared intersection with Hamden. When I arrive, the cars involved in the collision have been moved. One is parked in North Haven and the other in Hamden. The car parked in North Haven has damage on the front passenger side bumper and fender. The car parked in Hamden has damage on the rear passenger side fender. I determine immediately that this collision has occurred on the Hamden side of the intersection. I notify my dispatcher, and she advises me that the Hamden police are occupied and will arrive in approximately twenty minutes. As a courtesy to the Hamden police, I collect the licenses and registrations from these two drivers so that he can complete his accident report.

The driver of the car parked in Hamden is a young male of college age. He has parked his car in the service station located on the southeast corner of the intersection. I ask him to surrender his paperwork and inquire how the collision occurred. He tells me he was traveling south on Whitney Avenue and had to stop midway in the intersection because two vehicles ahead of him were turning right into the service station. The traffic signal was "green" when he passed through the intersection. He could not completely get his vehicle clear of the intersection because of the turning traffic in front of him. While he was stopped, the other car collided with him. He could not tell me where that car was coming from when the collision occurred.

The driver of the car that was parked in North Haven had observed that I was talking with this man. She was a 61-year-old woman who was upset that I was talking to the other driver. She crossed the intersection demanding to know what we had been discussing. I calmly explained what I was doing and that the accident had occurred in Hamden. We would have to wait for them to arrive to complete the accident report and investigation. I asked her to surrender her license and registration to me. She refused to do so at first and insisted on explaining how the accident occurred. She started the explanation in the following way. She said that she was stopped behind the white line because her traffic signal was red. She was in the furthest eastbound lane of the three in the intersection. When the light changed to green signaling she could go, she accelerated and drove into the intersection. She also drove right into the rear passenger side of the other vehicle.

I questioned her about looking to make sure that there was nothing in her way before entering the intersection so that a collision like this would not occur. I explained, "Just because the light grants you access to the intersection, you do not have the right of way because it is necessary for the operator of the vehicle to allow the entire intersection to clear." I tried my best to explain you just can't push the vehicles in the intersection out of the way without consequences.

This cute old lady became enraged, telling me I had no idea what I was talking about. She insisted, "The traffic signal was green for me, and therefore I have the right of way. The other driver should not have stopped where he did." She asked me about my experience with conducting accident investigations. While my experience was not very much as a police officer, common sense and the way the law is written clearly point to the fact she violated the law and was at fault for the collision. She would not accept my conclusion and began to badger me. The tirade continued for 20 minutes. She told me I was incompetent, too young to be able to make a rational decision and ranted on and on.

I investigated this accident completely on my own. I know it technically has occurred in another jurisdiction, but as soon as that officer arrives, I will just turn over my findings to him. He will read what I have done, thank me, and just sign off on the report. I wanted to ensure she would receive enforcement action showing the accident was caused directly by her action. I even wrote an infraction violation ticket that carries a monetary fine.

The Hamden police arrive at the scene 45 minutes later. The officer and I agree my report is accurate and concise. However, he is a veteran, and he convinces me there would be no jurisdictional issues with my completing the accident report on my own. We use my report as the official legal report of the incident, and everyone leaves the scene. Case closed.

The very next day, the captain in charge of my division orders me to report to his office immediately upon the completion of roll call. I report to his office as requested. He explains he has received a complaint from a civilian regarding the way I handled an accident investigation. The elderly woman from the accident at Whitney Avenue and Skiff Street had written a two-page letter of complaint about my demeanor and actions during the investigation.

The letter serves as evidence in my defense that I conducted the investigation exactly the way it should have been done. The only mistake noted was the location of the collision occurring in another town.

The captain has me read the letter and then asks me to explain why she was making a complaint. I tell him that I could not determine any reason why she would complain except for the ticket for the violation. I just believe she is upset over being charged with a violation.

The captain looks at me and begins to speak. "This is one of the best, most concise accident reports I have seen in years." He stands up from his chair and asks, "Why did you do such a good job on this?" Without hesitation, I tell him I take pride in my work and complete all my work that way. Deep down inside, I have a feeling the woman would not agree with any of my findings. What should have been routine needed to have a little more attention paid to it. He becomes emotionless, looks me in the eye and says, "Did you know that this took place in Hamden?" My response is, "Yes I did." The captain then chuckles, "Why in God's name did you do all that work and not just wait for the Hamden police?" My response, "That little old lady pissed me off, and I wanted to make sure she was dealt with. I made sure she got a ticket by writing it myself."

The captain could not hold back his laugh, and he exclaims, "Well, at least you are honest, and you didn't try to make up a story." He ends the meeting with a lecture about not investigating anything that occurs in any other town. I should also keep my emotions out of investigations.

I am slightly puzzled upon leaving this meeting. The captain said something about being honest. Why wouldn't I be honest? Why would I want to make up a story when I had not done anything wrong? When I attain the rank that conducts investigations involving misconduct by police officers, this statement would make perfect sense.

It will take approximately six to eight years for me to become totally comfortable with being a police officer. The daily routine of preparing for work and writing reports is similar to what was done in the Marines. The incidents, however, are different every day.

High speed pursuits are common events in the early 1980s. There is growing sentiment and a movement to have those kinds of police actions reduced or stopped completely. The moment you determine a person in a vehicle is going to attempt to evade your attempt as a police officer to apprehend them, the adrenaline kicks in. Driving a car at high rates of speed through rural areas is extremely difficult.

Every pursuit I am involved in ends in the vehicle being pursued and crashing into something. Only by the grace of God did the pursuits I initiated all end with only the suspect being injured. The most serious crime I pursued a suspect for was a robbery with a firearm.

On an evening shift in early June, I was assigned to patrol the west side of town. A broadcast was received from North Branford, a neighboring town that an armed robbery had just occurred in their town. The lone, white male who committed the robbery had fled the scene in a blue colored Volkswagen Rabbit. There was no marker plate visible on the car as it was observed leaving the scene of the robbery.

The business robbed was a liquor store. The perpetrator of the robbery was described as a white male in his late teens or early twenties. He was in possession of a rifle, and the police gave a description of his clothing. The business that he had robbed was only about three miles away from the edge of my patrol boundary. There were two roadways that led directly to that business.

When a broadcast like this is received, officers are taught to take up a position that the suspect might use as an escape route. I did just that. While I was taking up that position on the only road that could possibly be used to get to my patrol area, a North Haven police detective, who was driving nearby in an unmarked car, radioed that he was following a blue Volkswagen Rabbit, and they were on the road I was on.

I parked my police car in the parking lot of a business on the opposite side of a railroad crossing from the direction they were traveling. The detective gave a detailed description of the car and the lone occupant as they approached my position. Had they turned off the main road at any time, they would have just gone into a dead-end road or a business driveway.

I was hoping that this was in fact the person who committed the robbery, but he was not speeding or making a move to get away from the detective. I could see approximately a quarter of a mile down the road and was able to see both vehicles at that distance. As they approached my position, the detective instructed me to pull the police car out directly behind the Volkswagen. He also instructed as soon as I pull out to activate my emergency lights.

I did as instructed, and the Volkswagen pulled over to the right-hand side of the road almost immediately. I was surprised by this and thought, "If this guy just robbed a store why isn't he running?" I felt real danger and believed if I got out of my police car, he was going to ambush me. I kept my transmission in drive and held my foot on the brake. I picked up the radio microphone and advised headquarters and my supervisors the vehicle was stopped. I then opened my door, and as soon as I did, the Volkswagen drove away at a high rate of speed.

With the microphone still in my hand, I closed the door and said, "And we're off," like an announcer starting a race. This pursuit traveled 300 feet westbound, turned right, and traveled three quarters of a mile south on a multiple lane main road. It would turn west again on a cut-through roadway for a short distance. The horsepower difference between a police car and a Volkswagen Rabbit is significantly in favor of the police car. All I was doing was keeping up with him until he crashed or ran out of gas.

He then turned right onto a straight two-lane road known as Hartford Turnpike. In approximately seven-tenths of a mile, there was a major intersection where he could enter a limited access highway. The radio was full of chatter, and I was advised that two police cars were in position to help at that intersection. When I got closer to the intersection, I could see the other police cars taking up a position to assist. The Volkswagen began to slow as if he was looking for another way to go. There was no way for him to change direction to the right, but there were two residential streets on the left side of the road. The detective and another police car were behind me, and two police cars were in front of me.

I made a maneuver to get alongside of his car as a moving roadblock, which proved to be a bad choice. As I came along the side of him, he looked at me, and I saw the barrel of his gun. For some reason, he did not shoot, but he suddenly slammed on his brakes. I did the same but found myself already in front of where he was. My car began to fishtail to the left, and it ended up blocking the roadway. The vehicle being pursued was able to make a left turn onto the residential street. My police car engine suddenly stalled. While I was getting it started and back into the fray, two other police cars were in front of me, engaged in the pursuit.

This residential street was a small cul-de-sac with only six houses on it. This made me believe the pursuit was ending with me facing the wrong way and attempting to get my engine started. When the engine roared to life, I made a quick maneuver and headed back in the direction the rest of the parade had traveled. A stalled Chrysler Plymouth Fury II had let me down. I was sure the apprehension was made. My role now would be cleaning up the mess.

The road had a small "S" curve with a slight incline of a hill and then it descended out of sight and ended. The police car gained speed to get to the end as I was trying to get "back in the fight," when the Volkswagen appeared in front of me on the front lawn of a residence. It was headed on a direct path to collide with me. I now made the conscious decision to use my police car to stop this car any way I could.

I turned the car to the left, and the Volkswagen attempted to get away from my move. The Volkswagen was bouncing wildly due to the position on the lawn. I again turned in the direction the Volkswagen had gone, and the two vehicles collided in the roadway. The cruiser was hit on the front passenger side wheel well, making it impossible to steer. The Volkswagen was heavily damaged but continued down the roadway, making an escape. There were no other police cars immediately in sight as the Volkswagen traveled away from me.

I stopped the police car, put the transmission into park, and watched as the Volkswagen was failing rapidly and unable to travel in a straight line. As I got out and ran to the rear of the police car, I could see the suspect. He was now preparing to get out of his car and flee on foot. I could see he had the rifle in his hand. I drew my revolver and took aim at his silhouette. I could only see the back of his head, his right shoulder, and part of his upper arm. He was still moving away from me.

I was focused on the fact the suspect was still mobile and escaping. My car was wrecked. I was starting to get out of the car when I remembered stories being told by Marines and police officers who had been involved in shootings in the past. As the action is taking place, you will be so focused on the incident you could experience tunnel vision. This phenomenon causes a person to just see one extremely concise item or individual person.

When I drew the revolver from my holster, my experience was much different as every sense in my body was amplified. I could smell the anti-freeze that was spilling from the wrecked car, and I could also smell the rubber from the tires that had skidded on the road. There were birds singing, police radios still chattering, sirens still wailing and people starting to gather to watch the action. Tunnel vision would not be my problem; it was more like system overload.

I got myself into a two-handed standing shooting position. I concentrated on my marksmanship, sight alignment, sight picture, hand position, trigger squeeze. Suddenly, I could see people behind my target! Oh, shit! I can't stop the trigger from firing the gun. I consciously push the revolver to the left as it fires. I fire one round of ammunition and hit a branch of a bush on a lawn. As I came back on target, a police car was there. I holster the pistol.

My attention now turns back to my car. I shut off the engine, overhead lights, and siren. I grab my nightstick and run down the hill to where the Volkswagen has come to a stop. I am met by my lieutenant who grabs me around the waist to stop me. He then explains to me the suspect is in custody and seated in one of the other officer's cars. The arrested man did admit to the robbery of the liquor store.

As the scene begins to quiet down, I realize my right wrist is swollen and sore. I sprained it as a result of the collision. Due to the pursuit, the collision involving the cruiser and the firing of my firearm, our department considered this a serious incident. The captain in charge of the Patrol Division, Hayes Gibson, responds to the scene. When he arrives on scene, he orders me to have my wrist examined at a hospital. I am transported by ambulance to a local hospital.

The captain interviews me in the front seat of his car prior to my trip to the hospital. He starts by asking me to tell him how the collision occurred. I explained the pursuit had gone onto a residential street, and by the suspect's actions, I believed he was not going to stop. I deliberately used the police car to stop him. He asked if there was a possibility the collision could have been avoided. I explained it became apparent this person was going to continue to flee. The only logical thing to do was use the police car as a roadblock.

The second question posed to me by Captain Gibson was, "What justification did you have to draw and fire a shot at him?" I explain, "After the collision occurred, I observed the suspect was bringing the car to a stop. When the car stopped, I could see the rifle in his hand." As soon as I completed the sentence, Captain Gibson stopped me from saying anything further.

My statement regarding the cause of the accident read in a manner making the collision unavoidable. I said the Volkswagen was headed straight for me as it was coming off the grass. When I turned to the left, it mirrored my movement. When I saw that happen, I turned in the opposite direction. The Volkswagen again followed me, and the collision resulted.

Captain Gibson announces from what he can determine to this point, the actions I had taken were proper. He thinks it is an example of excellent police work. I request someone telephone my wife because she would have been listening to the radio scanner. The chase occurred during the time when I would normally be heading home to eat dinner. My wife would listen on the scanner for when I requested permission to go to dinner. She would then put it on the table, ready for me to eat.

This will be the last time she listens to the police radio scanner. She had been tuned in to the entire incident. She was nervous I had been involved in a more serious collision or a shootout. It did not make her feel warm and fuzzy about my profession.

The "robber" is an eighteen-year-old senior in high school who lives in a neighboring town. This is the first crime he has ever committed. His take in the robbery was $417.00. His reason for turning to a life of crime is to use the money for a class trip his parents did not support. Being a full-time high school student wouldn't allow him time to work to earn the amount needed to take part in that trip.

I never heard from this young man again. There would be no court trial. He will make a plea bargain deal resulting in a felony conviction. He is never allowed to go on the class trip. Had he been completely successful with the robbery, he still would not have enough money to pay for the entire cost of the trip.

At this point in my career, I work a different shift every other week. Pursuits of people trying to escape after committing a crime are commonplace. Two weeks after the pursuit of the liquor store robbery suspect, I discover a burglary being committed at a residence in the Montowese section of town.

At approximately 9:45 a.m., while I am on a routine neighborhood patrol, I observe a young black male coming out of a window of a residence. He has in his hand what appears to be a stereo turntable. As he lands on the ground, turns, and notices the police car, he drops the record player and starts to run away. I report this to my dispatcher on my radio. My call goes like this: "Patrol 3 to headquarters, 51 in progress at 28 Beatrice Lane. In foot pursuit of lone black male headed south toward Middletown Avenue." I follow him a short distance and see he is running toward a car waiting for him.

I give up the foot pursuit and rush back to my police car. The waiting car will have to drive by my police car to leave this street and get back to a main road. I just get seated in the police car and start the engine when the suspect car passes me. I put the car in gear and begin to pursue the suspect. I advise headquarters I am now in a vehicle pursuit of a burglary suspect. Beatrice Lane leads directly to Route 17 (Middletown Ave.), a main roadway. The pursuit is high speed, and Route 17 leads directly to the city of New Haven. The vehicle I am pursuing is a dark blue Toyota Corolla. The license plate was reported stolen two days earlier and was not supposed to be on the car.

The Toyota does not have the power to go faster than the police car. I stay close to them into the city of New Haven. The car is driven at speeds higher than the speed limit. The person driving tries desperately to get away from my attempts to stop him by driving into a city-owned apartment complex. He collides with the corner of one of the buildings, and the car becomes disabled. Both suspects bail out of the car and run into two separate apartment buildings. I stop behind the vehicle and secure it. Both suspects are able to get away at this moment. A police canine used for tracking purposes arrives almost immediately. This dog is able to track down the driver of the getaway car. He is found hiding in a janitor's closet in the apartment building. The other suspect is found later in the day. He did not go to school on that day, but he had his backpack with him in the car. In his haste to get away, he failed to take his backpack with him. This backpack contained a student identification card with his name and photograph of his face. Detectives who investigated the incident are able to connect this person to the burglary. I am able to identify him when he is brought to the police department for questioning.

A couple months later, the department and town are experiencing a rash of street robberies and purse snatchings. They mostly occur in the commercial shopping centers. These robberies are being committed in the parking lots as people who have just finished their shopping are walking to or loading their purchases into the car.

The robbers either drive by the intended victim and grab the purse of the ladies by reaching out of the moving car, or one person will be walking or running by the victim and steal the purse. After they have a purse, the car used to flee the area will drive by, and they will pick up the person who committed the robbery.

During the commission of two of these robberies, the suspect approached the victim and confronted them with a handgun. The shopping centers are two strip malls on Washington Avenue. This allows for an easy escape route by traveling north or south. The interstate highway has two entrances less than seven-tenths of a mile apart.

On this evening shift, the Detective Division, in an unmarked car, is conducting surveillance of the stores. The weather has been much more challenging this evening. It is a hot, muggy late July evening. Thunderstorms and showers have failed to cool the night down.

I am assigned to the patrol sector in which these shopping areas are located. My instructions for the night are to remain close to these stores. The detectives will call me on the radio to stop any suspicious car or one that commits a robbery.

At 9:15 p.m., the detective asks me to stop a Honda Accord leaving the parking lot. The license plate entered into the computer system is stolen. The stolen license plate should be on a Toyota 4 Runner. The passenger has just committed an armed robbery in the parking lot. I get behind the Honda and turn on the overhead emergency lights. The driver ignores my attempt to stop them. There are three people inside the car. The driver accelerates and attempts to drive away from me. He turns right and is now driving westbound on the Route 22 connector. I am directly behind him with my emergency overhead lights and siren on.

The detectives are behind me as we drive west toward an entrance ramp that leads to southbound Interstate 91, a limited access highway. The road we are on consists of two lanes of traffic traveling in each direction. We must go over a bridge before there is anywhere to turn. The detective advises police headquarters that the pursuit is starting.

The entrance ramp is on the right-hand side of the road. I want to stay close to this car to get them to drive faster. The faster they are going, the more difficult it will be for the driver to make any turns. As we get to the point where they must turn or continue to drive straight, the driver begins to brake.

He is traveling too fast to make the ninety-degree right-hand turn. The car locks up all four wheels and cannot make the turn. I pass them because the driver has put the car into a panic skid. The front end collides head on into a steel guardrail, traveling at high speed. The man in the passenger seat is thrown through the front windshield. As the windshield breaks, the body is lifted out of the passenger seat and is wedged in between the partially removed windshield and the dashboard. The car continues to push into the guardrail, forcing the front wheels to leave the ground. The car, still connected to the guardrail, suddenly stops and crashes down onto the ground. The driver gets out of the wrecked car and begins to run away.

My police car has fishtailed and come to a stop. It is facing the car that just crashed into the guardrail. I watch the driver get out and vault over the guardrail as he is trying to run away. There are now three police cars arriving to help me, the two detective cars and another marked police car. As I get out of the police car to chase the driver who is now on his feet, I know that he is running down a hill and straight toward a river.

This man is suspected of committing an armed robbery with a firearm. At this time in American law enforcement, police officers are allowed to shoot fleeing felons or those people who have committed a felony. It does not matter the type of crime or if they are armed or not.

I run to a point at the guardrail and can see the man running down the hill. The street and hill are clearly visible as I draw my service revolver. I shout to the man to stop running or I will shoot him. I set myself into a kneeling firing position and begin to aim at the center of his back. I start to slowly squeeze the trigger.

The fleeing man suddenly and abruptly comes to a stop and flips headfirst into the ground. I do not shoot. "What the hell has just happened?" I think. He is down, and it looks as if he is unconscious. I holster my pistol and run the 25 feet to where he is lying.

There is a three-foot high fence made of metal not clearly visible in this low light, and he has run straight into it at full speed. His left leg is stuck in the fence and is broken at the ankle. He is semi-conscious and is grabbing at his leg. I immediately handcuff and search him. He is not holding anything, but right next to where he has fallen is a handgun. I leave it on the ground but move him away from it. My focus is on this one man. I can hear police officers shouting in the roadway.

I get control of the man who is now in my custody and start to lead him up to the road. One of our detectives comes over the guardrail to help me. He still has his gun drawn, and I find myself staring down the barrel of his gun. I tell him he could holster it, and I need his help with this arrestee. The arrested man has broken his left leg at the tibia and fibula. He is charged with several serious crimes and is released so he can receive medical assistance for his injuries. The passenger is also charged with several serious crimes. His injuries are life threatening as a result of being partially ejected through the windshield.

It is determined after an extensive investigation these two men were responsible for more than twenty separate armed robberies. Both were convicted on multiple incidents, and they will spend a long time in prison.

# CHAPTER 14

# DRUNK DRIVERS

My experience as an officer will continue to grow. Each day as a police officer brings something different. This is not a routine life or profession. Some days are spent on the midnight to 8:00 a.m. shift, and this shift produces the most drunk drivers.

The official charge for someone who is arrested while driving under the influence of alcohol or drugs will constantly change as my career continues. The war against drunk drivers begins to take hold in the 1990s. Driving while drunk will be debated more than gun control. In North Haven in 1983, there are more bars, restaurants, and taverns that serve alcohol than fast food restaurants and gas stations.

In 1983, to be considered "Legally Under the Influence of Alcohol" while driving, the Blood Alcohol Concentration or BAC had to be greater than .15 % to gain a conviction. For a human being to get the BAC elevated to that point depends on a variety of things. Without getting "all technical" about it, determining if someone was over that amount was difficult.

The entire process of the arrest, testing, processing, and paperwork involved with a suspected drunk driver makes most police officers less vigilant in enforcing it. I find myself unsure at times if the driver is drunk or not. The only time I would pursue an arrest would be when the effects of the alcohol were so obvious anyone could see it.

My father is part-owner of one of the establishments that serves alcoholic beverages. The restaurant is known as "Chefs." While I was serving in the Marines, the restaurant was the location of a homicide investigation. My younger brother discovered the body of a murder victim on the property on a Saturday morning while visiting with my father.

My father and mother have been divorced, and as part of the decree, my youngest brother has visitation with Dad on weekends. On Saturday morning, it is my father's responsibility to check the stock, gather the money for bank deposit, and clean the restaurant. There is a river to the rear of the restaurant my brother played in.

On this day, Andy walks into the rear yard near the river. He gathers some stones and begins to throw them into the river. While he is doing this, he is walking along the bank. When he reaches a point where there is a bush growing toward the river, he notices a sneaker hung up in this bush. As he investigates further, he determines it is an entire human body hung up in the bush. The chest and head of this body are under the water. Andy runs back to the front entrance of the restaurant and excitedly proclaims to our father there is a body outside. In disbelief, our father dismisses what he said and tells him to stop joking around. Andy persists with his discovery and convinces my father and several others to leave the building to go see.

They confirm that it is a human being and is in fact dead. The police are notified, and they respond in force. The first officer determines the report is real; there is a dead body at the restaurant. A detective is assigned to investigate the reason this person ended up here.

We learned this is a young man who has been shot and killed. The detectives assigned to the case are Stephen Smith and Joe DePoto. Steve Smith is the same officer who was there when I was involved in the motor vehicle accident as a child. A diver is brought in to search the river for evidence. This is the second homicide influential to and memorable for me before I become an officer.

It is determined this murder occurred in West Haven. The victim was a young man who allegedly had sexual relations with a girl who was several years younger and a minor. The father of the minor girl and a friend of his committed the murder. The friend was a resident of North Haven and was related to one of the bartenders.

The investigation will continue, and the trial of the suspects arrested for this murder will occur after I become a police officer. The police will eventually arrest two men responsible for committing the murder. I know one of these men personally and worked on several construction sites with him before the arrest.

The bartender is an employee of my father and his partners. This bartender who is working the night before my brother located the murder victim's body is related to the suspect. When the investigating officers interview him, he explains to them it was a busy, hectic night, but at approximately 11:00 p.m., his nephew entered the bar with a friend. His nephew is the suspect who will eventually be arrested. The two of them sat at the bar and ordered one beer each. They were both happy and laughing while they sat at the bar. He spoke with them briefly when his nephew proclaimed, "Hey, Uncle Bill, would it be okay if we disposed of a body out back?" The bartender, thinking it was a joke, responded with, "Sure, go throw it in the river."

The day the victim's body was found, this bartender was at the bar. Upon seeing the dead man, he became sick to his stomach, ran inside, and vomited. He now admitted the reason he was so sickened was because he believed his nephew was responsible for the killing.

The nephew was eventually arrested and convicted of this murder. He was sent to prison along with the other man who was in the bar that night. Apparently, they shot this young man while he sat in the rear seat of a car. They then brought him to North Haven and attempted to dispose of his body by throwing the victim into the river.

This part of the river is affected by ocean tides. When they threw his body into the water, the tide was rising or coming in. The investigators believe, as a result, he washed up stream first. When the tide began to fall or go out, the body moved and got entangled in the brush.

This murder will be solved, and arrests will be made. The two men will be convicted and sent to prison. The case will set legal precedence in the State of Connecticut, and I will become more familiar with many of the facts of this murder case than any other.

The fact that my father is a part-owner of an establishment that sells alcoholic beverages does not stop me from enforcing the drunk driving laws. On several occasions I will stop people who have come from and were drinking at my dad's bar. I will know some of these people personally and make some difficult decisions. I found being a small town police officer meant I had to arrest people I knew.

Upon my return from Cuba after leaving the Marine Corps, I brought my father two boxes of Cuban cigars. Cuban cigars were considered to be the best in the world. The United States government did not allow the importation of anything from Cuba. My dad shared those two boxes of cigars with his friends. I did not get much satisfaction from my time spent in Cuba. This night with my dad, enjoying the pleasure of a Sir Winston Cuban cigar with his friends, was something I could never put a price tag on.

Drunken driving is a serious deadly offense, but I would have many funny interactions with those people, many of whom should never have gotten behind the wheel to drive. One such incident involved the arrest of a young woman after a snowstorm.

This arrest occurs on the evening shift at approximately 10:30 p.m. It is nearing the end of the shift, so I am looking forward to going home more than I am looking for someone to arrest. I am driving on a main road cleared of snow with two-foot-high snowbanks on each side of the road.

On a straight stretch of roadway, this woman drove her car into one of the snowbanks, honestly believing she was still driving. The motor is running, and the rear tires are spinning, trying to gain traction. I stop behind her with the police car. The tires continue to spin, showing no signs of slowing. When I am even with the driver's window, I can see this woman concentrating on driving, yet she is going nowhere. I use my hand to knock on the glass. She is intent on driving, so she turns her head slowly to determine what the knocking noise is. Her head then snaps back and forth in a double take. She then acts as though she is pulling her car over to the side of the road. She continues to act as if she is still driving. I again knock on the window to gain her attention. This time she looks at me and smiles. I then yell at her and make a motion with my hand to have her open her window.

She believes she is still driving. I can tell by her movements that she applied the brakes, pulled the car to the right side of the roadway, and stopped. She reaches for the shifting handle located on the center console and moves it to the position of PARK. She then shuts off the motor by turning the key. While rolling down her window, she acts surprised I am standing next to her car.

I begin the conversation by asking her if she was okay. She says, "Where did you come from, and why did you stop me?" It is really hard not to start laughing, but with the straightest face I can muster, I say, "You are stuck in a snowbank on the side of the road. It looked to me like you needed some help." She responds, "I was not! You pulled me over; I stopped when I saw your flashing lights."

When she speaks to me it is obvious she has been drinking some type of alcoholic beverage. At this point, I ask my dispatcher to send a second car to assist me. Unfortunately, it would be for my protection as much as for hers. I stop talking with her and tell her to wait in her car. I knew she could not go anywhere anyhow.

When the back-up officer arrives, it is veteran patrolman, Don Harris, who had three more years of experience than I. I quickly fill him in, and we approach the car to speak to her again. When he talks to her, he agrees with my assessment – she is intoxicated. We both agree she should be taken into custody without administering a sobriety test due to the road conditions.

When I again speak to her I say, "I need you to step out of the car for me." She responds, "You may have to help me get up because I'm really drunk." In law enforcement, that is what is called a "clue." The legal term is a "spontaneous utterance." She just confessed she was intoxicated while driving. Most people involved with any kind of contact with police officers should keep their mouths shut.

She was removed from the scene, arrested, and charged with operating a motor vehicle under the influence of alcohol, drugs, or both. After completing the paperwork and processing of this young lady, I would never see her again. I am not aware of the final disposition of her case.

People who drive while they are intoxicated to the point they can't remember what they are doing are basically driving while they are unconscious. It would never cease to amaze me how many people would get behind the wheel of a 2500-pound rocket and think it was safe.

Here are some cases of driving while under the influence that were memorable without going into complete detail of each incident.

On a beautiful fall evening in October, as I was working on the west side of town on an evening shift, a very fancy, expensive car was being driven by a gorgeous woman on Route 5, the main road on that side of town, traveling north. While driving, the passenger side wheels were off the paved surface of the roadway over the curb. Fortunately for her and the car, in this stretch of road, there were no solid objects with which she could have collided. Her speed was about 20 miles per hour on a posted 45 miles per hour speed limit.

Slow speed is a good indicator of an intoxicated driver. This car had the unusual position of the tires over the curb indicating something was happening with this driver. She stopped her car immediately when I was behind her and activated the overhead emergency lights. When I got to the driver's side window and began to speak to her, it was obvious she was intoxicated. She was dressed in a skirt and sweater. The sweater was loosely knit, and this made it easy to see most of her chest area.

I immediately called for a backup officer to assist me and protect me from any false accusations. She was very lucid even though the effects of alcoholic consumption were obvious. When the backup officer arrived at the scene, we talked to her while both of us were next to her.

When I asked her to show me her license and registration, she began to negotiate with me. Her response to me was, "Officer, let's cut to the chase. You know I'm drunk."

I said, "I haven't determined that yet, young lady," to which she replied, "Well I am, and I don't want to get arrested tonight. I will do anything you and your partner want me to do. I really don't want to get arrested so what can I do for the two of you?"

This proposition was very tempting, and I decided to play along with her for a couple of minutes to see how far she was willing to go.

I asked, "What do you mean by that?" She immediately said, "I will give you both blow jobs, or we can go back to my apartment, and you can do whatever you want."

I explained to her that neither of us would be able to accept her offer. She was placed under arrest and taken into custody. I learned that she worked for a professional escort service and had a record for prostitution. I would never see or hear about her again.

Another notable intoxicated driver was a male subject that I observed leaving the McDonald's restaurant on the main street of our town. This arrest occurred on a midnight shift. I had just begun my shift when I was driving north on Washington Avenue. As I was driving past the McDonald's, a car was exiting the driveway of the restaurant. When he exited, he made a wide turn and drove over the curb. I turned around and began to follow the car south on Washington Avenue. The car was being operated very erratically. It swerved from lane to lane and did not stop for a red traffic signal.

He would not stop even after I had activated my emergency lights and siren. He made a right turn in the center of town onto Broadway. As he made that turn, he drove through a center traffic island with flowers planted on it. He did not stop and was now increasing his speed. We were traveling east on Broadway.

As I was communicating the direction of travel and description of the vehicle, two other officers made me aware they were on the side of town where we were. As we came to the intersection of State Street, the car turned left and was traveling south. He collided with an embankment while making this turn. We continued to travel south on State Street. When we got to the intersection of Dixwell Avenue, the two other officers joined in the pursuit. We executed a moving roadblock with the three police cars. Officer Jim Merrithew positioned his police car in front of the car. Officer Lou Nava drove to the side of the driver's door. I continued to follow behind. We all formed a roadblock, slowed down, and stopped him at a point where some trees blocked the fourth way for him to escape. When we had him stopped, he got out of his car and tried to run away. Officer Nava caught him instantly. They began to fight, and officer Nava ended it quickly.

The man was arrested. When he was being handcuffed, he was found to be bleeding from his hand, arm, and face. He was also missing two fingers on the hand that was bleeding. We began to look for his fingers, believing they had just been amputated. It was learned that he had lost his fingers in a previous accident while driving under the influence. His license was found to have been suspended because of the accident which caused him to lose his fingers. I do not know what happened to him after my case and never saw him again.

One drunk driver that I stopped had just exited the interstate highway at exit 13. I followed this car as it turned onto Toelles Road. Ninety percent of this road is in Wallingford, as is exit 13. As the vehicle was driving into North Haven, I was following it.

While I was following the car, it became apparent this person was lost or intoxicated. When the car began to travel southbound on Hartford Turnpike, a mostly straight road, it was more noticeable the driver was impaired in some way. The car swerved violently, avoiding a collision with a mailbox. Then, it crossed over the centerline of the road. When I activated the overhead lights to stop the car, it immediately turned into a residential driveway. A female exited the car, locked the door, and started to walk toward the front door of the residence. I called her and asked her to come back to her car. She immediately asked what was wrong as she was trying her key in the front door. She ignored me, acting as if I was not there at all.

After several attempts to open the door with her keys that would not fit the door, she realized I was standing next to her. She began to laugh when she said to me, "Where did you come from?" without stopping "I can't seem to open my front door. My key does not work." My response was, "Do you really live here? I notice that your car has Massachusetts license plates." Springfield, Massachusetts, is approximately 50 miles away from North Haven, Connecticut. There is an interstate highway that passes through the center of North Haven and also Springfield.

She opened her purse, reaching for her driver's license and said, "Yes, I live here. 1798 Chatham Avenue, Springfield, Mass." I told her she was not in Springfield, and this was not Chatham Avenue. She began to argue with me. I showed her my badge and shoulder patch and then placed her under arrest.

She explained to me that she had just gone to a friend's house in Agawam, Massachusetts, located just north of Springfield. She had a couple of drinks and then left to drive home. Fortunately, there were no reports of her vehicle being involved in or causing any accidents along the way. She was arrested after failing the sobriety tests. She kept on insisting she was in her own driveway. She insisted I needed a warrant to be on her property. She could not understand why a police officer from North Haven, Connecticut, was in her driveway.

When her husband came to the police department to bond her out, he was unable to understand how she was able to drive the 50 or so miles to North Haven while being intoxicated. He had received a telephone call from the friend in Agawam who was worried she had consumed too many glasses of wine. I never saw her again after this night.

The most notable case I had as a police officer occurred when I was a patrolman. I had made it a point to learn as much as I could about the law and science behind the effects of alcohol on the human body. I was one of the first officers in the state to receive advanced training. I knew the law as well as any officer could possibly know it.

On a day in July, during an evening shift, I would observe a vehicle involved in a collision being operated on Middletown Avenue. The front passenger side of the car was heavily damaged. The tire was flat and almost completely gone. I was able to get the operator to stop the car in a short distance. When I started to speak to the driver while he was still seated in the driver's seat, I could see a marijuana cigarette burning in the ashtray located in the center console. The smell of burning marijuana was intense. When he spoke to me, the familiar smell associated with someone who is under the influence of an alcoholic beverage was missing. He was obviously under the influence of an intoxicating drug, and it impaired his ability to drive. I arrested him for driving while under the influence of drugs or alcohol.

In the state of Connecticut, a person arrested for this charge must submit to a chemical analysis of his blood, breath, or urine to determine the blood alcohol concentration (BAC) or the type of drugs in their system. The type of test used is determined by the police officer.

Our police department had recently received the most advanced Intoximeter. This is the machine used to determine the BAC of a person by analyzing their breath. The hope was to make testing easier for the police so they would become more likely to arrest intoxicated drivers.

This driver was obviously under the influence of drugs. The breath test would be useless in this case. Drivers who had been arrested could not refuse to submit to the test requested by the arresting officer or they would have their license suspended. I was going to request he submit to a blood or urine test.

The sergeant on duty wanted to use the new Intoximeter. When I arrived at the police station, he greeted me at the rear door and informed me he had turned on the Intoximeter and it was "all warmed up and ready to go." When I told the Sergeant I was not going to use the machine, I think I either broke his heart or pissed him off.

I went in to secure my firearm and gather the required paperwork. When I got back to the arrestee, the sergeant was getting ready to have him submit to a breath test. I told the sergeant I was requesting a blood or urine test because I thought it was drugs. He replied, "You're not telling me what to do."

I was just about to make a mistake that would influence the rest of my career. This sergeant would eventually be promoted to chief of police, and I was going to tell him he was doing the wrong thing. I am not wrong with my assessment of the sergeant's actions, but I should have just let him do it and let his supervisor correct him, not me as a patrolman.

When he asked the arrestee to submit to a breath test, he allowed him to fulfill his requirement of submitting to a BAC test. Even though he was under the influence of marijuana, he knew that marijuana cannot be detected on a breath test. The arrestee was happy to put his lips on this machine and blow his lungs out.

I told the sergeant he should not be giving him a breath test. I explained there is no evidence to support the use of the machine to check for alcohol as I suspected drug use. I did not stop there. I would need him to write the report for this arrest. There was no way I could author a report to explain why this person was given a test for alcohol when I suspected drugs.

He ordered me to write the report, insisting I not tell him how to do his job. My report was written to put the sergeant in a very bad light. I made it appear as though he had no idea what he was doing, as it related to an arrest involving a driver suspected of being under the influence of a drug. I questioned his ability as a supervisor in the report.

When the lieutenant who was the commander of our platoon read the report, he thought it would be in my best interest to change the report. I refused to change any part of my report. This sergeant would eventually become the chief of the department. This caused a rift between us for the rest of my career. We would have difficulty finding common ground to work on. He would always outrank me, and our leadership and management styles would always conflict.

Police work is different each day. There are distinct characteristics to the types of crimes each officer deals with, dependent on the shift assignment and duties. Dayshift involved mostly minor fender bender accidents, residential burglaries, shoplifting from stores, minor drug offenses, and many medical emergency calls.

The midnight to 8:00 a.m. shift was usually quiet. When there was activity occurring, it was usually catastrophic. These would include serious motor vehicle accidents, a major structure fire, or some major crime. When it was quiet, the security of the town was our focus.

The evening shift was always the busiest and most unpredictable. Most of the important meaningful incidents that affected me during my career happened during this shift.

There was one incident occurring on this shift that made me realize I needed to be ready to defend myself at a moment's notice. There are individuals who want to hurt or kill police officers just because they wear a uniform. They are not afraid of the police, and they have no respect for the law.

On one evening shift, I learned this the hard way. The town had two apartment building complexes in the early 1980s. One of these was a long rectangle building that sits on a small ridge, off a main commercial roadway. It is set off the road approximately 1,000 feet. The roadway that leads to the parking lot meanders up a hill and then sharply turns to the right. It continues around the north end of the building.

The front of the apartments faces west in these apartment buildings. The rear of these apartments faces east with balconies or porches that overlook two ponds. There are four floors divided into thirty separate units. Each unit houses eight separate apartments. Number thirty was at the north end of the building with number one being at the south end. The management office was located on the ground floor of unit number five.

The parking lot was on the west side. There was capacity for each apartment to have one space with six extra spaces for each unit. The parking lot was on a slope. After a resident had parked, they would have to walk slightly downhill to their residence.

They were inexpensive for the area and always seemed to be full. I lived there for two years just before I was first married. The incident happened at approximately 8:15 p.m. on a fall day in October before Halloween.

The dispatcher calls me by my badge number and instructs me to check the Whitewood Pond Apartments for a Chevrolet pickup truck that has been involved in a hit-and-run accident. This pickup truck collided with a car in Wallingford.

Wallingford is the town bordering North Haven to the north. The Chevy pickup allegedly collided with the rear of a car on a side road and did not stop. The person in that car was able to note the license plate number as the pickup drove away. The plate matched the description of the pickup, and the registration showed the owner lived in Whitewood Pond Apartments # 21D.

The common procedure would be to go to inspect the parking lot to see if the vehicle was parked there. Most times, the vehicle would be in the parking lot. The owner, having fled, would be hiding and not answer the door. Sometimes, the car that is being sought is not found. This night would become something different.

I am parked a short distance away. I write the marker plate down and drive to the apartment parking lot, looking for the parking space for unit # 21. As I pull into the lot, I see the pickup truck immediately. It is parked in the fifth space, and steam is coming out of the front end. There is heavy damage from a recent collision. I park the police car directly behind the pickup truck. I notify the police dispatcher that the truck is in the parking lot. I also advise the dispatcher it is damaged, and I ask her to notify Wallingford Police. I tell her I will be checking the vehicle.

When I exit the police car, I slide my nightstick into the holster and grab my portable radio and flashlight. As I approach the driver's side door of the truck, I can see the window is open, and there is a person lying on the front seat. I notify the dispatcher the truck is occupied and request a backup officer be sent to assist me.

I don't know if the request is ever received or acknowledged, as things turn to shit immediately. As I am talking on the portable radio, the person in the front seat springs to life. It is a large man. The pickup truck is equipped with racks that carry multiple ladders. The body of the truck is filled with roofing supplies. I immediately think, "I hope this guy isn't drunk, and I hope he is calm."

The conversation starts out like this: "Hello, Officer, how are you?"

"I'm fine. I need to see your license and registration."

"Go Fuck yourself" is the response I get from the man in the pickup truck as he tries to open the door to get out. At first, the door is locked, and this slows him down slightly. I push my weight against the door to keep him in the truck. I try to reason with him and convince him to stay in the truck, to no avail. He begins to swing his arm out of the window, attempting to hit me. Nothing I am saying to him seems to be heard or make any difference. He wants nothing to do with me. He is focused on getting out of his truck. He pushes the door open and gets out. The entire time, I keep asking him to stay calm and remain seated. When he gets out, there is one thing on his mind, and it is to kick the shit out of the police officer standing in front of him.

He is obviously under the influence of some type of drug. Once he is free of the doorway of the truck, he begins punching mostly the air at first, but he soon gains his balance and is hitting me. I defend myself by fighting back. I land a couple of punches with my left hand, but my right hand is holding the portable radio. While grappling with him, I am trying to talk on the radio and then get the radio into the holder on my belt.

After a couple of punches are exchanged, I manage to get the radio secured. Once I have two free hands, I am able to take the fight to him. He is incredibly strong, and I need to use as much strength as I have to just keep him at bay. With the fight continuing, we are moving our way down the parking area toward the apartment building. We also move from #21 to #29 and are now on some grass.

I knock him to the ground, but he gets up quickly. I draw my nightstick and try to fend him off with it. He ducks down low and attempts to tackle me. A blow to his shoulder with the nightstick stops that, and he turns to run away in the opposite direction. I hit him again with the nightstick, but the force of it hitting him makes it fly out of my hand. He turns to run away toward his apartment, and I chase him the short distance. He is able to get to a point right in front of the apartments, and I am able to knock him to the ground. When he attempts to stand, I drive him into a ground floor window of an apartment. He is bent in half at the waist and stuck in the window with arms and legs stretched out in front of him. I am exhausted. I grab his legs and yank him out onto the ground. I then get on top of him, straddling his torso with my knees on his arms. We are in a small alcove, partially hidden from view. I pull out my radio, and as he continues to struggle, I check the dials, making sure it is on the correct channel and that it is turned on.

I radio in the following: "I NEED HELP NOW!"

As soon as I put the radio back into the carrier, I hear sirens. Sirens of all tones and styles are heading toward me. This is the first time in my life I have felt real fear. This man wanted to hurt me. This fight was not over yet. The cavalry have not yet arrived.

The first police car to arrive is Patrolman Mark Margolis. He drives right past me and stops where my cruiser is parked. The second officer to arrive right behind the first is State Police officer, Tom Shia. They are both yelling my name trying to locate me. I am yelling back at them as other police cars are arriving. I am approximately 250 feet away from my cruiser. Officer Margolis gets to me first.

He sees that I am bloodied and exhausted. He looks at me bewildered and yells, "What the hell happened? What do you need me to do?" I look at him and say, "I need to roll him over so that I can handcuff him." Mark is kneeling near his head. He looks at the two of us and is obviously shaken. He yells at the man to roll over. This man responds by yelling, "Fuck you," and spits at Officer Margolis. Officer Margolis responds by slapping him on the side of his head with his open hand.

I let my weight off him, and he rolls over. When I let the man up, there are four other police officers there: Officers Margolis, Debbie Pausig, and Albert Roan from North Haven, and Tom Shia from the State Police. The man who is now an arrestee has no more fight in him. By the time I walk back to my cruiser, two Hamden police, two New Haven police, a second State Trooper, the Wallingford officer, and the North Haven sergeant have arrived at the scene.

I learn two things that night.

1.  Police officers will be there for each other. No matter what age, sex, race, rank, organization. We are the Thin Blue Line.
2.  There are people who want to hurt police officers, just because they wear a badge.

There could not have been a more diverse and eclectic group of police officers that came to my rescue that night. Margolis is Jewish, Debbie is female, Al Roan is black, and I am white. The two police officers from New Haven are Latino, and the Hamden officer is of Irish decent. The two things I learned that night will never change.

My eyelid on the left side was scratched. I had a small cut on my lower lip, and two of the knuckles on my right hand were cut. The spit shine on my boots was destroyed. My shirt and trousers were filthy, and my hat was sitting on the pavement – crushed. There was a distinct trail of equipment and scuffmarks that showed the path of the fight.

The man was found to have used cocaine and alcohol prior to being involved in the hit-and-run collision in Wallingford. He was a contractor who specialized in replacing roof shingles and roofing damage repair. He would die due to a drug overdose just six months later.

My tactics will change after this incident. I no longer trust any individual I encounter professionally. I am starting to understand why police officers act the way they do. My thoughts drift back to the time when I found the missing man dead in his backyard. I remembered how I thought the police officers there were cold and callous on that day. That is the way I am now. Four other incidents will occur at this apartment complex that will always be in my memories.

# CHAPTER 15

# WHAT IT TAKES TO BE A POLICE OFFICER

O ne day in February, I am sent to investigate a domestic dispute involving an unmarried couple engaged in an argument. The man has leased the apartment, and he has allowed his girlfriend to live with him there for six months. Her name is not included on the rental agreement, and there is no written agreement.

On this day, there is a covering of snow outside, and the temperature is 28 degrees. The male has forcibly removed the female from the apartment and told her she is no longer allowed to stay with him. He believes she is seeing someone else. He has thrown her out in the cold with only the clothes on her back.

When I arrive, the woman is standing outside, wearing only a terrycloth bathrobe and fuzzy slippers. She is attractive, but boy, is she pissed off. I drive to a point, keeping the front end of my car between her and myself. Domestic disputes are among the most dangerous calls police officers will handle.

When I get out of my car, I ask her if she has any weapons. Her response is, "The bastard threw me out of the house in my bathrobe.

No, I don't have any fucking weapons." I wait for the backup officer to arrive before we go inside. While I am waiting, I offer her a seat in my police car to warm up. She refuses and remains standing in the cold.

When the backup officer arrives, we walk up the stairs to the third-floor apartment. The boyfriend reluctantly opens the door and then refuses the three of us entry into the apartment. He explains his ex-girlfriend is no longer welcome in the apartment. He apparently has had experience with the police and the criminal justice system because he tells us, "If you police officers don't have a warrant, you can stand in the hall, too."

After explaining the reasons a warrant is not necessary and he needs to allow the woman back inside because she is entitled under the law, the woman puts on a show for us. The area outside the apartment is small compared to any room inside. She begins to yell at her ex-boyfriend and points her finger at his face in an overly aggressive manner. As she is doing this, her robe opens exposing part of her chest. I make note of what she is and is not wearing. I point out to her she has come undone, and this distraction allows us to make our way into the apartment. The young woman is then allowed to get herself dressed. The two of them agree she will leave in her own car and visit a friend.

The man is arrested for his behavior. Connecticut law requires an arrest be made whenever there is any type of physical contact. He was considered to be the aggressor. While he was at the police department, he made a written complaint regarding my behavior. I am again required to answer questions from the captain in charge of the Patrol Division. Captain Peter Ori interviews me regarding the incident. He asks me ten useless questions about my past encounters with this couple. Then he comes to the reason for the citizen complaint regarding my behavior. Captain Ori's conversation goes like this: "While you were at this domestic dispute, was the female only wearing a terrycloth bathrobe?" My response is, "Yes and fuzzy slippers and white with pink polka dot bikini underwear." Captain Ori then asks, "Did the robe come open at some point, exposing the young lady's chest?" My response is, "Yes, sir, and they were beautiful."

I answered the question in that way because I knew the complaint was going to be about my remarks when her robe opened. I glimpsed briefly but tried to maintain professionalism. My comment was, "Please cover up."

Captain Ori begins to laugh out loud. He told me, "I can count on you for the truth no matter how bizarre it is. You are going to have to learn to temper your responses. Don't be so willing to volunteer information." The lecture did not stop there. He told me to limit my responses to "Yes" and "No" answers.

The reasons for this become very clear to me in the future. When it becomes important to remember details while testifying to a case in a court of law, lawyers will make sure every word, every explanation, every minute detail will be extracted from your memory banks.

The apartment complex will continue to be a place I must constantly be aware of. The third incident is not as dramatic but is very memorable. This time, the police have been notified of a loud argument taking place in one of the apartments on the third floor. When I am driving up the roadway, I can see into one of the apartments. Most of the other apartments are dark. What I see is something amazing. It is 11:30 p.m.

There is a completely unclothed female sitting on the floor with her legs crossed and arms dangling by her side. A man is standing in front of her screaming and pointing his finger at her. I am unable to hear what he is saying. When the back-up officer arrives, there is nothing he can add because he does not have any history of being there.

We make our way to the apartment while the man inside continues to scream abusive language. He is so consumed with cussing and belittling the female, he does not hear the doorbell or knocking at the door. We have the dispatcher search the computer to find a telephone number associated with this apartment number. The phone is called, and contact is finally made.

This man refuses to open the door for us. We argue with him about what he can and cannot do for approximately 15 minutes. During the entire conversation, he continues to threaten his girlfriend. He will not let her get up, and he will not open the door. Eventually, we convince him to open the door by explaining we will forcibly open it, and he will be responsible for paying for the damage. He then allows us into the apartment.

Fortunately, the girlfriend is not injured. As soon as we are inside, she finds the courage to get off the floor and make her way to the bedroom. She must come past us because of the floor plan, and she is totally naked. She is beautiful, and her body is like a model you'd see in a magazine. The man continues to insult her with derogatory words.

She is getting dressed while we are aggressively keeping him away from her. The man explains he caught his girlfriend having sexual relations with someone else. This guy claims everything the woman owns he has paid for and given to her. She does not work and used to be addicted to heroin. The man helped her get "clean" approximately four years prior to this incident. He knew her as a friend before her addiction and was now romantically involved with her. The relationship had just started three months ago. The man had been taking care of her to keep her straight for the four years prior to becoming romantically involved.

The reason he gave for treating her the way he was is that when he found her in trouble four years ago, she had nothing. No clothes, no home, no money, nothing. He found her being treated in a hospital. So, today, he had her strip and told her she could leave. She could leave with nothing because he had paid for everything she had. Unfortunately for him, the world does not work that way. She was allowed to remain in the residence and keep her clothes. He was arrested for his conduct on this night. I learned my lesson the last time a previous incident when a woman exposed herself. I kept my mouth shut and handed her a blanket so she could cover her body.

I never knew what happened to him until several years later. He had been involved in a motor vehicle accident that left him in a vegetative state, being kept alive by machines and drugs. She left him after this incident and went back to using drugs. She died ten years later.

Naked women, half-clothed females, people having sex, injured bodies, and death will be common happenings. Each time it happens, I don't believe it has any less of an impact on my feelings. I stare at every naked woman and evaluate what I see. Broken bones and lifeless bodies seem to have become common. I refuse to let those things change me.

I try to find hope and something funny in every event, no matter how tragic or devastating. Life as a police officer and being married prove to be difficult. My wife was able to start a career in the medical field, becoming a hospital administrator. As our professional careers advanced, she was the principal breadwinner in the family. I will cherish our marriage and life together forever. I make a promise to her to not bring the "JOB" home with me.

It is difficult to be a perfect police officer. There is no such thing. You fight a constant battle to keep it all together. Many books and articles have been written about how a police officer needs to be able to handle any situation. There should be no subject a police officer doesn't have some knowledge about.

I make sure I have an outlet to keep my emotions from interfering with our marriage. As a young boy, I became interested in guns and hunting. Hunting would serve as the best way for me to get away from everything. The woods would be my place of worship. Hunting deer would be the most common form of hunting I do. This is an ordinary day of hunting.

The crosshairs of the Leopold 4x10 telescopic sight is zeroed on the base of the skull. I am ready. I begin to slowly move the trigger to the rear, squeezing, easy, nice, and easy, think about your mechanics, steady, BANG! The round is on its way. My shoulder absorbs the recoil, and the bullet strikes the target almost in the same instant.

I had spent most of my life training and preparing for this moment. I cannot believe this is the way it is happening. It is true what they say about the feelings you experience when you finally get the opportunity. This adrenaline rush is like nothing I've ever experienced. I always thought it would feel different. I thought I was going to be nervous.

The 180 grain semi-jacketed boat tail round crashes into the base of the skull just above the neck. There is no doubt that he is dead. The skull is pierced, and the motor nerves are severed from the brain. His strong muscular body falls to the ground like a Raggedy Ann doll being tossed aside by a three-year-old during a childhood tantrum. He is dead.

I begin to think about how I ended up in this position. I begin to realize that it is cold, bitter cold. The snow had been falling steadily now for about two hours. This is November snow, a rarity, the first snowfall of the year. The first snowfall, like every first, is special and unique. I always loved when it would snow on these November days. The snow meant there would be good times during my annual pilgrimage to Pennsylvania for the opening day of deer season. The deer season always starts the first Monday after Thanksgiving. This year Thanksgiving is late in November, so the possibility of snow is greater.

Normally, deer hunters don't try to shoot the deer in the head or the neck. This deer would only offer this shot. He would only expose his head, and I had no intention of taking this deer to a taxidermist. There are few opportunities to harvest a deer on this trip each year. When the target becomes available, you cannot hesitate.

Once the deer is down, the work begins. After I climb down from my tree stand, I gather the equipment I will need to remove the internal organs. A deer needs to be "gutted" prior to being removed from the woods. While I get what is needed, several of the men I am hunting with hear the shot. Two of them come to see if they can be of any help. It is always easier to clean a deer when someone helps, and I welcome the assistance. Two friends have come to help. They are a brother police officer and a professional firefighter. As I start to cut into the chest of the deer, they begin to tell stories about accidents or shootings they had to investigate or perform some type of first aid.

As soon as the stories begin, I start to think of a motor vehicle accident I had witnessed while I was away in Vermont hunting with my German shorthaired pointer, Otto. I owned a small 13-acre piece of land near Mount Snow and had taken three days off from work to go bird hunting. The dog and I were camping out on the property.

We had just driven back from picking up some food to eat. I am on the main roadway driving from the local general store with our chow. Approximately 500 feet ahead of me, I see a car pulled over to the side of the road. The four-way hazard lights are activated. As I drive closer, I can see a motorcycle on its side.

Then, there is a body. The body is a man with a full-face covering helmet on. There are three people standing there looking at him. I stop the car and ask if I can help. I explain I am an out-of-state, off-duty police officer. An elderly woman looks at me and says, "I think he's dead." These are not the four words I need to hear right now. I hand her my car keys and tell her, "Go to the trunk of my car. There is a big red box with flares, a flashlight, and a medical kit in it." I look at the victim, point to him and say, "I'm going to see if I can help him."

I run to the body and quickly check for any bleeding or breathing. He is not in bad condition but is not breathing and there is no blood. I ask a bystander to help me remove his helmet. All I have this person do is stabilize his torso while I remove his helmet, keeping his neck stable. As I remove the helmet, I feel a vertebra sticking through the skin just below the skull. There is a large amount of blood pooled inside the helmet.

He has broken his neck and is dead. I did not even attempt to start CPR. As I stand up, the police, ambulance, and fire engine arrive. The woman had set up a beautiful flare pattern. The police officer immediately asks me about the accident.

I did not witness the accident, so I am of no help. There is a nurse on the ambulance that originally thought I should have begun CPR. Once she saw the damage to his neck, she understood why I chose not to begin. There are no witnesses to this accident. The only person who knows exactly what happened is dead. I learn that the motorcyclist was driving at an extremely high rate of speed just before the accident occurred. A woman who was sitting on her porch saw this and relayed that information to the investigating police officer. The investigation determines the motorcyclist was traveling too fast to safely execute a small twenty-five-degree turn. He lost control, flipping the motorcycle on the side, was ejected and launched directly into a utility pole face first. This probably killed him instantly.

While this was taking place, my dog Otto had been in my car alone for over an hour. When I stopped the car, he was asleep. When I finally get back to my car, he is definitely awake and is hungry or pissed off, or both. There is a snowstorm taking place in the interior of my car. White foam and bits of insulation are everywhere. The interior upholstery which was formerly green is now gone. Cold steel and fiberglass fibers are all that are visible. The little ears on Otto's head are wiggling wildly while his head moves from side to side. The white foam and fibers are filling the air inside the driver's compartment with each shake of his head.

The violence ends as soon as I open the door, and Otto sees me. The night was a wreck. My car needed a new interior. I just saw another dead body. The food I had bought was gone, including the paper it was wrapped in. I packed everything up and headed back to Connecticut.

I could not get away from death, even when I went to another state on my own personal time. I needed to learn how to deal with it. I was recently married, and I did not have any children at this point in my life. I made the determination I would keep these things to myself. I would internalize every incident and deal with death in my own way.

I was back in the woods with my deer. Even my hobby involved death. Hunting did not always involve taking a life. It is far more and will make me a better person. It will teach me patience and respect for the woods and wildlife. It will become my passion. Hunting will consume me and be the outlet to allow me the fortitude to get past the terrible things I will deal with.

The hunt was over, and it was back to reality. Back at work there is a fourth incident which occurred at the Whitewood Pond Apartments, three months after the contractor had assaulted me. I am working the midnight shift. While routinely patrolling, a car drives past me on Skiff Street while I'm waiting at a red light. As the car crosses in front of me, I notice it has a taillight out. When the light changes to green, I begin to turn in the same direction that the other car is traveling. The car starts to accelerate to an extremely high rate of speed. He then drives through the red traffic signal at the next intersection. He is attempting to get away from me.

Skiff Street leads downhill to State Street. I accelerate, and I can see him turning left onto State Street where he continues to drive fast. He suddenly executes a left turn into the driveway of the Whitewood Pond Apartments. This driveway turns in the opposite direction as Skiff Street. He is now traveling uphill. The driveway turns sharply to the right because there is a pond straight ahead. He is far enough ahead of me that I lose sight of him at the turn. The reason I lose sight of him has nothing to do with the turn. He has driven into the pond. This pond is only five feet deep, but the car is only partially submerged.

The driver has made his way out of the car as I am pulling the police car to the side of the road. The emergency overhead lights have already been activated, and he believes someone else has called me. He nonchalantly begins a conversation as if he had just driven off the road accidentally. He is acting as if he was not driving recklessly. He pretends that this is the first time he has seen a police car this evening.

He begins the conversation with a lie. "Hi, Officer, I was just coming from work in New Haven on State Street. I think I fell asleep at the wheel." He then continues, "Made that turn a hundred times before and never had any problem." At this point in the conversation, I hold up my hand in the stop position. I say that the worst thing he could be doing is lying to me.

I had checked his license plate through the Department of Motor Vehicles and determined that the car was registered to a Wallingford address. I then say, "That was my police car you passed on Skiff Street. Why would you be driving on Skiff Street if you work on State Street?"

Suddenly, his entire demeanor changes. I now get into a defensive stance and order him to stop walking and put his hands where I can see them. I have him walk to the front of my car and place his hands on the hood of the car. I am not taking any chances. Once he is in that position, I frisk him and place him in handcuffs.

I did not intend on fighting for my life again. Once he is handcuffed, I sit him in the rear seat of the police car and ask him if he wants to tell me the truth now. Instantly, he begins to tell me his life story. His license had been suspended because he had been arrested for driving while under the influence. His car was not registered or insured. He had just come from a bar where he had been drinking.

I do not feel sorry for him or show any empathy. I charge him with as many charges valid for this little incident. They included DUI, speeding, reckless driving, defective taillight, unregistered car, no insurance, suspended license, and failure to drive right.

Ten days later, I would investigate a legitimate accident where a car ended up in the pond. On this day, however, this man is lucky he is alive. I will never understand why people try to run from a police officer. The police car is equipped with a radio. There is usually more than one officer working at a time, so it is almost impossible to elude them. The drivers who try to flee are mostly inexperienced criminals who panic for one stupid reason or another.

They then make poor decisions. They start to exaggerate or make up stories and tell lies. They forget who they are and try to be someone they should not be. If they would just relax and drive normal, most police officers would not give them a second look. There is this look a person will give to a police officer that cannot be described. Only a seasoned officer can read the face of a person who is trying to hide something.

When it comes to drunken drivers, each of them is different. Alcohol affects every person in a different way, including the amount one consumes, the type of drink, the amount of food they have eaten, how much they weigh, and the amount of experience they have drinking. The science behind the way the human body reacts to alcohol will be something which will now be taught to the police.

In 1986, I will be trained in a new scientific technique that will improve the detection of a person under the influence of alcohol. This will be the first training session of this new method that will take place in Connecticut. It is known as Horizontal Gaze Nystagmus. Simply stated, it is an involuntary twitching of the eyeball.

When the eyeball is moved voluntarily to the extreme sides of the eye socket, it will cause pain and discomfort. When a body is sober, it can control the pain and keep the eyeball steady without any visible twitching. When the human brain has been compromised by drugs or alcohol, the eyeball will twitch. The reason behind this is the pain stimulus travels faster than the part of the brain that tells the person to hold the eyeball at its maximum deviation. The twitching is slight as the intoxication reaches a specific level. The more alcohol in the blood, the stronger and more pronounced the twitching gets.

When I complete the two-week course of study, I am certified to use this as an additional sobriety test. I am to show the officers I work with how to administer the test. This test will eventually become one phase of the standardized tests for all DUI suspects.

Officer Ted Stockmon is new to the police force in 1986. I have explained the test to him, and he is eager to see it performed on a suspect. We are both working on a midnight shift when he stops a female he believes to be intoxicated. He has stopped her on a side road, but there is ample room to conduct the tests.

There is really no need to use the new test because her level of intoxication is extreme. The test is used to determine those borderline cases and is not needed now. The woman is gorgeous. On a scale of 1 to 10, she is about nine and a half. The only reason she isn't a ten is because she is drunk.

She is dressed in a silk blouse that is buttoned down the front. Her waist and upper thighs are barely covered by a mini skirt. She has long blond hair with blue eyes. Her shoes are red high heels, and her legs are covered in flesh colored panty hose. The miniskirt has a zipper in the front that goes the entire length of the skirt. Her body is put together perfectly.

The sobriety tests are not standardized in 1986. The North Haven police require four simple tests. They are: 1. the walk and turn test, 2. the one leg stand test, 3. the stand straight, head tilt, and touch the finger to nose test, and 4. the stand and pick up an item such as a coin or a pen from the ground test.

Officer Stockmon requests I assist him. When he calls on the radio, he states, "Can I have Officer Genovese respond here and do the eye thing?" I respond along with Officer Grimaldi and Lieutenant Corazzini. We begin testing with the Horizontal Gaze Nystagmus. She fails the test, and the results indicate the intoxication is extreme. We continue to conduct additional tests. We do so because she is cooperative and is at the happy stage of intoxication. When we get to the test that requires her to pick up an item, I explain the test and demonstrate it to her. I then place a quarter in front of her and instruct her to pick up the quarter by bending at the waist and knees.

She has her own unique way of doing the test. As she starts her descent, she spreads her legs to the side. This causes that zipper to start an ascent to the top, exposing her private area. It makes that distinct Buzzzzzzzzzz sound of a zipper opening. The two officers I am with do not allow the zipper to make the complete trip. They both look in amazement and shout simultaneously, "Your zipper!"

She is obviously flustered. She stands up straight and pulls the zipper back to the closed position. I then point out that she failed to pick up the quarter. When she hears me, she bends her legs again, and the zipper begins to open Buzzzzzzz. The two officers again point this out to her. This sequence continues another four times.

She suddenly stops and exclaims, "You guys are fucking with me now!" She is obviously aware we are toying with her, so now it is time to stop. Once a suspect becomes uncooperative when conducting sobriety tests, the arrest phase will be difficult. The way I make it easy to handcuff a person I have decided to arrest for DUI is to ask if they will submit to one more test. Every person that I had tried this with has agreed to participate.

I require them to place both of their hands palm down on the fender of the police car. I then instruct them to spread their hands out. Once they have done it, I ask them to keep their hands on the car and walk backwards. This places them in a position to be searched or patted down before they realize it.

This young lady is cooperative until the first handcuff touched her wrist. Then, the wildest beast imaginable is released. Her wrists are too small for the handcuffs. Her hands are easily manipulated, making the bones smaller than the handcuffs can be adjusted. This young woman is now as fierce as a Marine in hand-to-hand combat. Her hand slides effortlessly out of the cuffs. She's flailing her arms violently, and the four of us quickly grab whatever part of her body we can reach. Each of us is able to get hold of an arm or a leg. We again restrain her, this time using plastic tie wrap handcuffs. She continues to fight. The septic tank that is in the position of her mouth is gushing language that would make hardened veterans blush.

We secure her in the rear seat of Officer Stockmon's police car. The young woman rolls around in the seat until she is able to position herself in a way to be able to kick out the windows. Lying on her back with her head against the passenger side door, she bends her knee up to her chest, and she kicks the driver's side door window until it shatters.

Officer Stockmon drives to headquarters before she can get her whole body out through the window. The police department is less than a mile away, and each of us follows him to headquarters. We have to pick her up out of the car and carry her into the building. She is constantly squirming and twisting. With all of the movement, her miniskirt is now hiked up to just under her breasts. There are now more runs in her panty hose than can be counted.

This is my first experience with an arrestee who lost complete control of her sensibilities. She fought as if she was a wild animal caught in a trap. There was no possibility of getting her to cooperate. All the officers involved had to hold her down in a chair. We ordered an ambulance to transport her to the hospital.

When an ambulance is ordered for any reason, the fire department is notified. In this case, an engine with four fire personnel responded, and there were two more people on the ambulance. There were now ten emergency service workers attending to this one out-of-control drunken lady. Each one of these ten men is now content to be involved.

With all the squirming, twisting, and fighting, her clothing is completely disheveled. Her blouse is missing all but one button. That specific button is the closure of the blouse centered on her cleavage. The lace bra that holds her breasts in place is not able to keep up with the struggle. As she is loaded onto the stretcher, she continues fighting.

She has to be restrained by being tied to the stretcher with several bed sheets. The fighting continues as she attempts to break free. She thrusts her hips off the cushion toward the sky. This is done over and over in a rhythmic fashion making it appear as if she is performing a sexual act. She is finally removed from the police department, humping some invisible being while tied to a hospital stretcher.

It was determined she had been under the influence of alcohol and a hallucinogenic. That led to a conviction for operating a motor vehicle while under the influence. The State of Connecticut has a special program which allows a person to have a conviction of this type erased from the permanent record. The arrested person is required to apologize to every police officer involved.

The next time I see her, the transformation is nothing short of miraculous. She is dressed in a navy blue Anne Klein business suit. Her hair is pulled into a tight bun. The contrast from the night of the arrest is heart stopping. Today she is an eleven on a scale of one to ten. She politely, in what can be described as the most lady-like performance imaginable, greets me in the lobby of the police department. I remember her name, but I am not prepared for the beautiful, feminine apology delivered. Her voice is sweet and soft. There are no four-letter words used to get her point across. This is completely opposite from the night of the arrest. I accept her apology and wish her all the best for the future. I never hear from her again and have no idea what happened to her.

Police work takes on a whole new life after this incident. A few weeks later, I have another violent encounter with an intoxicated driver. I am assigned to the four p.m. to midnight shift.

Interstate Highway 91 makes its way through the center of North Haven. This is a limited access highway patrolled by the CT State Police. Incidents that occur within the area of this roadway fall under their jurisdiction. There is one state trooper who is assigned to patrol the highway from Middletown to the end in New Haven. This is approximately 25 miles, covering both the north and southbound lanes.

Local officers are often dispatched to an incident as a first responder or to back up a state trooper. It is a warm summer night, and nothing has occurred yet this evening. The Hotline radio connects all the local law enforcement agencies. We always listen to it so we are aware of things taking place close to us.

A report is transmitted that there is a vehicle with heavy front-end damage being driven on Interstate 91. The car is said to be dragging something behind it. I am close to the highway, and the dispatcher has me respond to the highway.

As a police officer, we are allowed to enter highways from areas other than the paved entrance ramps. I enter the highway from an area near Elm Street and the Route 40 connector. I travel onto an entrance ramp and begin to travel northbound. The traffic in front of me is almost stopped, and every vehicle has moved to the two right-hand travel lanes.

I see a car stopped in the left-hand lane, enveloped in a cloud of steam. When I get closer, I see there is a steel cable guardrail with four wooden posts attached to the car. The car is not moving, and the engine is not running. There are approximately 75 feet of guardrail behind the car. I stop my police car there and leave it with the emergency lights lit. I set up a flare pattern and then approach the car.

I see the head of a man leaning against the driver's side window. He is either sleeping, unconscious, or dead. It is a four-door Jeep Wagoneer. With my flashlight, I quickly survey the interior to see if there are any other passengers. The jeep is empty, except for the driver.

I begin to bang on the window with my flashlight to arouse him. After several raps on the window, he awakens and begins to manually roll down his window. As he is turning the crank, he is speaking incoherently and reaches with his other hand for the ignition. As he turns the key, it is now obvious that the motor has ceased. The car will not start, and I don't have to worry about him driving away. I transmit on my portable radio what the situation is and advise the dispatcher the driver is apparently intoxicated. I want him to stay in the car until the State Police trooper arrives.

I begin talking with him through the open window. I do not want him out of the car because I am alone, and drunks are unpredictable. While he is sitting there, I notice there is some type of club next to his seat and the passenger seat near his back. Now, I am concerned when we attempt to get him out of the car, he is going to use the club.

I ask him for his license. He very calmly reaches into his pants pocket and removes a money clip. The driver's license is right on top. Instead of handing it to me, he places it on the dashboard. He sucks me right into his trap because I believe he does not understand my instructions. I reach into the car to get his license. When I reach in, he sucker punches me. I don't know how he got his hand around like he did, but it was a good punch which caught me on the right cheek.

The punch hurt but did nothing but motivate me. In one swift motion, I had removed my handcuffs from the holster and had one of his wrists locked up. I attempted to pull him out through the window. I knew this wasn't going to work because he was able to use his feet as leverage as he turned to face the door and push away from me. The fight and the struggle for control were now on. We exchanged a couple of rabbit punches until I let him loose. Then I opened the door and was again able to grab the handcuffed hand. I was still unable to pry him out of his car. Suddenly, the passenger door opened. A firefighter friend of mine pushed the man toward me, and I punched him four or five more times until he fell to the ground. I then finished handcuffing him. We had been fighting each other for about 40 seconds, but it seemed like 40 minutes. I searched him while he was on the ground.

At this moment, my nose is bleeding, and my cheek is sore. As I stand him up, two State Troopers arrive to take over. After my explanation of what occurred, they remove my handcuffs and replace them with a set of their own. The man is then seated in the rear seat of the state police car, which is also occupied by a police K-9 named King. The troopers are Joe Davis and Paul Hibson. We would work together many times during our careers.

The State Troopers handle the processing and paperwork for this case. The drunken driver had collided with a cable guardrail in East Haven, approximately 14 miles away. The connection rod for the cable became embedded in the radiator of the Jeep. The motor would eventually cease to run because the coolant ran out.

I do not know what happened to this man after he was transported by the State Police away from this accident scene. I was told that he was not willing to fight with the K-9 or attempt to make any sudden moves. I did learn he lived in a town by the shore approximately 40 miles away in the opposite direction he had traveled.

# CHAPTER 16

# THE DARK DAYS OF POLICE WORK

One of the darkest days of my police career was about to take place. I would be forced to arrest a commander of New Haven's Investigative Services Division.

March 17, 1986, I am assigned to the evening shift. My patrol is the Montowese section of town, patrol number 3. It is St. Patrick's Day. Police officers have a long tradition of celebrating this particular holiday. Parades, parties, celebrations, and the consumption of alcoholic beverages are common for the day. Drunken driving is also common on this day.

Unmarked police cars are usually fairly easy to spot during this time period. The Chrysler Grand Fury III has cornered the market by supplying municipalities with police cars. The same models that become marked cars will be unmarked. Fire departments will use the same vehicles for their chief officers to drive.

During my shift, just before I am going to eat dinner on Quinnipiac Avenue at the intersection of Middletown Avenue, a white Grand Fury passes in front of my marked car. The driver of this car has his head sticking out of the side window. He is flipping me the bird and yelling, "Fuck you" as he drives by. I try to ignore this behavior. I continue driving and return to this same location ten minutes later and find the same car parked on the side of the road. The motor is running, and the driver is asleep in the driver's seat. I park the police car behind him and turn on the overhead emergency lights. As I walk up to the car, the driver suddenly awakens and drives away.

I get back into the police car and see he has only traveled approximately 250 feet. I keep the lights on and again stop right behind him. I am on Quinnipiac Avenue, next to a small set of stores that has a small parking area for fifteen cars. I again approach the car, and this time, I get to the side by the open window.

The driver is again asleep. I can see a pair of fireman's boots and a bunker coat in the rear seat. There is also a case of beer. My first thought is this is a firefighter who is intoxicated. I reach into the car and shut the motor off. I now use my portable radio and ask for a back-up officer to assist me.

I attempt to wake the driver by yelling at him. He does not wake up. I continue to yell at him and then push on his shoulder. After three or four shoves, he wakes up. He is startled and begins to mumble incoherently. I ask him who he is, and he immediately begins yelling at me. "You know who I am. Why did you stop me? I'm going to have your badge for this."

I ask him over and over to show me some identification or his license, registration, a badge, anything to show me who I am dealing with. He refuses and just continues to argue with me. He is obviously intoxicated. While we are talking, he reaches the ignition and is able to get the car started.

I ask him to shut the engine off and try to reason with him. While I am talking with him, one of our North Haven police detectives stops his car next to me and asks what is happening. I tell him that the man will not show me any identification documents to me. He was stopped and is apparently intoxicated. The detective looks at me and says, "Do you know who you have stopped there?"

I reply, "No, I don't, but I think he is a fireman." At that moment, my back-up officer arrives. The detective says to me, "You should let him go because I know who it is." The detective then just drives away without telling me who this man is.

The back-up officer has only two years more experience than I. As he gets his car in a position to assist me, I am discussing with the man that he needs to shut off the motor. He begins to argue with me and becomes enraged. I am about to make a huge mistake. I reach into the car with my right hand to turn off the ignition.

When I do this, the driver grabs my hand, and at the same time, puts the car transmission into drive. The car starts to move forward. I am now in a predicament that I do not think I can get out of. I yell as loudly as I can for him to let go of me and to stop the car. I convince him quickly as he is only making this whole incident dangerous and worse for him.

I am able to shut the engine off while running alongside the car. We have only traveled approximately twenty-five feet, but this is the straw that breaks the camel's back. My mind is made up. No matter who this man is, he is under arrest. The back-up officer is now by my side. The car has stopped, and the keys are removed from the ignition.

We then remove the driver from the car. When he steps from the car, he goes down on one knee. As he is turning to get to his feet, there is a holstered revolver on his hip. I immediately force him to the rear of his car and reach to remove the revolver. When I put my hand over the gun, this man grabs my hand.

He is very large, standing at about 6 feet, 3 inches tall. He weighs approximately 290 pounds. When he puts his hand over mine, I speak to him and maneuver him to a position I can control him from behind. He is not cooperating with either of us. I can sense that he is uncomfortable with the way he is being treated. I continually talk to him, asking him over and over what his name is and what he does for a living. Now that I have located his revolver, I am no longer thinking he is a firefighter. He still refuses to tell me his name or point me in the direction of his identification. I advise him that I believe he is intoxicated and ask if he would submit to take some sobriety tests. He refuses and just verbally abuses me.

As I begin to search him, because I am intending to arrest him, I still find nothing in his pockets. I place him in the handcuffs and seat him in my police car in the rear seat. I secure his revolver in the trunk of my car.

I then go and look in his car for his identification. Lying on the driver's seat is his wallet. The wallet is opened and is exposing a gold badge, a New Haven police commander's badge. Next to the badge is a perfect identification picture of the person I have just arrested.

I have just arrested the Commander of the Investigative Services Division of the City of New Haven's Police Department. The head detective is in handcuffs, seated in my police car. When a person is arrested, the radio call is said in code. It is simply stated, "41 with 1."

My backup officer will take an inventory of the car and wait for a tow truck to come and remove the vehicle. During the entire drive to the police headquarters building, the commander abuses me verbally. He calls me all different types of vulgar names. He criticizes my appearance, my age, my uniform, and my department.

I am nervous about making sure I do everything necessary. I can't make any mistakes. I keep thinking that I wish I could have a video recording of his behavior. I also wonder why the detective just drove away and left me hanging.

When I get to the police department, I secure him and prepare to complete the arrest process and paperwork. My lieutenant stops me and pulls me into a back room. He asks me to explain why I have arrested a police officer from another municipality. After I have explained the entire incident, the lieutenant agrees my decision was the correct one due to the circumstances.

He leaves me to do the processing on my own. The arrested commander will not answer any questions and will not submit to any tests. He signs the forms he knows he is required to sign. A lieutenant from the New Haven police I personally know comes in to post the bond. When they leave the station together, the lieutenant lets me know he agrees with the action I have taken.

My lieutenant and the detective who are working refuse to get involved. They will not help in any way. They both want to distance themselves from this incident. Their names do not appear in any of the reports. There are no references made regarding those two officers.

The commander from New Haven is teaching me a valuable lesson. In order to convict someone of a crime, there has to be indisputable evidence. The evidence has to be something that can be seen, smelled, touched, or heard. It cannot be a thought or an assumption. The facts of this case are going to be my professional opinion of what occurred just now. It is going to be easy for a case to be made by a defense attorney proving my case wrong.

I am on my own. No other officer can help me. Not one of them wants to help me or be involved. I need to have all of my facts correct. There is no way I can afford to make any errors. It is imperative I "cross all my t's and dot all my i's."

So, what is my evidence? I had observed him driving erratically as he passed by me. The gesture of "flipping me the bird" and yelling obscenities at me would not prove he was intoxicated. I had to focus on what I had smelled and the observations I made of his actions.

There would be no sobriety tests considered as pass or fail. There would be no alcohol breath, blood, or urine test to show the BAC level. I was not even able to check his eyes for nystagmus. Observations were all I had. I describe his actions and my observations with as much detail as possible. I have no tangible evidence.

The court case against the commander would drag on for over a year, causing a rift between the two police departments. When the behavior of the commander on the night he was arrested was specifically explained to individual officers, the rift was closed. Any reasonable police officer realized he gave me no choice. The prosecutor for the State of Connecticut did not want to offer a plea deal.

For months after this incident had taken place, the more senior officers and police who held a rank in our department treated me in a different way. There is an uneasy feeling each time we work together. I believe those men thought I would arrest my own mother should I get the chance. These police officers believe I did not care who I was arresting. It did not matter that by arresting this officer, I was ruining his career and life. This was not the way I intended to be as a police officer. I had no intention of ever arresting any police officer.

I don't know the final disposition of this particular case. This commander had a drinking and driving problem. Approximately a year and a half after I had arrested him, he was involved in a major motor vehicle accident. In Hamden, he collided with another vehicle and then fled the scene. He was not able to travel far because of the damage.

He was found to be intoxicated at the time of the collision. He was arrested by a police officer of the Hamden police for fleeing the scene of the collision. I felt I had been vindicated for the action I had taken. I would tell everyone who asked me about this incident that the treatment that I was given by my peers was an injustice to me and just plain wrong. Every one of those officers would eventually apologize to me for the way they treated me.

I would continue to enforce the law without prejudice and would treat every person I came into contact the same. I would try to be color blind and be as open-minded as possible.

The police officer is not the one who is ruining a person when he or she is arrested. The actions of the individual are the cause of the demise. When the commander became intoxicated to the point he could not drive, this was the point when his career was ruined. The inability to take responsibility for his own actions led to his problems. I believe I am saving his life and allowing it to turn in a new direction.

I had no desire to take his position away from him or cause him any harm. I had no aspirations at this point in my career on being elevated in rank. My basic goals were to go home from my shift uninjured and do the best that I could. I would worry about promotions later. The destruction of careers would be left up to those other individuals.

This whole incident made me think back to my high school years. In the fall of 1973, I began my senior year of high school. I played football each of the four years that I attended high school. I was good enough to play on a high school team, but I lacked the talent to go on and play in college at any level. My classroom grades were not special in any way either. Football was my motivation for staying in school.

Playing football taught me about competition. Individual and team competition existed in sports as well as in every aspect of our lives. I never expected to be in competition with my peers as a police officer. There was never anything like this in the Marine Corps. The profession was difficult enough on its own. The added competition to gain favor would make this almost impossible. I was not in this profession to be in a competition. I just wanted to do the best I could be. Boredom was a major concern of mine. North Haven did not experience a large amount of crime. Most of the time was spent training and preparing for crimes that would never occur.

CHAPTER 17

# SOME GOOD LUCK

Some good things would happen during my career as a police officer. One time I recall occurs when I am working an overtime assignment, directing traffic while a utility company is repairing a utility pole damaged as a result of an automobile accident.

We are on Church Street next to the town hall. While I am directing traffic around this construction site located right at the town green, I am abruptly confronted with a married couple driving their car recklessly toward me. The husband is driving, and his wife is leaning over the front seat into the rear seat. The hazard lights are on, and he is sounding the horn. He is driving faster than the speed limit. The roadway is curved, and the tires are screeching as he approaches me.

Fortunately, I am able to get him to stop. The driver steps out of the car frantically pleading with me to help him. He is screaming, "My son has stopped breathing! Help me, my son is not breathing!" I immediately open the rear door and see a small boy strapped into a child's car seat.

His mother is trying to straighten his head and neck. In as calm a voice as I can muster, I reassure both parents everything will be okay.

On the inside, I do not have the slightest idea of what could have just happened to this child. I unbuckle this four-year-old from the car seat and pick him up. The adrenaline rushing through me makes his body feel as though I am handling a doll. When I pull the child out of the seat, his head tilts backward.

His body feels lifeless and flimsy. There is a space on the rear seat where I can lay him down as I prepare to resuscitate him. As soon as I straighten his neck out, he lets out a huge gasp for air and breathes on his own. Then he starts to cry.

I use my radio and call for assistance from the professional medical services. A fire rescue vehicle responds to the scene along with an ambulance. We would determine the little boy had fallen asleep after spiking a fever. With the configuration of the child seat and the straps, his throat had swollen, and his airway was cut off. Simply removing him from the seat saved his life.

The couple had lived in North Haven all their lives. The husband was a postal employee I had known as an acquaintance. We would become good friends over the years. The little boy would grow up to be a strong healthy adult and raise his own family. The husband and wife consider me the "one who saved their son's life." I did nothing but unbuckle his seatbelt. There are many little stories like this one that make the profession rewarding.

A second incident occurred on a beautiful, sunny Sunday morning in the early summer. I am on the midnight to eight in the morning shift on a routine patrol assignment in a residential neighborhood. Nothing had happened during the entire shift until 5:30 a.m.

While driving on this particular road, I see a small child wearing only a t-shirt and a diaper walking on the sidewalk. There are no adults around, and the child stops walking and waves his hand at me as if he is waving hello.

I stop driving and walk over to the young boy, thinking he could not have even been two years old. I try to have a conversation with him. My ability to understand baby talk or whatever language this little guy is speaking is getting me nowhere.

Something I have always done since I was a Marine is to have a supply of Tootsie Pops available for a snack. He takes my hand and the candy, and we start to walk to the closest house to see if he was missing from there.

It takes several minutes to awaken the people living there. They are of no help at all. They had never seen this child before. They did not know of anyone in the general vicinity who had a small child this age. I graciously apologize for waking them so early, and then we leave.

I walk to the house nearest to the direction from where he had come. I notice a minivan with out of state license plates. In the rear window hangs one of those little warning signs that proclaims, "BABY ON BOARD." As I approach the front door, I can see it is open. The storm door is closed, but the main door is open. I ring the doorbell and am greeted by a gentleman who is in his sixties. My first thought is "This is probably not the right house," but when he sees the child, he calls back into the house, "Susan!! SUSAN!!" He then asks, "Why do you have my grandson in my front yard?"

What we determine is the daughter of this elderly man is visiting from out of state, and it is her child who I have found. The baby boy is twenty-one months old and a bit of an escape artist and wanderer. There is no crib at Grandma and Grandpa's house. They do not have childproof door locks or any way to ensure the baby is secure in their house. He apparently woke up, went to the front door, opened it, and went for a walk. The family is mortified and believes I am going to arrest them. I am just pleased this child was returned home before he was seriously injured or something else happened.

This was one of the rewarding days. Then, there are those days you wish that you had some type of magical powers or you could turn back time. Good seemed to rarely happen. There was always something wrong or bad that would overshadow happiness.

One of the fringe benefits to becoming a police officer is you know about all the special events taking place in your area We are made aware of these events, including the visit by a celebrity or important politician. Police officers are used as traffic and crowd control and protection of the individual. This allows me to meet and speak with several amazing individuals.

I meet three governors of the State of Connecticut, two senators, a congressional representative, and the former First Lady, Hillary

Clinton. I would meet hundreds of athletes, including baseball, football, and basketball players from the college and professional ranks. From time to time, there would be some other famous entertainer or celebrity visiting town.

One famous television and movie actor who visited is Ernest Borgnine. He would visit often because his mother lived in North Haven. He would make a special trip to visit with the police officers of my department because of the way they treated his mother. One year, he was our guest at the Police Association of Connecticut's annual picnic.

Talking with these people always made me uncomfortable. When I meet them, it is always under formal conditions. I was usually working and in uniform complete with my gun belt and firearm. Most of the conversations were professional in nature. When I am working, I am extremely uncomfortable answering the questions asked of me. I know these people are just trying to be friendly and personable, but I am there to make sure that nothing happens to them. I am not there to talk about the weather or if I enjoy being a police officer. Politicians are the worst because they are always trying to get your vote.

There is one politician who worked his way up through the state legislative ranks that I worked with, guarded, protected, and escorted. Every time I am assigned to his detail, we have to be introduced. He has no memory of ever having been near me or knowing who I am or that we have met several times, carrying on multiple conversations. He is presently serving as one of Connecticut's senators.

The most fun I had on a protection detail is when the Walter Camp Football Foundation held their annual enshrinement banquet and awards ceremony in a venue in our town. I am assigned to guard and transport two college football players who would both go on to have professional careers in the National Football League. I am their personal driver/police officer for 12 hours. I meet several other former professional football players. The highlight of the night is when I take a picture with the "Bud Girls," two gorgeous models who promote Budweiser beer.

The town I live and work in has an annual agricultural fair. The North Haven Fair Association has held this event for 75 years. The association owns a large tract of land in the middle of the town where this event takes place. It is extremely popular and draws crowds of ten to fifteen thousand people on the weekend days and nights that it takes place. This is where I meet a few governors and many celebrities who entertain at the fair. I'm not famous so nobody really pays much attention to me at the fair. My one shining moment at this fair came when I am the chairperson for a fund-raising event.

I proposed and arranged for our Police Benevolent Association to raffle a Ford Mustang. The raffle ran for an entire year, and the winning ticket for the car was to be drawn as the last event of the fair. Tickets were sold at $5.00 apiece. The winner was a married couple who had just given birth to their first child. Several members of the PBA thought it was a huge mistake to raffle the car. They believed in the end, the PBA would lose money. When it was all said and done, the profit for the raffle was over $38,000 dollars. This would be one of the proudest and happiest moments of my career.

CHAPTER **18**

# LIFE CHANGING EVENTS

I n 1989, my son Steven Aaron Genovese is born on February 19. I consider this the happiest day of my life.

Two weeks after my son's birth, I am dispatched to a medical call involving a baby. I am working the day shift and have just gotten into the police car and signed on for duty. It is a bright sunny, beautiful day. There is not a cloud in the sky. The temperature is pleasant, and the humidity is low.

The dispatcher advises me I need to respond to the call using my lights and siren. I am a minimum of two minutes away from this residence. I activate the emergency lights and siren and drive the most direct route to the call. The house is two blocks away from my residence.

When I stop my police car in front of the house, a woman is coming out of the front door, holding a baby in her arms and performing CPR. I notify the dispatcher of this and tell them to have the medical personnel "step it up," meaning if you are not in a hurry, you need to be.

Once the process of CPR has been started, it means that the body has no palpable pulse and is not breathing. That human being is dead. You are hoping by a miracle of science or God somehow you can breathe life back into that dead body. My experiences with CPR have not been good. I know this woman who is carrying the baby. She is a friend and a registered nurse. I ask her if she needs me to take over for her, and she tells me that she is okay and is still able to continue. I get an oxygen bottle out of my car to saturate the air close to the baby. The ambulance arrives at the same time as the fire rescue truck. The paramedics take the baby from the nurse and leave as fast as they arrived.

The mother of the child has fainted at the sight of finding her lifeless child. While she is attended to, I need to notify our investigative services division. There will have to be an investigation as to the circumstances surrounding the death of this baby.

The investigation will determine the baby died of natural causes. He was six months old and died of what was known as SIDS (Sudden Infant Death Syndrome). This will affect me in a way for which I am not prepared. I watch my baby son until he is two years old. I will spend many sleepless nights in his room just watching him sleep.

In 1989, I am considered for promotion to the rank of sergeant. There is a testing requirement consisting of a written and oral phase. I finish second on the test, and at the time, there is only one sergeant position vacant. The list will remain in effect for one year.

In January 1990, a sergeant position becomes available, and I am promoted to sergeant. Life is good right now. The rank of sergeant in the police force is different from a sergeant in the Marine Corps. There are eight enlisted grades or ranks and eight officer ranks in the military. All officers outrank enlisted personnel. There is no enlisted rank higher than the lowest officer rank.

In the law enforcement, there is no standardized way ranks are given out or what they represent. In the small department I am a part of, there is a variety of ranks and titles that mostly just mean you receive more pay and have different responsibilities. Should you be assigned to the patrol division, the rank structure is simply low man is a patrolman. The next rank is sergeant, followed by lieutenant, captain, deputy chief, and chief of police.

When I receive my promotion to sergeant, we work a schedule where officers choose their respective shift by the seniority they hold.

There are nine sergeant positions in the entire police department, and six are assigned in the Patrol Division. One lieutenant and two sergeants would be assigned on each shift. In a five-day work schedule, sergeants work two or three days with another sergeant or a lieutenant.

I am the lowest man on the entire list of sergeants. I am therefore relegated to work the shift that no other sergeant wants. I would work the midnight to eight a.m. shift for the next nine years. On its face value, that sounds bad. And, for a normal human being, it is bad. It is impossible to get in any real good sleeping time. Professionally, though, it is the best possible scenario I could be in. I never have all of the bosses hanging around. I am able to be an independent thinker and figure things out on my own.

Sergeants are involved in more incidents. As a sergeant, I would respond to every incident and back up patrolmen on their motor vehicle stops. When I am assigned to supervise the entire shift on my own, I learn the dispatching procedures. I would see more, learn more, and do more on this shift as a sergeant than any other time as a police officer.

As a sergeant, you are considered a higher-ranking officer, more so than a patrolman. I don't know why it occurs or what the reasoning behind it is, but just showing up at a scene of an accident, a fight, or anything and wearing the sergeant stripes brings a sense of calm. When the sergeant is there, everything is going to be fine.

July 2, 1990, 12:15 a.m., I am working the midnight shift assigned as the road sergeant. The lieutenant is on his scheduled days off. I am junior in rank to the other sergeant so he will serve as the commander of the shift. I have just left the police station, and I am driving southbound on State Street.

The dispatcher notifies me and another patrol car that the State Police are requesting assistance with an accident that has occurred on Route 15. Route 15 is a limited access highway that runs through the west side of our town. It is the jurisdiction of the State Police, but we help them with accidents often.

I am less than 30 seconds away from this accident. It is reported to be located on the northbound lanes between the exit ramps # 62 and #63. I am entering the highway at #62 on ramp when the dispatcher completes the explanation of where this motor vehicle accident is.

I must drive up a short incline, then go down a hill about 250 yards, and I can see the scene of the accident. There are five cars stopped on the right-hand side of the road because I am approaching with my lights and siren. I stop my police car at the point where the vehicle left the roadway and collided with a cable and pole guardrail. The car has the passenger side facing the roadway with the nose of the car facing south. The nose should be facing north. The State Trooper is parked in the median on the southbound side of the road. He has his alley lights and a spotlight trained on the accident scene so the car is brightly illuminated.

There is a man seated in the rear seat of the State Police car. The State Trooper is seated in the front seat talking into his radio microphone. I advise our dispatcher of the exact location and let the other responding personnel know to use the #62 on ramp. When I get out of my car, I walk over to the trooper. I do not know him, so I introduce myself and ask what he needs help with. The response is, "They are both dead." I am speechless when he points to the car and says, "The two kids were in the car. They're both dead."

Without saying anything, I turn and run to the wrecked car. I turn on my flashlight, searching to find the children he is talking about. There is no body in the front seat. In the back seat, I find what once was a living four-year-old boy. He had obviously been thrown around the inside of the car violently. It looks as if his head is almost completely severed from the rest of his body. The bones of his legs and arms are protruding through his skin. There is blood everywhere.

I snap back to looking in the car. The trooper said that "They are both dead." There are two of them, so I am wondering where the second one is. Then, I look at the passenger side of the car. It is completely opened up. The sheet metal has been peeled right off the car and is hanging on the guardrail.

Just then, I look down on the ground to see two purple sneakers along the side of the car near the rear end. Partially buried in the dirt and debris is the second child. Her head is not visible. The rear tire had come to rest on top of it. The rest of her body is intact, and there is no visible bleeding. The body is lifeless though.

As I turn away, a firefighter from the rescue truck is standing next to me. He looks at me and says, "What do we have, Sergeant Genovese?

Where are the victims?" I look at him and reply, "You won't need your medical bag. We are going to need two body bags. There are two dead children over there, and it is not a very pleasant sight."

Fortunately, I do not have to stay there or write any reports about this. However, this day will haunt me for the rest of my life. I have visions of those two children almost every day. Nothing I do or any treatment that I've sought has made that accident disappear.

I have never been sick and thrown up from the sight of blood or a mangled body. By this point in my career, if it was going to happen, it would have happened then.

CHAPTER 19

# MY PROFESSIONAL CAREER

I become an emergency medical technician for two reasons. The town paid $500 extra each year incentive, and the town would pay overtime rates when you needed to attend any training. So, money was reason number one.

I also believe it would be important to have the medical training due to the assignment of being a first responder. I am on the SWAT team and feel the need to have as much training as I can. I hate classrooms and homework. It seems I am destined to spend many hours training for one thing or another.

Training is usually voluntary, just as it was in the Marine Corps. There are not any special assignments that come from having more training. The training I would receive as an EMT prepares me to better serve my family. My resume would consist of many training seminars and specialized subjects.

I would graduate from the University of New Haven with a Bachelor of Science degree in Public Administration and a minor in Criminal Justice. I would also have enough extra credits to earn an Associate's Degree in Criminal Justice. This would all come to fruition in 1990.

Two years prior to becoming a sergeant, I received training as a firearms instructor for training police officers. I had taught myself how to be a better, more proficient shooter. I was able to determine what mistakes were made while firing a handgun that would affect an individual's marksmanship. I became incredibly good at this and was recognized by the instructors at the police academy.

The police department would send me away for several SWAT training courses. The most involved was a two-week FBI sniper course. Prior to the sniper course, the other courses involved tactics, long guns, and building entry techniques. I would be deployed as a sniper four times in my career.

The most memorable deployment came on a nice, warm summer day in July. The North Haven police had a shared tactical team with a neighboring town. The North Branford police department was a 31-man department, so it made sense for the two departments to share resources. Eventually, there would be a multi-town tactical team.

On this particular day in North Branford, two officers are dispatched to a residence for a complaint of a family dispute. A wife had filed for a divorce from her husband. He became enraged and began to smash the furniture in their house. When the wife attempted to stop him, he threatened to kill her. The wife left the house and drove to a convenience store and telephoned the police from there. This was the age before cell phones were common. When the police responded to the residence, they found the man had barricaded himself in the house.

When the police officers try to make contact with him, he shouts, "If any police officers come in here, I will kill them." This is followed by the distinct, one-of-a-kind sound of the pump action of a shotgun chambering a round. It is commonly referred to as "the racking of a round." There is no other sound like it.

The police, knowing their lives are in danger, retreat to a safe area with cover. They call for assistance in the form of the SWAT team. The house is secured, and innocent bystanders are moved out of range. The house is located on a busy street, so traffic has to be rerouted.

While this is taking place, the enraged husband is dismantling his house. He has smashed out several windows by throwing furniture from inside the house through them. A microwave oven and two chairs are lying outside of the kitchen window. From the living room window, a rocking chair has been ejected. There is a sun porch attached to the front of the house. The windows were once the louvered glass type. He has managed to break every single pane of glass in every window.

I am deployed with my sniper rifle in a neighboring yard, approximately 120 yards away. I have a complete unobstructed view of the front and side of his house. The house faces east so I am observing the south and east sides of the house. The driveway runs along the south side of the house. His work truck is parked in the garage, which is unattached behind the house.

I arrive on the scene and am deployed to my position by 7:30 p.m. It is summer, so it is still light out. When I am set up properly, it is almost impossible for the untrained eye to see me. I am in range to hear and see everything this man does when he goes past a window.

The rest of the team and other police officers are deployed in a safe area or in a perimeter, making sure he does not leave. There is a negotiator who will make contact any way he can. The negotiator will attempt to reason with the man and have the matter end peacefully.

On this night, the man will not talk to the negotiator. The phone rings, but he picks it up, says hello, and then hangs up. This scenario is repeated over and over. In between the ringing and hanging up of the phone, pieces of furniture are thrown out of different windows.

While he is making his way around the house, he is singing, "I'm breaking the law. Breaking the law. I'm breaking the law. Breaking the law. The police are here, and I'm breaking the law. Breaking the law." This singing is continuous during the night. This goes on well past midnight.

While he walks back and forth, our radio continues to communicate with all the members of the SWAT team. No gun has ever been seen. The deputy chief of our department and the chief of the North Branford police advise me specifically to "take the suspect out" and "You have a green light should he present himself in a window with a gun."

This means they are authorizing me to shoot and kill this man if I see him holding a gun. I make a conscious decision at this point that he will not be shot unless he shoots first. Mere possession of the gun would not constitute a death sentence.

I could not justify the taking of this young man's life because he was just served with divorce papers and decided to take it out on his house. He was kind of entertaining and to this point had not hurt anyone. I believed that he would be asleep soon.

At about midnight, he stops singing and begins to watch television. He is seated on the only chair left in one piece inside the house, watching the only television left in the house. The phone is no longer ringing because it had been thrown through the window. One door is barricaded with the refrigerator and the other with the washing machine. The dryer is in the driveway.

Every window is demolished. Barricading the doors serves no purpose at all. The SWAT team is planning to make an entry before sunrise. Sometime around 3:20 a.m., a plan is set in motion to have two separate teams of four officers on each team enter the house.

One group will enter through the kitchen, and the other will make a frontal assault directly into the room where he is seated. He is seated in a large, puffy leather chair, watching the television in a room just behind the front door. We soon learn those are the only pieces of good furniture left inside.

The furniture from inside of the house has been completely emptied into the yard. The windows are all smashed. It would be simple to get into the house. The problem is how to provide adequate cover and concealment for the whole police SWAT entry Team.

The decision is made to "flash bang" the house from two distinct sides using the cover of darkness. I am able to observe the entire assault. The first explosion is set off in the kitchen. The second is ignited only a second later, which is only three feet away from the chair the subject is seated in.

He is heard muttering the words, "Oh, shit. I'm fucked," just before he is removed from his chair by two SWAT officers. The National Football League would have been proud of the perfectly executed tackle they performed.

No shotgun is ever located in the residence. He divorced his wife, and she let him keep the house. He still lives in the house after repairing all the damage. My decision to not just shoot and wait was the right one.

I continue on the SWAT team for several years, serving as the sniper. Eventually, my promotions in the police department coincide with my operational duties on the team. When I attain the rank of lieutenant, I also become the commander of the SWAT team.

In the beginning of my career, life as a police officer is becoming easier. I am gaining confidence in my abilities to handle any type of situation the public and my supervisors throw at me. Then, an incident occurs that will set me back.

While my wife is pregnant with our first child, I will be sued for the alleged use of excessive force. The suit stems from an incident which really should not have gotten to this point. The police should never have been involved in the first place. It is an example of a spoiled rotten rich kid who was never disciplined, believing the laws did not apply to her.

I was found not guilty of all the civil rights violations they claimed I committed. I thought this lawsuit was more frivolous than the guinea hen lawsuit when I was a kid. My wife is pregnant with my son. She comes to the court with me each day, so I thought it was worth mentioning.

The rank of sergeant is the most educational and interesting of all the positions I will hold. One of the more interesting events of my career occurs while I hold this rank. I am also now the person in charge of the firearms training for our department. Along with this comes the responsibility of maintaining the firearms and related equipment.

I am expected to attend the firearms training sessions held at the police academy whenever our department hires a new officer. As a result of attending several classes in consecutive months, the staff recognizes my abilities to teach and my knowledge of firearms are extensive. They request I become an adjunct firearms instructor.

Our chief of police allows this, and I attend an intensive two-week course that will serve to certify me as a firearms instructor to teach future instructors. My chief and I see this as a great asset to our department. It will mean that we will always have free access to a firing range and a direct connection to the police academy.

As a result, I am allowed to be at the academy twice a year to train new instructors. I still must be at the academy when a new recruit is receiving his firearms training and the department training. This requires I be away from my duties as a patrol supervisor often.

The biggest reason I am removed from my patrol duties is the cost of paying my overtime. My shift is the midnight to eight in the morning shift. I could easily do both assignments, but the budget would not allow for that amount of overtime pay.

I have also been assigned to the SWAT team. I received training at the FBI for Law Enforcement Snipers. I am the only officer in our department who has this specialized training. When I advise the chief I am required to shoot at a minimum of once a month with the department rifle in order to stay certified, the department informs me they will not pay me to do this. I work out an agreement with the chief where he would allow me to take the department rifle out once a month, and the town would pay any range fees and purchase the ammunition.

I was deployed four times with the Swat team as a sniper. I am very happy to say I was never required to shoot the rifle at any human being.

CHAPTER **20**

# THE SUBWAY HOMICIDE

N orth Haven would only experience a homicide approximately once every twelve years. Most of my time as a sergeant is spent as desk commander. This assignment requires dispatching duties more than any other duties. I work with a lieutenant who would claim that he needed to be on the road to properly supervise his men.

On this specific day when I arrive at the police station, the prior shift has had an action-packed night. They are presently involved in an incident where a young man had been assaulted. The assault occurred in the North Haven Shopping Center allegedly carried out by three unidentified men. They are now being actively sought by police officers in our department. The man who has been assaulted is well known to our police department.

The night is just about to become one of the most confusing and intense nights of my entire career. Lieutenant Tim Mulroy is assigned as my shift commander. He orders me to remain in police headquarters and assume the duties as the desk supervisor.

The two officers who are assigned as "early men" are already engaged in activity. There are three other patrolmen who will start their shift at midnight. They will be asked to load their vehicles immediately upon arrival at the police station due to a backlog of complaints.

Lieutenant Mulroy drives his police car northbound on Washington Avenue after leaving the police department. When he passes the area of 77-79 Washington Avenue, he watches three men run across the roadway from the west side of the road to the east side. The three men are running to the rear of a bank building located at number 76.

The lieutenant radios the location and the description of the three men. He then explains he is turning his car around at Franklin Street. The lieutenant is operating south on Washington Avenue and then east on route #22. As the lieutenant is advising dispatch, a telephone call is being received.

We immediately receive a telephone complaint from a motorist who claims a tractor trailer truck has collided with a pedestrian in front of the Subway restaurant. The tractor trailer does not stop and is continuing to drive north on Washington Avenue. This person also tells the dispatcher a police car just drove past the pedestrian lying in the street, traveling in the opposite direction as the tractor trailer.

The tractor trailer now makes a left turn into the shopping center at # 79 Washington Avenue. The truck is clearly marked with the grocery store markings of Stop & Shop. There is a Stop & Shop store located there. I have already dispatched two patrolmen to this incident, while the dispatcher was taking the information over the telephone.

The lieutenant has turned around and is driving back to where the alleged pedestrian has been struck by the truck. Officer Michael Kasperzyki arrives next to the pedestrian and confirms a body lying in the street. As he arrives, he also observes a vehicle exit the bank parking lot at #76, traveling north with no lights illuminated.

The lieutenant believes the car is possibly the vehicle the three men ran to. He attempts to catch up to the vehicle and effect a motor vehicle stop. Officer Kasperzyki requests the traffic accident investigation team be notified to respond because he believes a fatal hit and run accident has occurred.

Officer Kevin Kelly then arrives at the scene where the alleged pedestrian has been killed. He immediately recognizes this person is wearing a Subway Restaurant uniform. He also knows him personally as the manager of the Subway Restaurant. The lieutenant has not been able to find or catch up to the other car and is now returning to the alleged accident scene.

I have dispatched the fire department, ambulance, and two police officers to the alleged accident scene. I also dispatched a police officer to the Stop & Shop store to secure the alleged hit and run truck. The dispatcher and I have notified the surrounding towns and the State Police of the vehicle description that fled from the lieutenant.

Officer Kelly believes the Subway Restaurant manager has been killed some other way. He inspects the inside and finds a trail of blood leading to the alleged pedestrian. When he tells the lieutenant who has finally arrived on scene, the lieutenant contacts me by radio.

The lieutenant sounds like he has never been involved in police work. He begins to scream like a scared child at a horror movie. He repeats dispatch instructions that had already been completed. He requests we call the detectives and traffic division to investigate two separate incidents. His instructions are garbled and incoherent. He is obviously overexcited and irrational.

I calmly and clearly speak into the radio microphone and say, "When you calm down and can determine what you have there, I will dispatch the appropriate personnel. At this time, everything you need is on the way."

There is a long pause of silence on the radio. The next form of communication I get is a telephone call from Officer Kevin Kelly. He called from the inside of the Subway restaurant. His explanation of what happened is this:

The manager of the Subway Restaurant has been killed in some way after a robbery was committed. He is bleeding from the mouth area. The medical personnel believe the wound was made by a gunshot. The cash register to the restaurant is open, and the money is missing, except for a small amount of change.

There is a trail of blood that leads to the point where the manager ended up in the road. Officer Kelly believes he was wounded and walked into the road to find help. Officer Kelly thinks the manager was attempting to get help from the truck when he collapsed in the street.

Apparently, the three men who ran across the street to the bank parking lot are the suspects who have committed this crime. The vehicle that fled the scene with the lights off needs to be found. There was no motor vehicle accident involving a pedestrian.

North Haven had just experienced a robbery homicide. The assignment as desk officer is about to become extremely busy. The supervisor of the detective bureau is notified first. He will be the commander of the investigation. The entire staff of detectives is ordered into work as soon as they can get in. The roadway and area are closed off, and traffic is detoured around the scene.

The investigation moves quickly, and an arrest is made in less than 24 hours. What has happened is this:

A street gang had given a task to three young men as initiation into the gang. Their assignment was to complete an armed robbery of a suburban restaurant or convenience store and bring the money back to their sponsor.

The armed robbery did not have to include the murder of anyone during the commission of the robbery. It was, however, an unfortunate result of this one. The three young men who committed this robbery entered the store and acted as if they intended to purchase a meal.

When they determined the attendant was alone in the restaurant, they committed the robbery. As they were demanding money from the restaurant employee, they forced him to open the cash register. While he was attempting to open the cash register, it began to make a beeping sound.

The young men who were committing the robbery believed this was a "hold-up" alarm. They shot the restaurant employee in the mouth because of this. This wound did not kill him immediately. Because they believed an alarm had been set off and the police were being notified, the three armed robbers fled the building.

Their car was parked behind a parking lot occupied by a bank, located directly across the street. When they were crossing the street, coincidently, it was the same time the police lieutenant was driving past them. The restaurant attendant who was mortally wounded had now made his way to the street. He was dying and fell down in the road while a tractor trailer truck was driving by.

A witness was in a car driving in the opposite direction as the truck saw the man lying in the street. This witness telephoned the police reporting, "A pedestrian has just been hit by a passing truck." This report was wrong, but the witness believed this is what had happened.

The civilian dispatcher, who received the telephone call during the time of the robbery, could only focus on speaking to the witness who reported the pedestrian accident. There were no other customers in the store. The restaurant did not have any camera or security system. All of what happened was not witnessed by anyone who was still alive.

The three robbers were able to get into their car and leave. They left the parking lot without being observed by anyone.

The original assault victim gave false information to the police when he made his complaint. He was beaten by an acquaintance of his. He had been selling him some marijuana and had mixed in some oregano. His story about being assaulted by three men was a total fabrication. Nothing was true.

The lieutenant was on system overload. He believed all three incidents had occurred, and he was going on the road to search for three assailants. When he drives by the Subway Restaurant, he sees three men running to their car. What he doesn't know is they have just robbed and murdered the restaurant employee. When the lieutenant turned his car around to look for the three men, he drove right past the robbery suspects. The robbery suspects were able to leave and drive back to their home.

Officer Kevin Kelly was the calmest of the officers on the scene. He was able to determine what had occurred. He knew the night shift manager of the Subway Restaurant and identified him in the street. Officer Kelly was able to determine that there was a blood trail leading from the person in the street to the rear door of the Subway.

Arrests were made that afternoon. The three young men were taken into custody later in the day. After that day, the lieutenant stopped going out on the road when he worked with me. He would suffer a stroke on duty one day on an evening shift and retired a short time later. He was never married and lived by himself. He was never the same after the stroke.

Steve Smith would again be the lead detective on this case. He was able to make the arrest so quickly because a detective in the Waterbury police department had an informant who had been talking to the three men who had committed the robbery and killed the manager.

They were bragging they had robbed a Subway Restaurant in New Haven and had killed the manager. Every time a major crime is committed, a message is sent to all the police departments in the state. The detective from Waterbury saw this message and contacted our detectives.

This is the one murder that occurred while I was a police officer in which I had the most involvement. I never was able to leave the police station and go to the scene of the crime. We all had to be available for court and were subpoenaed when the suspects were scheduled for trial. A plea bargain agreement was arranged before a court trial ever took place. The three suspects admitted to committing the robbery. The one who had the gun and pulled the trigger confessed he did it. They were all sentenced to jail time.

# Chapter 21

# MOVING ON

I would finally get off the midnight shift as a sergeant and begin work on an evening shift. An incident would occur on this shift that would make me realize there are some dangerous people living amongst us.

I was a sergeant assigned as the commander of an evening shift. Normally, there would be two supervisors scheduled on each shift. It would be a lieutenant and a sergeant or two. When one of them was sick or on vacation, they would not be replaced. I was working as a lone supervisor that day.

A woman drove to our police station and was met by a patrolman in the parking lot. This woman said she had left her house on Upper State Street because her partner had threatened to kill everyone in the house and herself. This woman had two young children in the car with her.

When the patrolman tried to question her further about the friend, this woman drove away. The patrolman followed her, attempting to stop her using his emergency lights and siren. The house on Upper State Street is only two miles away. The officer who reported this is

Officer Michael Correia. When he arrives at Upper State Street, the woman has entered the house and is talking to her partner.

When the partner notices Officer Correia, she proclaims she is armed and the police should stay away. The officer notifies the police department this is happening. He requests a supervisor respond to the scene. I have a full complement of six officers working that night.

One of the officers is already inside the police department. I order him to man the desk, and I get a car to respond to Upper State Streer. When I arrive, there is a very masculine looking woman-man standing at the doorway to the second-floor bathroom, holding two pairs of scissors in her hands. She is threatening should anyone come close, she will stab them and commit suicide.

Officer Correia is approximately eight feet away trying to convince her to drop the scissors and come out and talk. Officer John Mulhern is right behind him. Officer Correia allows me to take over negotiating with her. He explains to her a supervisor has arrived and will be able to make promises and decisions.

I begin to speak with her from approximately six feet away. She is standing in the doorway of the bathroom. Her hands are held up in a defensive position, and each hand is grasping a pair of scissors. I tell her who I am and ask her to explain why we are in this position.

I learn immediately she is a lesbian living with the woman downstairs. She is upset because her partner has told her to leave, that she no longer loves her. I negotiate with her for approximately 15 minutes when a trained North Haven police negotiator arrives at the house. It is Officer Debbie Pausig.

I allow her to take over the negotiations. Officer Pausig and the woman do not get along, and the woman attempts to stab her. Officer Pausig retreats, and I take over talking to her. She has now retreated into the bathroom and is in the bathtub behind a glass enclosure. I take up a position on the left side of the doorway. Officer Mulhern is on the right.

I tell her she has changed the conditions for the way she is to be treated. She needs to surrender calmly, or we will remove her by force. She refuses to comply with any of these requests and charges toward us. I draw my firearm while kicking the bathtub door. Officer

Mulhern hits her hands with his nightstick knocking the scissors out of them. Officers Mulhern, Correia, Anne Regan, and I charge into the bathroom, wrestle her to the floor, and are able to handcuff her.

The bathtub door is destroyed in the process. She continues to fight with all of us at once. The woman is eventually subdued. I holster my firearm as soon as I determine she no longer had any weapons. The officers who ended this standoff were now the brunt of her verbal abuse. She was not able to physically fight any longer. There were enough police with a hold of one part of her body or another to keep her from moving. She is removed from the residence by being carried out.

No officer has been injured as a result of this encounter. This is amazing considering the small confined area this confrontation took place in. The officers get this woman to a hospital for treatment. Two officers will be by her side for the entire examination. I will never see her again and do not know what happened with this case.

My ability to negotiate with people to get them to give up weapons has always ended with a standoff. They have always been face to face, and I knew when they heard me talk, there was no bullshit coming out of my mouth. They would also know by my body language I had no intention of retreating or backing down.

Another similar incident will occur in a halfway house for recovering alcoholics on the east side of town. It is Christmas Day, 1993, and the department has received a call that a man is in the facility with a rifle, threatening to kill everyone and commit suicide.

All the officers on duty at this time have been dispatched to that location. I am fortunate to be the sergeant assigned as the road supervisor. I arrive there after the patrolman assigned to the area has already arrived along with a backup car.

There is a group of people standing outside the building, all behind a solid brick wall. The two police cars are parked behind the wall. I don't see the officers and call them on the radio. One of them answers, and he advises that the man with the gun has retreated to a common room within the facility. This room is located in the rear of the building. It is only accessible by a hallway where the officers have taken up positions of cover and are attempting to talk to him. The room he is in has no outside access or windows.

After parking my car and getting into the building, I will begin to negotiate with him. I learn right away he has a friend in the room with him who is afraid to leave because the man has told him if he tries to leave, he will shoot him. The two police officers have taken up defensive positions. One is on the right side of the room, and the other is on the left.

When I get into a safe position, I begin to speak to him and find out immediately he is an Army veteran. This gives me some common ground to begin to negotiate.

I learn that he served in Vietnam in 1968 and 1969. When he came home after the war, he was able to get employment with a construction company as a dump truck driver. He was married but has a problem with alcoholism. This caused him to lose his license and his job. His wife divorced him recently. He is armed with a Mossberg bolt action .22 caliber rifle.

I start the conversation by telling him I was in the Marine Corps. I tell him I am the person in charge on this day. I let him know that even on Christmas, the police are prepared to take care of people like him, and we are not here to harm him.

He immediately breaks down crying and tells me he does not want to die. He walks toward the door with the rifle and throws it into the hallway. I don't know what magic words I used or why he surrendered so easily. The young man was transported to the hospital by ambulance, and I never saw him again.

This man was different; he just had a problem. That problem was he could not deal with what had happened to him as a result of his addiction to alcohol. He could not deal with or handle the mental stress that had occurred in his life. He drank himself to the point of no return.

I had no intention of arresting this man for his actions on this day. Not because it was Christmas, or because he was a veteran. He just needed somebody who would talk to him and listen to his problem, someone who would tell him the truth.

I would have another such encounter with a man who I had known for several years. He had recently married a girl he had gotten pregnant. He did not intend on marrying this girl. He had taken responsibility for his indiscretion and was taking care of the infant child.

He was involved in a relationship with another woman at the same time he was involved with his wife. The wife had just learned of his affair and confronted him regarding this affair.

His wife had made arrangements to leave him and move back to her parents' house. On this day, she is packing her belongings and preparing to move out of his house. He has the baby and tries to get her to stay by threatening to kill the baby.

Two officers and I are sent to the house, not knowing all of these facts. The dispatcher just sends us there for a "boyfriend versus girlfriend fight." The dispatcher has no details of what this fight is about. Officer Mike Kasperzki is the first to arrive, and he learns the boyfriend is inside threatening harm to the baby. The girlfriend has made her way out of the house.

Officer Anne Regan and I arrive at approximately the same time. Officer Kasperzki makes his way inside the residence. When I get inside, I find the man has the baby in his arms and is holding it in a way that he could cause great harm to his neck and head should we try to grab the baby or try to take him into custody.

The negotiation is again face-to-face, and it is difficult for me because his demands are not logical and do not make any sense to me. It takes me about a half an hour to convince him the baby has done nothing to deserve this treatment. Should he hurt the baby, he would only make things worse, and nothing good would come from this. Eventually he surrenders the baby, after which he is immediately arrested. He then becomes combative, and we have to use some force to get him handcuffed and into the police car so he can be taken to jail. Officer Regan and I do a quick "pat down" to check for weapons. Officer Kasperzki transports him to the police department. He begins the arrest paperwork process.

The man is wearing a tight leather jacket, and when he is asked to remove it or take it off, he refuses. He then reaches into an inside breast pocket and pulls out a gun. Officer Kasperzki is able to grab this gun before it can be fired or used.

I will receive a letter of reprimand by the chief of police for failing to locate the firearm during my "pat down" because I should have searched him. We were unable to complete a full search because of the way he was fighting. We just wanted to get him to the police department where we could conduct a search while in restraints. He paid the court a fine for the charges issued as a result of his arrest that night.

Our job as police officers is to enforce the law. The law also mandates police officers arrest those people who are observed committing a crime. We do not have a choice. A police officer has discretion to determine how severe a charge can be for the crime committed, but they must act.

People who use marijuana forget it has a very distinct odor. In one of the best cases I was involved in, we were summoned to an apartment house for a loud argument taking place in an adjacent apartment.

When the patrolman and I arrived, we were greeted by the husband who was surprised to see us at his door. Upon our arrival, the argument had stopped. The husband was polite and allowed us to come into the apartment. The moment we entered, the smell of marijuana was in the air.

I could clearly see two marijuana cigarette butts, commonly referred to as "roaches," in an ashtray on the coffee table in the living room. When we turned our backs on the husband to speak with his wife, he removed those roaches from the ashtray.

The husband and wife assured us they were only involved in a verbal disagreement which was over, and they would both be going to bed soon. We were assured by them there would be no further arguing for the rest of the night.

When we left, I instructed the officers to apply for a search warrant to search for marijuana. We had enough evidence to establish a standard of probable cause already. We simply are looking for the marijuana that made the two cigarettes.

We leave the residence and are back in forty-five minutes. We search the entire apartment and find packaging material, a scale, and a stolen handgun. There are also empty plastic bags with marijuana residue. No large quantity of the plant is found.

Before we leave, one of the police officers notices a car with out-of-state license plates. He checks this car and learns it is stolen. The car is not locked, and we begin to search it. The interior is immaculate and looks brand new. The trunk is found to have a large suitcase. The suitcase is filled with 22 pounds of marijuana in neatly packaged single one-pound bags. In the outside pocket of this suitcase is the husband's driver's license.

This allows us to arrest him and charge him with multiple charges, including but not limited to, operating a drug factory. The driver's license in the stolen car with the marijuana was the only way we could connect this man to any crimes.

This is just one of those events that happens in the course of the everyday monotony of law enforcement. We knew there was some type of activity involving the illegal use of marijuana being committed at this apartment. Only the luck and persistence of the individual police officers brought the proper conclusion to this day.

While I hold the rank of sergeant, it becomes obvious the opportunities in this small-town police department will be few. I decide to look to another agency to continue my career in law enforcement. It does not appear anyone in our department will be retiring soon. I have served long enough to qualify for a pension from this department. I apply and continue through the application and testing phases to become a State of Connecticut police officer.

I will continue my work in the police department and not accept a position with the State Police. I will soon be promoted to lieutenant and decide I do not want to go through "Boot Camp" again. I will also be promoted to Captain and serve in the department for 35 years. I will end the book at this point. Future years hold material for additional books.

THE END (ALMOST)

Mark Robert Genovese

Praise for *I'm Not Famous*

*"I'm Not Famous" is exactly what it says. A reflection and retelling of life. No spin, no agenda, just a tale of life."*

**Paul Kalsbeek,**
Former Chairman,
Marine Corps Heritage Foundation

*"A descriptive and interesting journey of an American dedicated to Country, Community and family."*

**Ralph Black,**
Operations Chief (Ret),
New Haven CT Fire Dept.

Printed in the USA
CPSIA information can be obtained
at www.ICGtesting.com
LVHW041222061223
765454LV00056B/1193